Fragmenting modernism

MANCHESTER
UNIVERSITY PRESS

Fragmenting modernism

Ford Madox Ford, the novel and the Great War

SARA HASLAM

Manchester University Press
Manchester and New York

distributed exclusively in the USA by Palgrave

Published by Manchester University Press
Oxford Road, Manchester M13 9NR, UK
and Room 400, 175 Fifth Avenue, New York, NY 10010, USA
www.manchesteruniversitypress.co.uk

Distributed exclusively in the USA by
Palgrave, 175 Fifth Avenue, New York,
NY 10010, USA

Distributed exclusively in Canada by
UBC Press, University of British Columbia, 2029 West Mall,
Vancouver, BC, Canada V6T 1Z2

British Library Cataloguing-in-Publication Data
A catalogue record for this book is available from the British Library

Library of Congress Cataloging-in-Publication Data applied for

ISBN 0 7190 6055 9 *hardback*

First published 2002

10 09 08 07 06 05 04 03 02   10 9 8 7 6 5 4 3 2 1

Typeset in Minion
by Action Publishing Technology Ltd, Gloucester
Printed in Great Britain
by Bookcraft (Bath) Ltd, Midsomer Norton

It is above all to make you see.
(Ford Madox Ford, *Joseph Conrad: A Personal Remembrance* (1924))

It was perhaps Turgenev's extreme misfortune, it was certainly his supreme and beautiful gift – that he had the seeing eye to such an extent he could see that two opposing truths were equally true.
(Ford Madox Ford, *Mightier Than the Sword* (1938))

For my parents

Contents

Acknowledgements

I should like to thank Chris Walsh, at Chester College of Higher Education, for finding me some valuable time to write, and Bob Owens, at the Open University, for encouraging me in the final stages of this book. I am very grateful to those who have commented at various points on the manuscript: Bernard Bergonzi, Arthur Bradley, Paul Clark, Sarah Cooke, Olwen Haslam, Phil Horne, David Mason, Max Saunders, Sita Schutt and Paul Skinner. For kind permission to reproduce copyright material I am grateful to Michael Schmidt and Max Saunders. I remain in Phil Davis' debt for introducing me to Ford in inspiring circumstances as an undergraduate. My thanks also go to Anna Symon for her support during early drafts of the book. Members of the Ford Madox Ford Society have helped to provide a stimulating environment for my research, and I should like to thank Michela Calderaro, Vita Fortunati, Robert Hampson, Elena Lamberti, Roger Poole, Joe Wiesenfarth and Angus Wrenn. Max Saunders has offered generous and sustaining advice throughout the project and I am particularly grateful to him. Finally, to Paul, my reader, without whom this book would not have been completed, go my thanks and love.

Biography-in-brief of
Ford Madox Ford

Ford Madox Ford was born in Merton, Surrey, to an artistic and bohemian clan on 17 December 1873 – the first child of Catherine Madox Brown's marriage to Franz Hüffer (or Francis Hueffer, to which he anglicised his name) in 1872. He was Ford Madox Brown's first grandchild. When Lucy Madox Brown, Catherine's sister, married William Rossetti, brother to Dante Gabriel and Christina, two years later, Ford's relationship to significant literary figures of the day, and to the Pre-Raphaelites, was confirmed. There was money, coming mainly from publishing, on his father's devoutly Catholic side of the family (based in Münster); unfortunately, very little of it filtered down to Francis, the youngest of seventeen children. Although Ford's father was an atheist, Ford himself entered the Church in November 1892, following a visit to his continental relatives. His conversion was important in artistic terms; though his practice was irregular, his struggle with religious belief and the sense of tradition Catholicism bestowed was to ferment in much of his writing. However, his relationship with his pan-European family had a deeper impact on his development: it fostered a belief in a common Western culture.

Following Ford's birth, and his christening as Ford Hermann Hueffer, the Hueffers moved to Hammersmith. Ford's initial, cosmopolitan, schooling was to suit him well. He boarded at the Praetoriuses' school at Folkstone, with his younger brother Oliver. The Praetoriuses were from Frankfurt, and French and German were spoken on alternate days. But it could be said that Ford's real and abiding education had started much earlier. From a young age, because of his connections, Ford had been surrounded by what he later called the Victorian, and Pre-Raphaelite, Great Figures. Such figures would visit Madox Brown; the stories of these visits would be told and retold. When coupled with the experience of spending time with the Rossetti children, as well as the young Edward and Olive Garnett (with whom Ford and his sister Juliet mingled after Richard Garnett was made keeper of printed books at the British Museum in February 1890), the shadow that these figures threw would instil in him a sense of his own inferiority that would haunt him throughout his adult life.

Francis Hueffer died suddenly in 1889, leaving no money. Ford went with his mother and brother to live at Ford Madox Brown's home in Primrose Hill, two doors away from that of William and Lucy Rossetti where Juliet was lodged. The bond he formed with his grandfather would prove to be one of the most significant of his life, in personal and in artistic terms (perhaps it provided a model for those other, highly significant, relationships with Joseph Conrad, Arthur Marwood and C. F. G. Masterman). Ford is an exceptionally visual artist, one who depicts scenes and textures, colours and images in his work; this applies to his treatment of time as well as of space. In his essay 'On Impressionism', published in 1914, he describes this technique, one that he developed with Conrad after meeting and beginning to collaborate with him in 1898.

Ford left Pretoria House school after the death of his father, but a relationship with a fellow pupil, Elsie Martindale, was to continue. It led to an elopement in March 1894. Elsie's parents did not approve of Ford, partly because of the Rossetti dalliance with anarchism and his own attendance at socialist meetings at Kelmscott House; more seriously, however, he was not thought to be a sound financial prospect. Dr Martindale was not wrong in this opinion of Ford's earning power; the inability to earn sufficient funds was to dog Ford mercilessly for the next forty years. The only brief respite from financial stresses was to come in New York in the 1920s when, as the acclaimed author of *Parade's End*, Ford was fêted, and rewarded, as the great man of letters that he was.

Elsie and Ford spent their short honeymoon in Germany, and then settled in the Romney Marsh area of southern Kent – their geographical locus for the next ten years. Significantly for Ford's life as a writer, the area also laid claim to Henry James, Stephen Crane, Joseph Conrad and H. G. Wells. Ford would never lose his love of the country and his sense of the healing power of rural existence. After the war (in which he was an officer, a second lieutenant, with the Welch Regiment), suffering from shell-shock, his instinct would take him back there, to grow vegetables at Red Ford in West Sussex and allow the ghosts of the previous four years to do their worst. (It was after the war, in 1919, that he changed his name to Ford Madox Ford.) For the time being, though, his energies were taken up with trying to earn a living by his pen, a task that was made easier in some senses, and more challenging in others, when Edward Garnett brought Conrad to call. Despite Conrad's seniority (he was 41, Ford was 24), he suggested collaboration. Though the novels that they produced do not seem adequately to describe the sum of their two parts, Ford learnt much of his craft from this difficult, admirable, demanding and great writer. Their relationship wasn't easy (they broke with one another in 1909 – Ford still published Conrad's biography in 1924), and nor was Ford's with Henry James. Ford also eventually quarrelled with his great friend Arthur Marwood, the figure often credited with being the model for Ford's wartime hero, Christopher Tietjens in *Parade's End*.

These friendships seemed to founder due either to Ford's relationship with money or to his relationship with women. The *English Review*, Ford's initial foray into editing, emerged from discussions with Marwood, Conrad, Edward Garnett and H. G. Wells after the Hueffers moved to London. Though it is often assessed as a great magazine of the period, this opinion is not ubiquitous, primarily because for the eight or nine months of Ford's editorship, in 1908, it was a financial disaster. Ford would never have dreamed of beginning a literary review solely, or even particularly, to make money. Yet his financial mismanagement was perhaps related to other kinds of carelessness, and when his marriage began to suffer and Violet Hunt appeared on the scene, he fell out badly with Garnett and the others. The stress of his personal life, never kept very, if at all, separate from his professional life, began to take its toll. His thirst for editing was not quenched, however; he began the *transatlantic review* in Paris in 1924.

Ford was with Violet Hunt for many years, and aimed to marry her in Germany, after leaving Elsie and trying to divorce her. In perhaps the most dramatic development in this long and painful saga, Ford was briefly imprisoned for bigamy at Brixton Gaol in 1911. Other important relationships include that with the Australian painter Stella Bowen (he had two daughters with Elsie, Katherine and Christina, and one with Stella, Esther Julia) and the novelist Jean Rhys. His final relationship was with the Polish-American painter Janice Biala, with whom he lived for the last years of his life, mostly in Provence, which he loved. With Janice he came to know some peace.

Social codes being what they were, Ford lost friends and supporters through the chaotic nature of his personal life. Yet his indefatigable literary spirit, his knowledge and production of poetry, and the greatness of much of his prose, meant that Ezra Pound, amongst many others, would acknowledge the power of his influence on prose and poetry of this century. Ford died on 26 June 1939 at Deauville, France, where he is buried.

[This biography is an abridged version of my entry in *The Literary Dictionary*, edited by Robert Clark (http://www.literarydictionary.com). A full list of Ford's publications is given in Max Saunders's biography, *Ford Madox Ford: A Dual Life*, 2 vols (Oxford, Oxford University Press, 1996).]

Introduction

The title of this book, *Fragmenting Modernism*, describes my dual intention in relation to its subject: novelist, poet, editor and critic Ford Madox Ford.[1] Isaiah Berlin writes in *Four Essays on Liberty* that 'historians of ideas cannot avoid perceiving their material in terms of some kind of pattern'.[2] Where modernism is credited with a pattern, and it usually is, it is more than likely that the concept of fragmentation is prominent in it.[3] I put Ford in context in what follows, and this necessitates placing him in this movement, in which, as editor of the *English Review*, author of *The Good Soldier* and transformer of Ezra Pound's verse, he performed a vital part. Indeed, Max Saunders writes in his magisterial biography of Ford that 'the period of literary modernism is "the Ford era" as much as it is Pound's, or T. S. Eliot's, or Joyce's'; Ford was 'at the centre of the three most innovative groups of writers this century'.[4] In addition, the language of decline, collapse and fragmentation is commonly applied by historical analysts to events and developments of the early twentieth century. These were the years during which modernist artists lived. As artists they responded to, and also helped to shape, such events and perceptions of them (in degrees that vary according to perspective); Ford must be placed in this context too.

But it is hard to talk about 'modernism' (or history) as a homogeneous mass, as will emerge in this Introduction. In my approach to Ford, then, I also fragment modernism itself. I focus on aspects of the modernist aesthetic that are particularly relevant to him and to his work; in so doing, I also demonstrate the fact that there is more to modernism than meets the eye. The prevailing wisdom concerning modernism and fragmentation (the 'pattern') is challenged in what follows. Ford, an advocate and cultivator of key modernist techniques, both uses these techniques to represent the fragmented experience and perception of modern life (in a text like *The Good Soldier*) and counters them (in what I call his positive fictions, like *The 'Half Moon'*).

In the remainder of this Introduction I will discuss these two sets of ideas in more detail, and sketch the related parameters of the chapters that proceed from them. When I use the term 'modernism', it is to refer to the more or less radical movements in the arts, especially in literature, that were prominent from the turn of the twentieth century to the years immediately succeeding the First World War.[5]

Fragmenting modernism I

'Modernism is not so much a revolution', according to Herbert Read, writing in 1933, but is 'rather a break-up, a devolution, some would say a dissolution. Its character is catastrophic'.[6] Later critics have followed this descriptive lead, identifying 'not just change but crisis' in modernist literature,[7] 'revolution' too (unlike Read), and 'the principles of fragmentation and discontinuity'.[8] Gabriel Josipovici writes of the predominantly 'fragmented form' of modernist texts (p. 124), David Tracy of the 'fragmented character of our times' (p. 174) as emblematised by Eliot's poetic fragments. Adopting typically violent topographical language, Frederic Jameson describes Conrad as a 'strategic fault line' in the emergence of the narrative form that will make up modernism.[9] David Trotter states, in a similar vein, that the very concept of modernism encourages us 'to think of literary experiment ... as the product of a specific crisis',[10] in its own case a rupture in which writers dissociated themselves from nineteenth-century 'assumptions' and practices, in Peter Faulkner's view.[11] Michael Levenson is not so sure about the cleanness of the break with the nineteenth century (some critics do stress the tradition behind modernist artistic principles[12]), but in his study of fourteen crucial years (1908–22) he attests that the literary modernists regularly broke with their own newly formed doctrinal principles.[13] Crucially, in cultural terms, it is the experience 'of fragmentation, of nearness to an edge, or dissolution of self' that produces what Helen McNeil calls the 'characteristic modernist terror' of T. S. Eliot, as represented primarily in *The Waste Land*, but elsewhere too.[14]

Post-war, the pattern can be discerned more clearly still: 'the modernists who followed after World War I were more noticeable for their pessimism and their sense of a failed, fragmented, society'.[15] Peter

Conrad affirms Childs's judgement, claiming that the war gave renewed impetus to modernism (particularly futurism) by releasing 'energies which the new physics had shown to be caged inside matter'.[16] 'Narrative relativity', related by Childs, Randall Stevenson and others to Einstein's work,[17] is described by Childs as 'the most striking aspect to modernist fiction'. Its characteristics are 'instability, unreliability, anti-absolutism' and subjectivity as seen in Conrad, James, Ford, Proust and Woolf, amongst others.[18] For Randall Stevenson, the war ruptured 'the sense of a stream of time', thus adding powerfully and quantifiably to the modernist urge to represent time as 'divided or fractured' (p. 147).

Criticism of modernist art (of a visual kind), in which the 'representation of modernity' has been said to hinge upon the 'fragmentation of the whole' often adopts a similar conceptual framework.[19] Catriona Miller relates the development of cubism, and its 'revolutionary impact' (one that is relevant to study of Ford), to the 'new theories of relativity and of the nuclear atom', as well as to the 'stream of consciousness philosophy of Henri Bergson'.[20] She deduces that 'in Paris in 1905 and 1907' the 'artistic death knell' was sounded when 'two separate and very different events ensured that the cultural traditions and certainties of the previous centuries were swept away for good … [fauvism and cubism] kickstarted modernism into existence'.[21]

With the exception of Read, all those quoted above are late twentieth-century critics, guilty, possibly, of imposing a pattern instead of deducing one. Use of the term 'modernism' itself, implying as it does a coherent movement, post-dated many texts later seen as crucial to it: The Nigger of the 'Narcissus', Heart of Darkness, The Ambassadors, The Good Soldier, The Waste Land, Ulysses and Mrs Dalloway. Stan Smith asserts that the term had its 'formal christening' in 1927, although it had been 'in circulation' informally for some time.[22] Allowing for, or even trying to discount, this general 'naming' time lag, however, and the retrospective critical tendency to discern a pattern, modernism still emerges as closely tied to fragmentation. The language employed by those artists who actually inhabited the times illustrates a remarkably similar perspective.

In 1914 Ezra Pound likened the passage of the modern movement to that of Attila, sweeping across Europe.[23] It had left many of its key figures grasping at fragments. Writing in 1918, Ford tried to reassemble the 'fragments' that were coming into his mind, 'as in a cubist picture', in narrative.[24] His most famous narrator struggles to give an 'all-round impression' as he tortuously and retrospectively constructs multiple examples of the 'minutest fragment' of the truth.[25] Woolf, too, in *Orlando*, tries to work with the 'thousand odd, disconnected fragments' thrown up by memory.[26] The idea of wrestling with fragments of memory, and time, is crucial to all these examples (and will prove crucial in this study as a whole): in 1897 Conrad had set it out as the task of the creative artist to work with the 'fragments' of experience that could be rescued from the 'remorseless rush of time'.[27] This image is echoed in the fragments that Eliot calls on in *The Waste Land* – a poem that originally had a Conradian epigraph – as well as in those that Ford reassembles (Ford and Conrad wrote together over many years[28]). Pound called *The Waste Land* 'the justification of the movement, of our modern experiment, since 1900'; coming close to naming 'the movement', then, in 1922, he also made Eliot's style and language in this poem emblematic of literary modernism.[29]

Max Nordau set himself in 1895 to diagnose the 'fin-de-siècle disposition' of 'degeneration and hysteria'.[30] He did so in eccentric (though influential) fashion, finding its cause in the fragmentary demands of modern life. Every letter written, every call made, every sight seen, every railway journey taken, wore away more nervous tissue by demanding too much of it, he decided; he blamed artists for projecting and deepening the problem (those involved with 'fashionable literary tendencies' were demonstrating an 'unhealthy mental condition').[31] In a futurist manifesto in 1913, Marinetti picked up where Nordau left off, writing (with excitement and approval) of the 'complete renewal of human sensibility brought about by the great discoveries of science [the telegraph, the telephone, the train, the phonograph etc.]' and their 'decisive influence on the psyche'.[32] Related concepts are seen in texts by H. G. Wells, Bram Stoker and Oscar Wilde, as well as, modified and extended, in those by Joseph Conrad and Ford Madox Ford.[33]

Cultural critics and historians display a sense of the time that is similar to that of these modernists and their literary critics. 'Modern forms of life', writes Anthony Elliot, echoing Nordau 100 years later, 'are increasingly marked by kaleidoscopic variety'. He goes on to say that cultural experience becomes 'permeated by fragmentation' as a result.[34] Jay Winter charts the 'cataclysmic record of European history in this [twentieth] century' and its 'bloody disintegration'.[35] So fragmentation figures in the historical picture, although this picture is more complex than many observers, looking for a regular pattern, might expect. In *The Bourgeois Experience: Victoria to Freud*, Peter Gay declares that the 'need to live by secure, sharply etched classifications is buried deep in the human mind and one of its earliest demands'.[36] Most historians agree that during the early twentieth century, classifications changed beyond all recognition. A. J. P. Taylor cites August 1914 as the catalytic date;[37] George Dangerfield offers a range of alternatives, but finds most significance in the Liberal landslide in the elections of 1906.[38] To his mind this victory heralded the struggle between 'two doomed powers: between the middle-class philosophy that was Liberalism and the landed wealth that passed for aristocracy'.[39] Samuel Hynes agrees that the metaphorically seismic shock of that event was wide-reaching; he suggests that the rule of the 'established orders' (Church, aristocracy, Tory party) was terminated by this election result.[40] David Cannadine, too, dwells on the significance of the political and social struggle between the 'Liberal Commons and the Tory Lords'.[41] He also adopts, in places, the language of destruction and fragmentation (especially when quoting aristocrats like the Duke of Northumberland on democracy, for whom the placing of political power in the hands of the many was anathema). But Cannadine dates the struggle, in its most bitter manifestations, both earlier, to the Liberal victory in 1880, at which point Frederick Calvert warned that 'all our institutions are on trial', and later, to the final 'emasculation' of the Lords in 1910–11 (pp. 39, 54).[42] Likewise attending to earlier dates, Asa Briggs describes the 'precipice' that followed a mid-Victorian plateau, after about 1880. This cultural landscape was precipitated, he affirms, by 'late Victorian rebels' (Wilde and Edward Carpenter amongst them) who 'pulled down' the 'pillars of society'.[43] In analyses like these, despite the occasional irregularity of the pattern, the contemporary turmoil and fragmentation of the social system are revealed. Ford's varied and imaginative written responses to such turmoil, detailed throughout this book, demand a reader's close attention to their texture, as well as to their content.

Historians and cultural critics disagree upon the constitutive effects of the First World War on this general tenor of collapse. A. J. P. Taylor writes of the distinctive division established at the outset of the conflict (then were the systems by which a 'law-abiding Englishman' would organise his life altered absolutely).[44] Winston Churchill uses apocalyptic language to record the way in which things were changed, when 'all the horrors of all the ages were brought together' in 1914.[45] Paul Fussell unequivocally states that 'the Great War took place in what was, compared with ours, a static world, where the values appeared stable and where the meanings of abstractions seemed permanent and reliable. Everyone knew what Glory was, and what Honor meant'.[46] Others recently quoted, like David Cannadine, have been more equivocal – certainly than Peter Conrad, who writes of the war that 'it marked a breach in consciousness like the fall of man'[47] – preferring to trace the sense of upheaval back into the pre-war years (I flesh out this argument in Chapter 1). The war unquestionably represents, however, the nadir of dissolution and collapse. In her preface to *Tendencies in Modernist Poetry* in 1917, without the benefit of hindsight, Amy Lowell binds the war firmly to modernist writing, stating that it is 'impossible for anyone writing to-day not to be affected by the war. It has overwhelmed us like a tidal wave. It is the equinoctial storm which bounds a period'.[48] Ford writes of the war in these terms, despite an acute awareness of fragmentation pre-1914. He variously opposes pre-war empiricists to post-war theorists, pre-war 'personal liberty' to (in terms which resonate with those of Taylor) post-war restriction. He even writes of pre-war sanity that opposed a form of post-war general madness amongst those who had 'taken physical part in the war'.[49] Chapter 4 of this book, 'In sight of war', is concerned with this understanding of the war, and with Ford's war writing, as well as that of others. It begins with a discussion of the linguistic fragmentation that war engendered. 'Large words' have gone,[50] as has the understanding of, and reliance upon, what they meant – a concept introduced by Fussell above, and also found in Ford, Hemingway and Henri Barbusse. In ways like this, the first four chapters of this book, and, differently, the final chapter, engage with Ford's subjects, style and language in this context of fragmentation.

Peter Gay locates the source of the need for systems as the 'human mind'. My first chapter examines the relationship between cultural, political and psychological investigations of fragmentation. Nineteenth-century realist and naturalist novelists, such as Flaubert (Ford's chosen climax to his *March of Literature*, along with James and Conrad) and Balzac, thought it necessary to keep abreast of developments in medical science, particularly psychology. This 'medico-literary collaboration', as Gunnar Brandell says it became, culminated in Paris of the 1880s when Charcot was professor of neuroscience at the Salpêtrière. In fact, Brandell continues, Charcot was 'associated more often with writers such as Daudet and Turgenev than with his medical colleagues', and writers regularly attended his lectures and demonstrations.[51] As Freud advanced psychology (and William

James told him in a visit to the United States in 1909 that 'the future of psychology' belonged to his work[52]), it became more intense still. Edith Kurzweil deduces that themes of modernist literature, such as 'loneliness, self-doubt, hypersensitivity, perversities of all kinds, estrangement from the community', all have their counterparts 'among the common neuroses'.[53] Historians analogise similarly. Dangerfield suggests that England was in a 'dangerous state of hysteria' in the years 1912–14.[54] Daniel Pick also conflates (although more obliquely) the language of psychology with that of history. He claims that 'it is in the period from 1870 to 1914 that we can locate the [...] circulation and escalation of a cultural critique in which war is at once the symptom and potential ruin of modernity'.[55] In Chapter 1 I describe Freud as 'at least emblematic' of modernism, and pursue the idea of a relationship between psychoanalysis and modernist literary subject matter and techniques.

Ford's literary technique is the subject of the second chapter. It is a wide-ranging (in terms of his *oeuvre*) and a general one, examining the way Ford explores what the novel, as genre, can achieve. A key Fordian modernist image is that of the kaleidoscope. 'You carry away from [a train]', he writes in 1905, a 'vague kaleidoscope picture – lights in clusters, the bare shoulders of women, white flannel on green turf in the sunlight, darkened drawing rooms'.[56] He translates these endlessly changing pictures, built of reflective fragments, into his prose. Chapter 2 here, 'Novel perspectives', examines the resultant dramatic thrust of the contemporary *Fifth Queen* trilogy, the eye for colour, for detail, for patterns. Ford watches, and he sees his characters vividly, as in a play. My reading of *The Good Soldier*, his great modernist text, continues this theme of visual reckoning. Dowell self-diagnoses as a cubist narrator, aiming at an 'all-round impression'; he is psychologically unfit for the task (also self-diagnosing 'the repression of my instinct'), and remains unable to grasp the whole (pp. 83, 101). As another manifestation of modernist fragmentation, one fomented by psychoanalysis and sexology, the four main characters are read partly as four parts of the same psyche, individually and oppositionally gaining (at times violent) expression.[57]

Chapter 3 concentrates the analysis of fragmentation on Ford's Edwardian novel, *A Call*, in what is essentially an exploration of the changing nature of sexual behaviour and roles. Ford's modernist credentials, as editor and as novelist, were closely bound to this issue.[58] Sexual radicalism pre-dated the war. Though some commentators thought that conventions for men and women had broken down under this strain, as Cate Haste points out,[59] the new twentieth century had been named the 'vaginal century' before war began.[60] The relationship between the sexes is cited by Hynes, by Gay and by Dangerfield, amongst others, as one of the extreme indicators of cultural upheaval in the Edwardian era.[61] Gay states that in 'the anguished and inconclusive debate over woman's true place, the fear of woman and the fear of change met and merged'.[62] Heightened visual sensitivity goes with the territory here, too: what characters see (and how they see it) in A Call, ability that is gender specific, is fundamental to Ford's plot, and is also symbolically important.

The four chapters detailed so far, and the way in which I discuss Ford within them, support the first part of my aim with regard to my title – assessing the fragmentation endemic to modernist writing. In these chapters I hope the fragmenting pattern of modernism will be clearly, though variously, discerned and shown. The three chapters that remain support the second part of my aim: to challenge this almost ubiquitous, catastrophic, slant to the pattern. Here, in closely analysing aspects of Ford's modernist aesthetic, I find and assess fragments that shore against ruins, and that give him the opportunity instead to rejoice in the multiplicitous nature of the modernist quest.

Fragmenting modernism II

It is, perhaps, clear by now that the visual aspects of the modernist aesthetic are particularly relevant to a study of Ford. Sight is therefore a governing theme in this study as a whole. What and how Ford, and by extension his characters, see (in imagination, in fact, as visions or impressions) emerges in analysis as the most consistent method of evoking modernist sensibility:

> That was how his past life came back to him, in those scenes of strong colours, remembered with strong emotions [...]. He was a record of coloured and connected scenes; and all he possessed was just those memories of scenes, highly enough coloured since he recollected with an extreme vividness alike the gilt amorini of the Venetian hotel and the seven, blue, momentarily immobilised Very lights over Kemmel hill and the stretched, slightly agonised eyebrows of Hilda Cohen and the lady in the olive tree...[63]

The kaleidoscope, with its coloured, textured shards of reflected glass, helps Ford to describe vivid experience that is always changing, always made new (Ezra Pound's artistic invocation was to 'make it new'). With its reliance on reflection, it also serves to confirm the related modernist emphasis of memory: what Gabriel Morton sees, in the above extract, what he *is*, in fact, is these shifting, non-hierarchical, bizarrely (though not obviously) 'connected' coloured scenes from his past life (think of the Woolf quotation here). Ford's job is to make those visions work in prose, even when the picture is far less clear than it is for Gabriel: it is a task he took to with a unique talent. In his obituary of Ford, Pound termed him 'an halluciné', an apt epithet for this extraordinarily visual writer.[64]

In the dedication to his first book of memoirs, published in 1911, Ford states his intention to present to his progeny the sum of his knowledge of life. He seeks a deep gift, one that is not 'outward and visible' but is, rather, buried and 'spiritual'. It is a gift that will be presented in narrative. He will write it from his memory, from his search for his past, from his attempt to come to understand the gaps between his past and present self. Gradually, as the picture develops, the children are forgotten. Unwittingly, Ford betrays the need to represent his personal narrative as his own:[65]

> To tell you the strict truth, I made for myself the somewhat singular discovery that I can only be said to have grown up a very short time ago – perhaps three months, perhaps six. I discovered that I had grown up only when I discovered quite suddenly that I was forgetting my own childhood. My own childhood was a thing so vivid that it certainly influenced me, that it certainly rendered me timid, incapable of self-assertion, and as it were perpetually conscious of original sin until only just the other day. For you ought to consider that upon the one hand as a child I was very severely disciplined, and when I was not being severely disciplined I moved amongst somewhat distinguished people who all appeared to me to be morally and physically twenty-five feet high.[66]

In the shadow of the 'Victorian Greats', as Ford also calls them, he continues to detail a distinct and powerful memory. As a small child, he incurred the wrath of his grandmother by stumbling upon the 'panting morsels of flesh' that were newly born Barbary doves, being kept in a window box at Ford Madox Brown's London house. He was fascinated by what he saw in the 'breeding box' (and he remains fascinated by the awe-struck picture of himself that his visual memory returns to him). The wonder, and the sexual disgust, that Ford experienced at that moment are fixed in memory with the punishing words of his grandmother. Furious, she told him that the mother dove would certainly eat her young if disturbed in this way. Ford's encounter with the forces of mother nature – he calls this the 'first surprise' and the 'first wonder' of his life – are thus cemented to an unconscious understanding of the castrating and murderous power of woman.[67] Here, this scene provides a powerful example of the way in which Ford visualises the past's existence in the present. In the detailed discussion of it in Chapter 5, it is recast as a source of the regenerative imagery found in his positive fictions.

Max Saunders identifies this kind of vision in Ford as versions of '"eidetic images": powerfully visual imaginings ... possibly the kind of visions that Freud understood as regressions to childhood memories.'[68] On one level this is probably so, and I consider this reading in more detail in Chapter 1. But more importantly here, Ford adapted his modernist theory in order to account for, and fully to use, these visions – most obviously in impressionism, the 'modernist doctrine' developed with Conrad, which I discuss in detail in Chapter 7.[69] He also based his most famous modernist text on a cubist aesthetic that allowed him both to incorporate art theory, and to show Dowell's monumental displacement in the modern world. Sight spoke for Ford; prose was 'a matter of looking things in the face'.[70] Cubism was the modernist language it used.

Cubism, already described by Catriona Miller as 'kickstarting modernism', was prompted by 'the desire of Picasso and Braque to find an alternative to the fixed certainty of one-point perspective' (Miller, p. 163). Cubists are known for their 'multiple viewpoints', their multiple perspectives.[71] Works of literary modernism are dedicated to the same task.[72] John Dowell, narrator of *The Good Soldier* (I give a summary of this novel at the beginning of Chapter 2), declares himself as a cubist narrator in the first pages of the text. But what can he mean? And is he right?

Struck by the sexual, emotional and psychological horror that he has come to see and know, Dowell writes in order to get the sight out of his head. But instead of showing it from all points of view, as one might expect, he shows it strangely, incompletely. He admits that 'the whole world for me is like spots of colour on an immense canvas' (p. 17);[73] his narrative is supposed to join the dots, to show the multiple relationships between the places and the people that he has seen and known. It doesn't do that for the reader until the very last minute (and maybe not at all on the first reading; see the discussion of the novel in Chapter 2).

It doesn't do that for Dowell at all: 'so here I am very much where I started thirteen years ago', he writes, twelve pages before the end of the text. Immediately, incredibly, he states that he 'should really like to be a polygamist', but then confesses that 'probably because of my American origin I am fainter' (p. 151). Thus he abandons a new existence as a rampant polygamist and proves he is as he was when the story began. If sexuality means 'sexual activity', offered by Bristow as one definition, then Dowell lacks it entirely.[74] (Interestingly, too, in the text as a whole there is precious little sight of the issue of the 'sex drive': children.[75]) He can't learn about the 'glove' that Ford teases him with in the first paragraph of the text ('we had known the Ashburnhams for nine seasons of the town of Nauheim ... with an acquaintance-ship as loose and easy and yet as close as a good glove's with your hand'). Setting the tone here, Ford uses a sexual image the meaning of which is hidden from Dowell: his multiple perspective is a joke from the start. Dowell's text is, in effect, one long confessional as to his physical, cognitive, experiential inadequacy as a man, as a husband and as a cubist narrator. This is not so for the narrators and protagonists of Ford's positive fictions. Here Ford establishes characters who see, and know, it all – usually in glorious technicolour.

In Chapter 5 I introduce the concept of Fordian 'positive fictions' (my phrase), and offer a way of reading Ford's dedication to his grandfather, and to his grandfather's circle (especially the Pre-Raphaelites), that feeds into the content and the visual style of these texts. The new things the protagonists see here might be painful, but they tend to be reclamatory too. As part of its analysis, this chapter, 'Imaginative visions', also reintroduces the 'woman question': the four novels to be studied reconstruct worlds of alternative systems which emanate from the fragmented consciousness of men such as Grimshaw. Having taken them apart, Ford will put them back together again (*The New Humpty-Dumpty* (1912) is one of the texts I examine). The displacement of primitive needs and their necessary reinstitution, as indicated late in the period by Vilfredo Pareto, is symbolised powerfully by the debate on women and religion: 'It is a curious fact that while the Christian, and especially the Catholic, Church denounces amorous pleasures, it is from them in the main that it derives the metaphors through which it expresses manifestations of faith. The Church is the Bride of Christ [...] the vision of woman hovers before [churchmen's] eyes. Banished in one direction, back she comes from the other'.[76] Ford traces ways in which the vision of woman returns, made powerful and rejuvenating by mythical investment and reclamation, and by the improved ability of male sexual response. In some texts Ford investigates the contemporary rage/fear in male reactions to women. (It is easy to forget the violence done to women for wearing bloomers, not to mention for demanding the vote. Pareto writes of women being beaten in Paris in February 1911 for wearing *jupe-culottes* in public; similar incidents occurred in Spain and Italy.[77]) He also explores the healing qualities of what Jung termed the female archetypes. Jung's theories, and Robert Graves's writings, are used as part of an illuminatory test of Jung's assertion that 'our world seems to be dis-infected of witches',[78] when the world is Ford's positive fictions.[79]

Developing the discussion of religion, Chapter 6 compares Ford's fantasy novel, *The Young Lovell* (1913), with the poem 'On Heaven', written at the same period. It seeks the religious equivalent of the symbolic healing of women to be found in Chapter 5, and investigates the peculiarly Fordian notion of peace. 'Fantasies are scenarios of desire', according to Gay; they are 'in touch with the deepest motions of the mind, principally its unmet needs'.[80] In 'Creative Writers and Day-Dreaming' Freud examines the often ordinarily sublimated extension of the childhood need for fantasy and play as expressed in creative writing.[81] In *The Young Lovell* and 'On Heaven' Ford's desire, his fantasy, is to do with being seen. Not for these characters Dowell's 'mortifying' experience of having Leonora's 'lighthouse glare' turned upon him (*The Good Soldier*, p. 29); here characters are seen and known in their entirety, in their complexity, and in this there is peace.

My final chapter is an analysis of Ford's theoretical, modernist stances (and considers impressionism, and Ford's position in the modernist subjectivity versus objectivity debate). It also engages with Ford's faith in the novel as a modernist tool; this faith emerges as one that is both necessary to, and threatened by, the times. Concluding with an analysis of memory and its role in the modernist quest, this chapter also returns the book to its beginnings, and a writer who believed in pictures of the past, and the present, and sought to write them, however difficult. Sometimes both past and present were too terrible for Ford's brain to countenance: 'nothing is more difficult, nothing is more terrible than to look things in the face' he wrote in 1910 (although this was what prose had to do).[82] This was years before the war was to make it maddening to try to remember and to make sense of the world in this way.

As well as revealing the fear and suffering that were a result of fragmentation, Ford also embraced what was, in more positive ways, the essence of the early twentieth century (Christopher Tietjens is made whole through war). This is the primary duality that demands attention in the reading of Ford. There are others, for there are energies in his writing which often seem to pull in opposing directions: the search for solidity is qualified by excitement in the apprehension of chaos and what can be learned through it; the need for peace is qualified by a degree of authorial integrity which recognises that peace is momentary; the attention to the trauma of self-discovery is offset by a character who shamelessly invented the 'facts' of his own life; ultimately, faith in the novel is tested to the extreme by the act of writing itself. This book reflects Ford's dynamic structure in its form as well as in its content: some chapters will be seen to discuss these dualities. What they should all display is Ford's response to the challenge of modernism, a pluralistic challenge to which he rises with the magic of his words.

Notes

1 Ford, as I have said in the biography-in-brief, was christened Ford Hermann Hueffer. He took the middle name Madox in the late nineteenth century, and adopted Ford (a maternal name) as a surname in June 1919. Throughout this book, I have used Ford Madox Ford as his authorial name.

2 Isaiah Berlin, *Four Essays on Liberty* (Oxford, Oxford University Press, 1979), p. 1.

3 'Fragmentation' in the catastrophist sense of the experience or perception (and thus representation in artistic terms) of disunity where there had been unity, but also in the sense of the experience or perception of new aspects of existence. See David Tracy's article, 'Fragments: The Spiritual Situation of Our Times' in John D. Caputo and Michael J. Scanlon (eds), *God, the Gift and Post-Modernism* (Bloomington, Indiana University Press, 1999), pp. 170–84, for both a discussion of the primacy, early in this century, of the language of fragmentation, and an assessment of its complex nature.

4 The groups of writers to which Saunders refers are the Sussex 'ring of conspirators', including Henry James, Joseph Conrad, Stephen Crane; the *English Review* contributors, including D. H. Lawrence, Ezra Pound, Wyndham Lewis; and finally those who wrote for his later, Paris-based, *transatlantic review* in the 1920s, including James Joyce, Gertrude Stein, Jean Rhys and Ernest Hemingway (*Ford Madox Ford: A Dual Life*, Vol. 1, Oxford, Oxford University Press, 1996, p. v). Hereafter cited as Saunders I (or, for volume 2, Saunders II).

5 My subject here is Ford, and these dates provide parameters for his works that I discuss. I don't accept, in general, the idea of a time-bound period of modernism. Some critics do, however, often citing 1908–22 as the critical period (though dates are always a matter for debate), climaxing in the publication of *The Waste Land* in 1922. See the first pages of Peter Childs, *Modernism* (London, Routledge, 2000); Stan Smith, *The Origins of Modernism: Eliot, Pound, Yeats and the Rhetoric of Renewal* (Hemel Hempsted, Harvester Wheatsheaf, 1994); Michael Levenson, *A Genealogy of Modernism* (Cambridge, Cambridge University Press, 1984).

6 Herbert Read, *Art Now: An Introduction to the Theory of Modern Painting and Sculpture* (London, Faber & Faber, 1933), p. 59.

7 Peter Childs, *Modernism*, p. 14.

8 Gabriel Josipovici, *The Lessons of Modernism* (London, Macmillan, 1977), pp. xiv, 138.

9 Frederic Jameson, *The Political Unconscious: Narrative as a Socially Symbolic Act* (London, Methuen, 1981), p. 206.

10 David Trotter, *The English Novel in History 1895–1920* (London, Routledge, 1993), p. 3.

11 Faulkner, *Modernism* (London, Methuen, 1977), p. 1.

12 Levenson suggests that while the modernists themselves 'repeatedly announced a clean break with the immediate past' there are, in fact, grounds for finding continuity with the Victorian era too (*Genealogy of Modernism*, pp. ix–x). 'Modernists didn't obliterate traditions; they stretched, explored, and reconfigured them', Jay Winter states in *Sites of Memory, Sites of Mourning: The Great War in European Cultural History*, before examining literary modernism (Cambridge, Cambridge University Press, 2000, pp. 2–5). See also Randall Stevenson's *Modernist Fiction: An Introduction* (Hemel Hempstead, Prentice Hall, 1998) (especially the introduction).

13 Levenson, *Genealogy of Modernism*, p. x.

14 Introduction to H.D.'s *Her* (London, Virago, 1984), p. vii.

15 Childs, *Modernism*, p. 27. See also Faulkner, *Modernism*, p. 14.

16 Peter Conrad, *Modern Times, Modern Places: Life and Art in the Twentieth Century* (London, Thames & Hudson, 1998), p. 217.

17 Though the Theory of Relativity emerged in 1905, it wasn't until several years later that it was confirmed (1919), and began to prove its literary currency. D. H. Lawrence remarked in 1923 that 'everybody catches fire at the word Relativity. There must be something in the mere suggestion which we have been waiting for ... Relativity means ... there is no one single absolute principle governing the world', *Fantasia and the Unconscious and Psychoanalysis and the Unconscious* (London, Heinemann, 1963), p. 177.

18 Childs, *Modernism*, p. 66. See also Stevenson, *Modernist Fiction*, pp. 74–5, 110–13.

19 Briony Fer, introduction to *Modernity and Modernism: French Painting in the Nineteenth Century*, ed. F. Frascina *et al.* (New Haven, Yale University Press, 1993), p. 11.

20 The work of this French philosopher was also important in developments in modernist treatments in narrative – especially in his thoughts concerning 'clock-time' when opposed to the 'psychological time' of the individual (his influence can perhaps most obviously be seen in a text like Woolf's *Mrs Dalloway* (1925)): 'When I follow with my eyes on the dial of a clock the movement of the hands ... I do not measure duration ... Outside of me, in space, there is never more than a single position of the hand ... Within myself a process of organisation or interpretation of conscious states is going on, which constitutes true duration' (Henri Bergson, *Time and Free Will: An Essay on the Immediate Data of Consciousness* (1889) (London, George Allen & Unwin, 1971).

21 Catriona Miller, 'Modernism and Modernity' in Shearer West (ed.), *The Bloomsbury Guide to Art* (London, Bloomsbury, 1996), pp. 163, 159.

22 Smith, *Origins of Modernism*, p. 1. R. A. Scott-James used the term in *Modernism and Romance* in 1908 (London, John Lane, 1908), title, p. ix.

23 Ezra Pound, 'Wyndham Lewis', *Egoist*, 1 (15 June 1914), p. 234.

24 Ford Madox Ford, 'Pon... ti... pri... ith' [1918], tr. Max Saunders, in Max Saunders (ed.), *Ford Madox Ford: War Prose* (Manchester, Carcanet, 1999), p. 32.

25 Ford Madox Ford, *The Good Soldier* (1915), ed. Martin Stannard (New York, Norton, 1995), pp. 101, 70. All references throughout this book are to this excellent and comprehensive critical edition.

26 Virginia Woolf, *Orlando* (Harmondsworth, Penguin, 1975), p. 55.

27 This comes in Conrad's preface to *The Nigger of the 'Narcissus'*, taken by Levenson as a 'representative text' with which to illustrate early modernism (*Genealogy of Modernism*, p. 2).

28 *Romance* was published in 1903.

29 Ezra Pound to Felix E. Schelling, July 1922, ed. D. D. Paige, *The Letters of Ezra Pound 1907–1941* (New York, Harcourt, Brace, 1950), p. 180.

30 Max Nordau, *Degeneration* (London, Heinemann, 1895), pp. 38–9, 506.

31 Freud considers the view that modernity has produced a general condition of neurosis in 'Civilized Sexual Morality and Modern Nervous Illness' in 1908 in the *Standard Edition of the Complete Psychological Works*, tr. and ed. James Strachey *et al.*, 24 vols (London, The Hogarth Press, 1953–74), Vol. ix. Hereafter, throughout this book, simply SE, to indicate Standard Edition, and the volume and page numbers will be cited; all Freud references (except where stipulated) are to the Standard Edition.

32 F. T. Marinetti, 'Destruction of Syntax – Imagination without Strings – Words-in-Freedom' in Umbro Apollonio (ed.), *Futurist Manifestos* (London, Thames & Hudson, 1973), p. 96.

33 Think of *The Time Machine* and *Tono-Bungay* by Wells, *Dracula* by Stoker, and *The Picture of Dorian Gray* by Wilde.

34 Anthony Elliott, *Psychoanalytic Theory: An Introduction* (Oxford, Blackwell, 1994), p. 7.

35 Winter, *Sites of Memory, Sites of Mourning*, p. 1.

36 Peter Gay, *The Bourgeois Experience: Victoria to Freud*, Vol. I, *The Education of the Senses* (Oxford, Oxford University Press, 1984), p. 31.

37 A. J. P. Taylor, *English History 1914–1945* (Oxford, Oxford University Press, 1965), p. 1.

38 Although dated, Dangerfield's book was cited in 1997 by Peter Stansky as drawing the relation between politics and modernity 'brilliantly' (*On or About 1910: Early Bloomsbury and Its Intimate World*, Cambridge, MA, Harvard University Press, 1997, p. 4).

39 George Dangerfield, *The Strange Death of Liberal England* (London, Constable & Co., 1936), pp. 29–30.

40 Samuel Hynes, *The Edwardian Turn of Mind* (Princeton, Princeton University Press, 1968), p. 11.

41 David Cannadine, *The Decline and Fall of the British Aristocracy* (London, Macmillan, 1996), p. 45.

42 The decline in the fortunes of the landed aristocracy (Christopher Tietjens, of *Parade's End*, is one of their number) began, according to Cannadine, in the 1870s due to the collapse of the agricultural base of the European economy, the rise in plutocratic fortunes and the Third Reform Act of 1884–85 (pp. 26–7).

43 Asa Briggs, 'The Later Victorian Age' in Boris Ford (ed.), *Victorian Britain*, *The Cambridge Cultural History of Britain*, Vol. 7 (Cambridge, Cambridge University Press, 1992), pp. 10–13.

44 Taylor, *English History 1914–1945*, p. 1.

45 Winston S. Churchill, *The World Crisis 1911–1918* (1923–27) (London, New English Library, 1964), p. 8.

46 Paul Fussell, *The Great War and Modern Memory* (Oxford, Oxford University Press, 1975), p. 21.

47 Conrad, *Modern Times, Modern Places*, p. 203.

48 Quoted in Vassiliki Kolokotroni, Jane Goldman and Olga Taxidou (eds), *Modernism: An Anthology of Sources and Documents* (Edinburgh, Edinburgh University Press, 1998), p. 342. Lowell joined the 'Imagistes' after coming to England from Boston in 1914.

49 Ford Madox Ford, *It Was the Nightingale* (1934) (New York, Ecco, 1984) pp. 65–9, 24–5, 63.

50 'Large words' (also called 'Big Words', and referred to in *The Good Soldier* as 'big words', p. 25) such as 'Courage, Loyalty, God' (*It Was the Nightingale*, p. 70).

51 Gunnar Brandell, *Freud: A Man of His Century* (Sussex, Harvester Press,

1979), pp. 8–9. A result of this cross-fertilisation was the 'rich literature of psychopathological characters that sprang up around 1890' (p. 14).

52 B. R. Hergenhahn, *An Introduction to the History of Psychology*, 2nd edn (Pacific Grove, CA, Wadsworth, 1992), p. 470.

53 Edith Kurzweil and William Phillips (eds), *Literature and Psychoanalysis* (New York, Columbia University Press, 1983), p. 18.

54 Dangerfield, *The Strange Death of Liberal England*, p. 90.

55 Daniel Pick, *War Machine: The Rationalization of Slaughter in the Modern Age* (New Haven, Yale University Press, 1993), p. 110.

56 Ford Madox Ford, *The Soul of London* (London, Alston Rivers, 1905), p. 120.

57 I also discuss Ford's progression from the nineteenth-century idea, via Otto Weininger, that the sexes were polar opposites. See Joseph Bristow's discussion of sexual classifications in the first chapter of *Sexuality* (London, Routledge, 1997), pp. 12–46.

58 Refer to Samuel Hynes's discussion in Chapter 5 of *The Edwardian Turn of Mind*. *The Good Soldier* was to be an 'analysis of the polygamous desires that underlie all men', as Ford put it in a letter to his publisher John Lane (Saunders I, p. 403). As editor of the *English Review*, Ford promoted French writers, thus forcing consideration of new literary techniques and of 'sexuality without the distortions of bourgeois sentimentality' (Saunders I, p. 242).

59 Cate Haste, *Rules of Desire: Sex in Britain World War I to the Present* (London, Pimlico, 1992), p. 43.

60 Viennese playwright and author Karl Kraus (who knew Freud) quoted in Mike Jay and Michael Neve (eds), *1900* (Harmondsworth, Penguin, 1999), p. 223.

61 Hynes titles a chapter 'The Trouble with Women', Gay calls one 'Offensive Women and Defensive Men'. These analyses do not concentrate solely upon the most obvious example of this upheaval, the suffrage/suffragette movement, but also illuminate the more subtle, personal and psychologi-cal perceived threats to the status quo of which the suffragette struggle was a precipitate form.

62 Gay, *The Education of the Senses*, p. 225.

63 Ford Madox Ford, *True Love and a G[eneral] C[ourt] M[artial]*, in Saunders (ed.), *Ford Madox Ford: War Prose*, p. 138. Though this extract is quintessential Ford, this novel, begun in 1918, was unfinished.

64 Ezra Pound's obituary ('Ford Madox (Hueffer) Ford: Obit.') was published in *Nineteenth Century and After*, CXXVII, August 1939, pp. 178–81.

65 Adam Phillips muses thus upon the comparisons between the writer of autobiography and the patient in analysis: 'Interpreting the patient's life-story means, among other things, revealing the implied listeners to it. (And

it might be an interesting question to ask of an autobiography: who is its implied ideal reader?)', *On Flirtation* (London, Faber & Faber, 1994), p. 71.

66 Ford Madox Ford, *Ancient Lights and Certain New Reflections* (London, Chapman & Hall, 1911), pp. vii–viii.

67 Thomas Moser calls the passage a 'Freudian's delight' in *The Life in the Fiction of Ford Madox Ford* (Princeton, Princeton University Press, 1980), p. 134.

68 Saunders I, p. 386.

69 The other 'doctrines', so named by Levenson, include imagism, vorticism, and classicism (*Genealogy of Modernism*, p. vii).

70 Ford Madox Ford, *Outlook* 33, 17 January 1914.

71 West (ed.), *Bloomsbury Guide to Art*, Cézanne entry.

72 All analyses of modernism stress this technique. I have quoted from some in this respect already in this introduction. Josipovici puts the literary fragmentation of form alongside cubist and serialist works as expressions of the human need to 'escape from linearity' (*Lessons of Modernism*, p. 124).

73 This is the case, too, for a later Fordian modernist narrator – Jessop in *The Marsden Case* (London, Duckworth & Co., 1923). He writes that he is forced 'to tell the story in spots – as the spots come back to my mind' (p. 18), though he knows that 'it would confuse anyone if I put all those visions, as they really return, one on top of the other' (p. 111).

74 Bristow, *Sexuality*, p. 16.

75 Obviously there are many ways of approaching sexuality other than the linear.

76 Vilfredo Pareto, *The Mind and Society*, tr. Andrew Bongiorno and Arthur Livingston (London, Jonathan Cape, 1935), Vol. II, *Analysis of Sentiment* (*Theory of Residues*), p. 844.

77 See Pareto, p. 1130. Ford's own account of this violence can be found in *Some Do Not...* (Volume 1 of the *Parade's End* tetralogy), when the 'city men' abuse the suffragettes on the golf course. '"Strip the bitch naked!... Ugh... Strip the bitch stark naked!"', they shrill (*Parade's End*, Harmondsworth, Penguin, 1988), p. 67.

78 Carl Jung, *Man and His Symbols* (London, Picador, 1978), p. 85.

79 His fantasy novels are made the entire subject of Timothy Weiss's study of Ford, so significant did he judge them to be. 'Superficially insignificant stories', writes Weiss of the early fairy-tales, 'are actually latent expressions of Ford's inner "story", of his fascination with the anima' (*Fairy Tale and Romance in the Works of Ford Madox Ford*, Lanham, MD, University Press of America, 1984, p. 9). Later texts, as I have been arguing, also fulfil this function.

80 Gay, *The Bourgeois Experience*, Vol. II, *The Tender Passion* (Oxford, Oxford University Press, 1986), p. 139.

81 Sigmund Freud, 'Creative Writers and Day-Dreaming', SE ix, p. 143.
82 This quotation comes from the last volume of the *English Review* that Ford
    edited, in February 1910 (p. 534).

1

The narrative push

In this chapter the relationship between fragmentation, repression and writing will be explored. Some of the less obvious contributing factors for Ford's first volume of autobiography (*Ancient Lights*) will also be examined. Close attention will be paid to the historical context that helped to produce *Ancient Lights* – discussed briefly in the Introduction and again in Chapter 5. Necessarily brief in its attention to some major issues (notably the First World War, addressed in Chapter 4), this is primarily a survey chapter that begins to trace, in broad terms, ideas and thought patterns that can be used helpfully to contextualise and to read Ford. Many of these issues, ideas and thought patterns will be returned to in greater detail later in the book.

The attempt to recognise gaps between parts of the self is powerfully resonant in the early modernist era: 'For both James and Dostoevsky, reality lay in human consciousness and the fathomless workings of the mind'.[1] We know from James's 'Chamber of Consciousness', in which suspends the spider-web of experience 'catching every air-borne particle',[2] and from discussion in the Introduction, that consciousness alone manifests multiple and distinct strands. When 'the fathomless workings of the mind' are introduced, the image becomes more complex still.

Psychology, psychoanalysis, literature

Psychology was the new science in this period. (It needed to be; Roy Porter points out that 'by 1900, it was fashionable to be neurasthenic', and that 'eminent Victorians positively revelled in hypochondria ... and hysteria'.[3]) Even William James, who described consciousness as 'a stream' that 'does not appear to itself to be chopped up in bits', posed a model of the self divided into three components: material, social and spiritual – and he said to Freud in 1909 that 'the future of psychology belongs to your work'.[4] Psychoanalysis emerged as simply 'a psychology that emphasised the unconscious mind',[5] rather than its conscious counterpart. Indeed, Richard Slobodin has claimed that 'in the pre-war years there was no great gulf between psychoanalysis and the experimental forms of neurology and psychology', reminding us that Freud had been a neurologist.[6] But the business of psychoanalysis is those 'fathomless workings', which it seeks to make known – a process that has always been in thrall to literature. The literary influences on Freud are regularly expounded (and usually include Shakespeare, Goethe, Flaubert and Schopenhauer);[7] Freud acknowledges that Sophocles himself introduces male fantasies of maternal incest into his story of Oedipus (quoting Jocasta's lines 'Many a man ere now in dreams hath lain / With her who bare him').[8] Psychoanalysis has been identified as a 'true child of literature', and Edith Kurzweil cites a tradition of a 'coupling of literature and psychoanalysis' going back to Freud.[9] In 1914, in a review of Brill's translation of *The Psychology of Everyday Life*, Leonard Woolf promoted a reading of the Freudian text as literature; the result, according to Elizabeth Abel, was that 'the characterization of psychoanalysis as a literary rather than a scientific discourse became a leitmotiv in England'.[10]

Steven Marcus calls the relation between psychoanalysis and narrative writing 'an ancient and venerable one',[11] and Freud himself stated in *Studies on Hysteria* that 'it still strikes myself as strange that the case histories I write should read like short stories'.[12] As Marcus then deduces, 'On this reading, human life is, ideally, a connected and coherent story, with all the details in explanatory place, and with everything [...] accounted for, in its proper causal or other sequence. And inversely, illness amounts at least in part to suffering from an incoherent story or an inadequate narrative account of oneself' (p. 61). There is an obvious modernist challenge to this kind of coherence; my theory is that Ford's autobiography both makes this challenge (through its prosaic rendering of multiplicity and fragmentation) and also emerges from an implicit understanding of the ideal function of narrative as described by Marcus. Ford is looking for a coherent story, an explanatory narrative for himself, as subject, in a rapidly altering world. (As a secondary process, he also searches for a complete narrative for his children.) Writing to his wife during a German cure for his 1904 breakdown, he analyses himself: 'I have the feeling that if I could be back with you my troubles would vanish, but alas they probably would not being deep within my nature'.[13] He establishes another curative method, one more attuned to the depths of his troubles, by writing about them. This theory, of the combined modernist challenge and belief in the ideal function of narrative found in *Ancient Lights*, will be expanded upon as I examine events of Ford's own life, and his time, in this book. But the *motivation* for *Ancient Lights* remains fragmentation, Ford's catalytic experience of spaces opening up between the past and the present. Marcus, in his understanding of Freud as a modernist writer, indicates the impossibility of such a writer ever knowing all – whether one's subject is one's patient, one's character or oneself. Marcus writes of Freud as 'like some "unreliable narrator" in modernist fiction' who 'pauses at regular intervals to remind the reader of this case history [Dora] that "my insight into the complex of events composing it [has] remained fragmentary", that his understanding of it remains in some essential sense permanently occluded' (p. 55). In addition, as a writer of short stories rather than novels (the former appropriate to the modernist era, the latter the high Victorian genre), Freud would have to release his characters into a future which he cannot know.[14] Ford also acknowledges this necessity at the end of his short novel, *A Call*.[15] Certain kinds of knowledge must remain hidden from view.

Foucault takes issue with what he terms the modern 'Repressive Hypothesis' (arguing that Victorian sexual behaviour was not as 'restrained', 'mute' and needful of excavation as has been assumed). And yet, 'medicine, psychiatry and psychology' are disciplines defined by him as instigators of diversification.[16] Fragmentation is part of the heightening of consciousness (perhaps due to the sense of what remains unknown): knowledge, scientific and psychological, refracts. By the time of Heisenberg's Uncertainty Principle (1923), Childs states, relativity was 'widely and excitedly debated in artistic circles as ... the scientific backing for modernist fiction ... in its use of perspective, unreliability, anti-absolutism, instability' (Childs, p. 66).[17] Writing, in as far as it disseminates knowledge, refracts too. Ford returns to the incident of the Barbary doves (see Chapter 5 for a full analysis) many times in his writing career, retelling it, always furnishing his reader with new information, with new parts of the memory. It is never complete, never known. In a way it is always unstable. Wayne C. Booth urges us to 'remind ourselves that any sustained inside view, of what-ever depth, temporarily turns the character whose mind is shown into

a narrator',[18] suggesting that a side-effect of the inside view is fragmentation and simultaneous multiplication of the point of view. It is a
view of which Ford is very fond, and which results partly in the production of such unreliable narrators as Dowell. In the writing of
autobiography it becomes a more confusing issue. Ford is writing the
processes of his memory, establishing a multiplicity of narrative
personae: Ford as narrator, Ford as implied author, Ford as subject,
Ford as child. Reading his text in the way I have done can reveal
another: his unconscious narrative persona.

The boundary between fiction and autobiography has already
become conflated. Ford did also misrepresent some of the facts of his
life in prose, and whilst telling stories – some of these 'untruths' will be
detailed as I proceed. Yet the anti-modernist idea of one objective truth
or reality is reductive as well as outdated and won't have much place
here; Ford's psychology, as well as his position in history, his subject
matter, his choice of narrative technique, and his appetite for autobiography, contributed towards his specific insight of multiplying,
fragmenting, levels of knowledge.[19]

Ford's psychology

Ford's first serious nervous breakdown occurred in 1904. The three or
four months at the beginning of 1904 were, as Ford said, 'the most
terrible period of Conrad's life, and of the writer's'.[20] In May it was
decided that he should go to Germany, 'the usual recourse at this time
for anyone with nervous troubles' (Mizener, p. 93).[21] He suffered
particularly from agoraphobia and anxiety about things at home (he
was, after all, a 'homo duplex'[22]), and when he was moved from
Boppard to Basel in October for further treatment he suffered his worst
breakdown. Saunders analyses Ford's agoraphobia as a 'metaphorical
repetition of a scene' (Saunders I, p. 186). The scene is that of being
overshadowed when a child by the Victorian Great Figures (Turgenev,
Rossetti, Swinburne amongst them), an intensely visual scene that
recurs throughout his autobiography (for Virginia Woolf, too, there
was a strongly visual component to mental collapse[23]). It was the imagined sight of an 'Implacable Face' that precipitated his second major
breakdown in 1911; Ford's ability as an 'halluciné', one that extended
into his often intensely visual prose, was at times a crippling one.
Ancient Lights was published in this year, and it is a text in which
the Victorian Great Figures make many appearances. Saunders also

describes *Ladies Whose Bright Eyes*, Ford's novel of the period, as a Pre-Raphaelite pastiche, an attempt to 're-imagine the medieval past Madox Brown and Rossetti painted' (I, p. 324), thus bringing those Great Figures to life.

Ford's visions could be described as further disturbing examples of those 'eidetic images' discussed in the Introduction; their impact was unmediated by his doctors. His 'treatment' – cold baths, teeth pulling, soda-water douches, pork-and-ice-cream diets – at Kurabstalt and Mammern at Boppard, and the Marienberg Kaltwasser at Basel, was ineffective. Ford described the Kaltwasser as 'the most horrible of all the monstrous institutions' that had tortured him yet, perhaps because of the German doctors' insistence that his disease was sexual in origin (Mizener, p. 100). Kraepelin's classification of psychological disease was in the ascendant at this time in Germany, and Ford would not have experienced much subtlety at the doctors' hands.[24] His sufferings poisoned his mind against mental specialists in general, including psychoanalysts. The intellectual dissemination of Freud's therapeutic ideas, based on the power of words, amongst Ford's contemporaries and some of his friends had not filtered to the practical level at which he could benefit from them (even the British Society for the Study of Sex and Psychology was not formed until 1914[25]). Psychoanalysis was born out of the failure of the hydropathic institutions (Freud had 'little faith' in hydropathy[26]); it sprang from the need to bring help to neurotic patients who had found no relief through rest-cures through the arts of hydropathy or through electricity.[27] Ford knew that the root of his problems lay deep within his nature; he intuited that he needed to bring it out. This he has shown in his reconstruction of these trau-matic memories in narrative. He was to be restricted to these attempts at 'self-analysis', for in his treatment he received no analysis.

In terms of contemporary medicine this was not surprising.[28] However, many commentators indicate a formative cultural status for Freud's theories.[29] This status (Dorothy Richardson commented on a whole atmosphere of 'Freudianity' by 1918[30]), added to the equating of its methods with narrative, is what makes psychoanalytic theory a crit-ical tool in the progress of this study. Such theory 'became in late Victorian and Edwardian times the liberating movement in science', writes Hynes, as he begins to establish his argument for its partial func-tion as a new faith.[31] He posits the theory that the recruitment of Frederick Myers to the banner of Freudianism was less to do with a professional dedication than with a personal quest for a replacement system of belief.[32] Myers wanted, Hynes states unequivocally, to fill the gap left when Darwinism deprived him of his Christianity. Carl Jung, who collaborated with Freud in his early work,[33] assesses this deprivation as a far more extensive problem of generic 'man', who 'today is painfully aware of the fact that neither his great religions nor his various philosophies seem to provide him with the "security" he needs in face of the present condition of the world'.[34] This 'condition', bred of increasing doubt and awareness of surrounding and increasing existential gaps, gradually intensified throughout the Edwardian period.

The pre-war condition

C. F. G. Masterman wrote the following words in 1905:

> Here is a civilisation becoming ever more divorced from Nature and the ancient sanities, protesting through its literature a kind of cosmic weariness [...]. Faith in the invisible seems dying, and faith in the visible is proving inadequate to the hunger of the soul [...]. And I think I am not alone in longing for a time when literature will once more be concerned with life, and politics with the welfare of the people: and religion will fall back again upon reality: and pity and laughter return into the common ways of men.[35]

Masterman was a great friend of Ford's.[36] He also knew and worked with Frederick Myers at Cambridge.[37] His elegy here concerns the movement away from ancient wisdoms and sanities, unconscious certainties that provided a framework for living as revealed in the literature of the day. This disappearance of ancient sanities is what Jung would term the loss of the primitive psyche, which he compares with the loss of childhood memory – what Ford is recovering in *Ancient Lights*. Freud too resorts to similar vocabulary when he terms psychotherapy the 'most ancient form of therapy in medicine' in an attempt to silence his modern detractors.[38] It is a talking cure, one that is also written. In his autobiography Ford sought out his 'spiritual heredity', his past, in order to give himself, unconsciously, and his children, consciously, a more whole, and therefore stronger, chance at life. The cure he finds seems to be to go back, at least to sites of conscious memory.[39] Adam Phillips highlights the common sense of this approach: 'Despite the new kind of resolute suspicion that Freud's work creates about autobiographical narrative – the suggestion that we trust the untold tale, not the teller – psychoanalysis is clearly akin to

autobiography in the sense that it involves a self-telling, and the belief
that there is nowhere else to go but the past for the story of our lives'.[40]
It is of note that he uses the word 'belief' – the past can be a provider
of faith. Ford's work does go back, but he does not only find the stuff
of fiction/autobiography in his own past; many historical periods fuel
his writing. Such writing combats the loss of 'ancient sanities', as well
as revealing the effects of their absence.

The need to make whole what is fragmenting is implicit in
Masterman's words: restore wisdom to its roots, imagination to faith,
compassion to politics, reality to literature, a knowledge of joy and
sadness to life. The divorce of such pairings, as well as the fear of immi-
nent and active change, can be seen to make itself felt in the paranoid
contemporary obsession with invasion. From 1900 to 1914 there were
'as many books and pamphlets' published on this issue 'as during the
previous thirty years'. This fear of invasion has obvious political, as well
as metaphorical and literal, manifestations. Concerning the political
contribution to the atmosphere, Hynes has suggested that 'England's
relation to Europe changed during the Edwardian years, and that
change is probably the most important of all the transformations that
took place in England before the war. It was a change that was vigorously resisted by the conservative forces of society, for whom Europe
was an infection and isolation was splendid'.[41] I would contend that it
is difficult to describe as 'most important' any of the categories of
change in this era, primarily due to the complexity of the interweaving,
of politics, say, and literature or psychology. But political language and
consciousness of the issues surrounding invasion informed the
language and concepts used in the literal spheres more relevant to the
current discussion. One was necessary to the other. What I want to do
at this point is begin to explore the contemporary imagery of the self as
under siege; the upsurge in national bellicosity was precipitated by the
rising apprehension of far more personal fragmentation.[42] Daniel Pick
isolates one particularly effective issue, transformed into metaphor: the
turn of the century project for a Channel tunnel. Predictable fears of
war and conquest are remarked upon, but Pick talks of the more subtle
dreads that the possibility of a tunnel evoked: 'miscegenation, degeneration, sexual violation'.[43] The overt sexual imagery of the tunnel at
some level awakens, and comes to symbolise, the fear that the sexual
safety and sexual purity (and as a result sexual complacency) of the
time would be challenged.

Peter Gay's writing of the end of the Victorian era concentrates on

purely personal geography, in contrast to Pick's approach. 'All cultures
[...] place boundaries around the passions', he suggests; 'they
construct powerful defences against murder and incest, to say nothing
of derivative transgressions'.[44] But, as he shows in his analysis, the
personal map is being forced to change: what before was uncharted
territory is now being talked about, by scientists, analysts and psychol-
ogists, and simultaneously, novelists such as Ford Madox Ford. H. G.
Wells's sexual radicalism, in fiction and in fact, was only 'one stream',
according to Cate Haste, 'in a current of dissent from respectability,
convention and established principles of social order which, by the
turn of the century, was building up to a sense of crisis'.[45] Grimshaw,
in Sloane Square (see Chapter 3), and Tietjens, at war (see Chapter 4),
each illustrate aspects of the boundary shift.

That neurasthenia came from society, not the trenches, has been well
documented, not least by Freud himself, who diagnosed 'nervousness
(neurasthenia or hysteria)' as seen in patients from 1905. The British
psychiatrist Forbes Winslow credited spiritualism with being one of the
'principal causes of the increase in insanity in England' in 1877.[46] This
understanding is sometimes confused by the analysis of the pre-war
years by writers such as Paul Fussell and Geoff Dyer, who do not always
appreciate the fact that 'though the war dramatized and speeded the
changes from Victorian to modern England, it did not make them'.[47]
The Edwardian era had within it the seeds of its own destruction, a fact
that Dyer denotes by his language if not by his material in the following extract. In this passage he is challenging the inherited notion of the
pre-war years as paradise destroyed. 'Things were, of course,' he begins,

> less settled than the habitual view of pre-August 1914 tempts us to
> believe. For many contemporary observers the war tainted the past,
> revealing and making explicit a violence that had been latent in the
> preceding peace. Eighty years on, this sense of crouched and gathering
> violence has been all but totally filtered out of our perception of the pre-
> war period. Militant suffragettes, class unrest, strikes, Ireland teetering on
> the brink of civil war – all are shaded and softened by the long, elegiaic
> shadows cast by the war.[48]

This brooding sense of violence must be invested with its original
power, for, even in wartime, Ford could write of the 'immense public
convulsion' that overwhelmed the people of Ireland in July 1914.[49]

Political facts make this reinvestment a necessity, for between
January and July 1914 there were 937 strikes in various areas of British

industry. The parliamentary situation was such that this could occur, for in 1912, writes George Dangerfield, 'the Tories decided that a Parliament controlled by a Liberal majority was a bad thing. Everything they did in the next two years was aimed [...] against the very existence of Parliament itself [...] [the Tories] set out to wreck the Constitution, and they very nearly succeeded'.[50] Such sabotage of a Liberal legislative programme was not unprecedented, as Cannadine points out,[51] and Wilson states of the general political picture that 'all the forms of upheaval that were reputedly racking British society in 1914 had developed in the previous five or six years'.[52] Despite the pertinence of these political facts, Dangerfield's analysis is persuasive, particularly in its attention to the psychological mood of 1912–14. He attributes the extent of the action undertaken by the suffragettes to 'the unconscious desires of all Englishwomen', suggesting that their challenge to the status quo was compounded by the militancy it made possible: a militancy initially generated by the unconscious. (Interestingly, some prominent pre-war suffragettes took up the cause of the National Vigilance Association; Christobel Pankhurst adopted the slogan, 'Votes for women, chastity for men'. A second generation of feminists – like Rebecca West, Wells's lover and friend to Ford – were more frank about their desire for sex.[53]) Dangerfield believes that this state of affairs also pertains to men, for the 'vagaries of pre-war English politicians' are also traced, in part, to 'irrational and unconscious' motives.[54] With the increasing apprehension at the quest for new power for women, the working classes, religious minorities, as the old systems collapsed, a concurrent suspicion was that the power of sexuality was coming to assert itself: certainly the growth of sexology and the rise of the 'new woman' were related. Dyer's words 'latent', 'crouched' and 'gathering' conjure up Henry James's 'beast in the jungle', sexual knowledge of self that will spring up and out, probably violently. Instinct has been sublimated to civilisation: as civilisation is shocked and changes, instinct begins to gain expression.

Freud, in his professional and authorial role, was at least emblematic of modernism. He reflects it: 'given the turbulence of modernity, Freud's social thought is an accurate reflection of the open, contingent and fragmented world in which we live'; and he could be said to instigate aspects of it, calling 'psychological research' (particularly the branch he instigated perhaps) 'the third and most wounding blow to the human megalomaniac'.[55] (The two previous blows, less grievous in Freud's opinion, were those instigated by Copernicus and Darwin.) In the relentless questioning of gaps lay the enforced recognition of what had been denied to the self, by the self. And it is in Freud's role as narrator of the human narrative, as writer, that this becomes most apparent.[56] Marcus traces Freud's culturally significant development to its culmination in his role as 'writer and humanist', when he became 'one of the paramount figures in the impulsion behind and the movement of the Western world into its decisive phase of twentieth-century modernity'.[57] Freud wielded catalytic knowledge. As well as being liberating, the relentlessness was also deeply disturbing. This confusing mixture of liberation and defensiveness, latency and awareness, exploded into the arena of the First World War, finding in it the perfect expression and concentration of itself – when for many the gaps in the personal narrative were forced home.[58] But this isn't only about shell-shock. 'Husbands, sons, fathers were missing. Facts were missing. Everywhere the overwhelming sense was one of lack', writes Geoff Dyer, suggesting that some kind of more general cultural narrative is under attack.[59] Jay Winter attests that 'the history of bereavement was universal history during and then after the Great War in France, Britain and Germany'; it was a history made more poignant by the lack of a body to bury.[60] The overwhelming sense was one of lack, but the factors that make up that sense are more complicated than the death of so many. They combine to inform my reading of the experience of the war as an obvious climax to the period.[61] As a metaphorical landscape, the war reanimated and heightened the fight between knowledge and ignorance, repression and liberation and opposing psychic manifestations and needs.

War

Masterman was the junior member of Asquith's cabinet in 1914 as war came. He says that his, and the more general, experience of the arrival of war was most like that of 'those persons who have walked on the solid ground and seen slight cracks and fissures appear, and these enlarge and run together and swell in size hour by hour until yawning apertures revealed the boiling up beneath them of the earth's central fires, destined to sweep away the forest and vineyards of its surface and all the kindly inhabitants of man'.[62] Anybody who knows Ford's post-war writing would find it very difficult not to see, feel and hear in Ford's talk of 'abysses of Chaos' and the 'frail shelters of the Line' the resonance of Masterman's visually apocalyptic prose.[63] Despite what has been learned of the instability of the Edwardian years, the shock to that changing civilisation caused by war was of course profound. What had been primarily – though by no means entirely – a 'mood' of the time, a subliminal seething gradually finding expression, is now out, and visible: the map of the Edwardian mind and experience is external and split between civilised society and the western front.[64]

War as essentially of its time in the exaggerated and enforced estrangement of self from self has been commented upon (I return to this subject in detail in Chapter 4). Shell-shock deprived men of their memories, of a complete personal narrative. Ford said that he suffered from failure of memory for a period after the first battle of the Somme, with the continuing result that his memory of events, for about a year after the war, was still extremely uncertain.[65] But what of the war in its less obvious, contradictory, and disturbing role as the potential liberator of repressed instinct? Can its extending geographical map be informatively linked in this sense to that of the individual? Perhaps the fight for acquisition of territory can be translated into the psychological sphere in the sense of rediscovery of the primitive psyche. In the way that some writers engage with these questions post-war, this would seem to be the case.

Gay says of the 'emergence of an exhilarating ability to enjoy sexual satisfaction' during marriage, an emergence that had its roots as far back as the pre-Edwardian years, that it was 'a liberating of repudiated knowledge, a kind of memory'.[66] Memory, yes – in Parade's End Macmaster describes his passion for his (married) lover like 'going into a room that you had long left and never ceased to love' (I summarise this text towards the end of Chapter 2).[67] The 'boundaries around the passions' are thus being tested in their elasticity, and as they are forced back room is being found for exhilaration, a word denoting experience that is uncontrolled. Gay's subjects, in their discovery, are not breaking new ground but rather finding that which had been forgotten, or more accurately, repressed. Freud's and Jung's theories would ascribe this discovery to the accessing of a more primitive nature. Freud states that 'Primitive men [...] are uninhibited: thought passes directly into action [...]. And that is why [...] I think [...] it may safely be assumed that "in the beginning was the Deed"'.[68] Through sex, in this manner, as well as in others that will be considered, the 'Hamlet' of incapacity could be challenged.[69] This critical inability to act, with which Ford, as well as others of his generation, laboured and fought, could also be seen to attain its height in the enforced passivity of the trenches. But concentration for the moment remains with the reinstitution of the power of the sex drive, a return to some of the 'ancient sanities' as a possible example of the restitution of the personal narrative to be found amid the fragmentation engendered by war.

In a chapter entitled 'Soldier Boys', Paul Fussell allies the sexual immaturity of the young recruits with their ability to experience sexual release during war. This is an issue that, as he admits, is controversial. 'Some relations between warfare and sexuality are [...] private and secret', he states, but goes on to reveal that there are 'numerous testimonies associating masturbation and exhibitionism with the fears and excitements of infantry fighting'.[70] This heightened awareness of the physicality of the self is what Frederic Manning testifies to, as a result of the 'extraordinary veracity in war, which strips a man of every conventional covering that he has, and leaves him to face a fact as naked and as inexorable as himself'.[71] War is a truth seeker then, a layer bare of facts that deprives men of their habitual clothing. Later in his novel Manning develops the sexual content of this idea, for Bourne is displayed in the blessed and the horrific presence of action: 'floundering in the viscous mud, [Bourne] was at once the most abject and the most exalted of God's creatures. The effort and the rage in him [...] made him pant and sob, but there was some strange intoxication of joy in it, and again all his mind seemed focused into one hard bright point of action. The extremities of pain and pleasure had met and coincided too'.[72] Manning's reader may infer a sexual source to this intense current of energy – the language seems to demand it – but there is no doubt as to the possibilities for catharsis in the event. The gratitude for necessary release, for action, becomes plain, and Fussell's later section, 'The Theatre of War', is reminiscent of Freud's thoughts on the subject. Freud recognises the human need for a world in 'fiction, in theatre, and in literature' that provides 'compensation for what has been lost in life'. In this world, Freud avers, 'we still find people who know how to die – who, indeed, even manage to kill someone else' – an explanation, perhaps, for Winter's view of a cultural tendency to '"cinematic" reduction of human suffering to the status of a performance during the war'.[73] Freud's word 'still' invokes the spirit of a time which sanctioned the less neurotic release of instinctual drives. Fussell develops Freud's image, stating that 'seeing warfare as theatre provides a psychic escape for the participant: with a sufficient sense of theatre, he can perform his duties without implicating his 'real' self and without impairing his innermost conviction that the world is still a rational place'.[74]

Freud writes on the experience of the closeness of death in war as a unification of the civilised man with the primitive urge to kill – now he can, and with impunity. The two forms of release (sexual and violently physical) are linked. In war, the 'final extension of the commandment ["Thou shalt not kill"] is no longer experienced by civilized man', says Freud, and modern man is thus allying himself much more closely with primeval man.[75] Manning expresses his study of his comrades in such terms, for 'men had reverted to a more primitive stage in their development, and had become nocturnal beasts of prey, hunting each other in packs'.[76] Manning isn't alone in his analysis; for Henri Barbusse, to be 'more wild, more primitive' is to be 'more human'. Peter Conrad suggests that 'war released the energies which the new physics had shown to be caged inside matter', whilst Niall Ferguson, citing Freud and the return to the 'primal man', raises the possibility that 'men kept fighting because they wanted to'.[77] Did men thus rediscover some ancient sanities in war? Were they in some horrific way thus more psychologically healthy? It is just this kind of hypothesis with which Daniel Pick has taken issue. He says in his introduction to *War Machine* that 'the writers I discuss are men, and often men for whom war evidently raises troubling questions of sexuality and gender, even though, at the same time, war is frequently said to resolve them'.[78] He asks critics to be wary of attributing a healing, relieving, power to war.

In some respects this healing does occur, and does so in Ford's wartime character of Christopher Tietjens. As explored in my fourth chapter, Tietjens is a sexually repressed and physically unaware man who is forced to extend himself, through the agency of war, in the most painful ways. And yet, in many other respects, of course, men were not more psychologically healthy; they did not always achieve, as did Tietjens, some final unification or incorporation of their new knowledge, of what they had seen. Such suffering was not due to the failed maintenance of a specific split in the psyche between the rational self and the self as actor in a theatre – the success of which, according to Fussell, would have resulted in 'psychic escape' – but to the abiding power of civilisation. It is expressed time and again through the medium of sight.

The power of civilisation is such that it prevents any ameliorative effect (however small when compared with the overwhelming destruction) being experienced due to the restoration of primitive drives. Any release that a soldier has felt must then be translated back into the civilised discourse of the time. Having had to rediscover their primitive urge to kill, the men were then hauled back to an old life that they could no longer inhabit with ease. An existential gap that could have been filled by a reunification of man with repressed urges is, rather, emphasised; the lack is felt more strongly as the men go home. Dyer writes that

> soldiers returned from this zone of obliteration [the western front] to an England virtually untouched by war. The Second World War left London and other cities cratered and ravaged by the Blitz. After the Great War the architecture and landscape of England were unchanged except, here and there, for relatively slight damage from air raids. Apart from the injured, there was no sign of a war having taken place.[79]

What the soldiers who were returning lacked was an external and reciprocal echo of that which they had seen and done and felt. They could see nothing around them on their coming home that answered or balanced what they had experienced in France. They had been changed, irreparably. Where was the subsequent change in their external landscape? It was not there.[80] The civilian population was a significant part of this problem.

Ford goes so far as to redraw the battle lines in his written analysis: 'more formidable than the frailness of the habitations was the attitude of the natives. We who returned were like wanderers coming back to our own shores to find our settlements occupied by a vindictive and savage tribe'. The lack of shelter, the lack of mental succour to be found on the return, was experienced as a paranoid perception of a new enemy – Ford does say that every one who had fought 'was then mad'.[81] Was it paranoid? Allyson Booth suggests that it was a normal response to 'the fracture between combatant experience and civilian perception of the war [that] was so profound that the idea of a homecoming became impossible'.[82] Her research in the diaries, memoirs and novels of many veterans has revealed that 'one of the most devastating consequences of fighting the war was combatants' discovery that the concept of home no longer existed as a geographical site'. One possible response was to 'abandon geography as the delineator of loyalty, replacing it with shared experience', hence emphasising the alienation between the two 'tribes' (pp. 31–2). Whatever the response, those who had not fought emphasised by their ignorance the cognitive abyss in the ex-soldiers, men who already had such difficulty equating what they had done and seen with the language they had for expressing it. This conflict – due also to what many of the veterans now looked like, for how were civilians to respond to the often horrific disfigurements with which *they* were faced?[83] – is like a new attack. Soldiers' new experiences, their new understanding, their additional primeval consciousness – a description encouraged by Ford's primal vocabulary of conquest, geographical and psychological – went unaffirmed by those who had waited. The gaps, the sense of fragmentation, were now, therefore, more powerful than ever.

In Henri Barbusse's novel *Le Feu* [*Under Fire*], a French soldier who is returning home on leave merges geographical and psychological approaches to landscape. His thought processes re-evoke the talk of maps, 'zones of obliteration' and the forgotten past, all of which affect the psyche deeply and are so appropriate to the time. Eudore is on a train: 'As we drew near in the dusk, through the carriage window of the little railway that still keeps going down there on some fag-ends of line, I recognised half the country, and the other half I didn't. Here and there I got the sense of it, all at once, and it came back all fresh to me, and melted away again, just as if it was talking to me'.[84] In this Wordsworthian image of the landscape of the mind, what is external really does inform that which is experienced internally. Eudore's semi-recognition of that which has always been the most familiar to him, his geographical location, is used to display his bewilderment at his strangeness from himself (he is unlike Dowell, who has never been able to root himself in this way). What used to fix Eudore, to remind him where he was, functions as such no longer – and he knows it has gone, he feels the lack, for fleetingly, every so often, a sense of the whole returns. He has become a modern Dipsychus, held in this position by an inability to recognise more than half of the landscape, internal and external, at any one time. His narrative is his illustration of this inability.

Fragmented psyches, a literature that expresses the crumbling faith in ancient wisdoms and exposes the splintering self, a war which is partly a climax to the dissolution of the sense of self, have been the matter of this chapter. Such considerations, as precipitately displayed in the novels of Ford Madox Ford, will be some of the matter of this book. The time was in many ways in crisis, and that crisis is expressed nowhere more than in the literature of that time, whether it be that of a novelist, of a politician or of a psychoanalyst. And maybe, as this is so, it is due to what Paul Michel, insane and brilliant author in the novel *Hallucinating Foucault*, formulates as a statement of belief: '"All writers are, somewhere or other, mad. Not *les grands fous*, like Rimbaud, but mad, yes mad. Because we do not believe in the stability of reality. We know that it can fragment, like a sheet of glass or a car's windscreen".[85] This visionary, prophetic knowledge – a modernist knowledge – persuades the writer to perceive, to sense and to expect instability. Fragmentations of reality, and the ways in which they are represented in Ford's novels, are the subject of the following chapter. His writing of his autobiography has been seen to be emblematic of the period in some ways: the attempt to come to terms with existential gaps which he believed were appearing in his memory, in his sense of himself; the feeling of fear, of certainties being lost; the need to tell his story, to write, to define himself are all mirrored by cultural and political events. Can the same be said for his fiction? This question will now be addressed.

Notes

1 Peter Childs, *Modernism* (London, Routledge, 2000), p. 45. The main impact of Dostoevsky's work in England followed the publication of Baring's *Landmarks in Russian Literature* in 1910 (*Oxford Companion to English Literature*, ed. Margaret Drabble, Oxford, Oxford University Press, 1985).

2 Henry James, 'The Art of Fiction' in William Veeder and Susan M. Griffin (eds), *The Art of Criticism: Henry James on the Theory and the Practice of Fiction* (Chicago, University of Chicago Press, 1986), pp. 165–83.

3 Roy Porter (ed.), *The Faber Book of Madness* (London, Faber & Faber, 1993), p. 62. Hereafter cited as *Madness*.

4 James also suggests that 'a man has as many social selves as there are individuals who recognize him' in *Psychology: The Briefer Course* (1892) (New York, Harper, 1963), pp. 45–6. He writes about the stream of consciousness in *The Principles of Psychology* (New York, Holt, 1890, p. 239). The remark to Freud was made during Freud's visit to America, see B. R. Hergenhahn, *An Introduction to the History of Psychology* (Pacific Grove, CA, Wadsworth, 1992), p. 470.

5 Hergenhahn, *Introduction to the History of Psychology*, p. 453.

6 *W. H. R. Rivers* (Stroud, Sutton Publishing, 1997), p. 53. In addition, like Kraepelin and Rivers, Freud had experimented on the effects of drugs. Despite the medical training Freud had, however (one in the positivist tradition of Helmholtz), psychoanalysis did, of course, develop along distinct lines.

7 See Hergenhahn, *Introduction to the History of Psychology*, pp. 453–8; Gunnar Brandell, *Freud: A Man of His Century* (Brighton, Harvester Press, 1979) throughout, but esp. pp. 62–82.

8   *The Interpretation of Dreams*, ed. Angela Richard, *The Penguin Freud Library*, Vol. 4 (Harmondsworth, Penguin, 1991), pp. 365–6.

9   Meg Harris Williams and Margot Wadell, *The Chamber of Maiden Thought: Literary Origins of the Psychoanalytic Model of the Mind* (London and New York, Tavistock/Routledge, 1991), p. 2; Edith Kurzweil and William Phillips (eds), *Literature and Psychoanalysis* (New York, Columbia University Press, 1983), p. 1.

10 Elizabeth Abel, *Virginia Woolf and the Fictions of Psychoanalysis* (Chicago, University of Chicago Press, 1993), p. 15.

11 Steven Marcus, *Freud and the Culture of Psychoanalysis: Studies in the Transition from Victorian Humanism to Modernity* (Boston, George Allen & Unwin, 1984), p. 244.

12 Josef Breuer and Sigmund Freud, *Studies on Hysteria 1893–95*, SE ii, pp. 160–1.

13 Saunders I, p. 99.

14 Peter Conrad, *Modern Times, Modern Places: Life and Art in the Twentieth Century* (London, Thames & Hudson, 1998), p. 257.

15 Ford Madox Ford, *A Call* (Manchester, Carcanet, 1984), epilogue, p. 161.

16 Michel Foucault, *The History of Sexuality, Volume 1: An Introduction* (Harmondsworth, Penguin, 1990), pp. 3, 33.

17 The sense of excitement at scientific progress was certainly not unqualified; it was sometimes regarded with horror. See *The Time Machine* and *The War of the Worlds* by H. G. Wells; R. L. Stevenson's 'A Plea for Gas Lamps'; Kelvin's calculations on the heat death of the sun (1892) for examples. In many instances narrative relativity is primarily disturbing – think of Marlow's encounter with Kurtz's fiancée in Conrad's *Heart of Darkness*, or the news of Andrew Ramsay's death in France in Woolf's *To the Lighthouse*.

18 Wayne C. Booth, *The Rhetoric of Fiction* (Chicago, University of Chicago Press, 1973), pp. 163–4.

19 In the terms and thought of Jacques Lacan, a psychoanalyst in the Freudian tradition, the psychology of any human has at its roots the dynamic relation of levels and the effects of a 'lack', or of gaps. See 'The Mirror Stage as Formative of the Function of the I as Revealed in Psychoanalytic Experience' in Douglas Tallack (ed.), *Critical Theory: A Reader* (Hemel Hempstead, Harvester Wheatsheaf, 1995), pp. 135–6.

20 Arthur Mizener, *The Saddest Story: A Biography of Ford Madox Ford* (New York, Carroll & Graf, 1985), p. 91.

21 Why was this the case? As Hergenhahn writes, 'the experimental psychology of consciousness was a product of Germany' (*Introduction to the History of Psychology*, p. 263); William James travelled there in 1867, bathed in mineral springs, and read German psychology. Germany was the home of 'the cure'.

22 See Saunders I, pp. 2, 12, 536; II, pp. 168, 197.

23 See 'Sketch of the Past' in *Moments of Being*, and chapter 10 of Hermione Lee's biography, *Virginia Woolf* (Harmondsworth, Penguin, 1996).

24 Hergenhahn writes that although Kraepelin 'brought order to an otherwise chaotic mass of clinical observations, his work is now seen by many as standing in the way of therapeutic progress ... People do not fall nicely into the categories that he created' (*Introduction to the History of Psychology*, p. 439).

25 It was formed in July, and Edward Carpenter was among its members. In early 1918 Virginia Woolf was considering joining and notes in her diary that some of the matter for discussion derived from Freud's work. (See *The Diary of Virginia Woolf*, vol. 1, *1915–19*, Harmondsworth, Penguin, 1979, p. 110.)

26 B. Zanuso, *The Young Freud* (Oxford, Blackwell, 1986), p. 101. Freud 'tried traditional methods of treating neurological disorders (including baths, massage, electro-therapy and rest cures) [all undergone by Ford] after setting up practice in Vienna in 1886'. He wasn't impressed with the results (Hergenhahn, *Introduction to the History of Psychology*, p. 461).

27 SE xvii, p. 259.

28 W. H. R. Rivers averred in 1920 that 'Freud's theory of psycho-neurosis was the subject of hostility exceptional even in the history of medicine' (*Instinct and the Unconscious: A Contribution to a Biological Theory of the Psycho-Neuroses*, 2nd edn, Cambridge, Cambridge University Press, 1922, p. 3). Samuel Hynes states that 'Freud's methods became acceptable only after they had been proved in wartime treatment of shell-shock cases' (*The Edwardian Turn of Mind*, Princeton, Princeton University Press, 1968, p. 114).

29 See Christopher Butler's discussion of, and regular reference to, Freud in his study of early modernism: *Early Modernism: Literature, Music and Painting in Europe 1900–1916* (Oxford, Clarendon Press, 1994). Elizabeth Abel quotes Bronislaw Malinowski on this subject: 'psychoanalysis has had within the last ten years [1917–27] a truly meteoric rise in popular favour. It has exercised a growing influence over contemporary literature, science and art' (*Virginia Woolf*, p. 15). Gunnar Brandell suggests that Freud's 'contribution has become every bit as important in the history of literature as in the history of psychotherapy' (*Freud*, p. 99).

30 Her comment comes in the first volume of *Pilgrimage* (London, Virago, 1979), p. 12.

31 *Edwardian Turn of Mind*, p. 138. His belief in its 'liberating' status is supported by the reviews of *Studies on Hysteria* in 1895–96. Whilst it was criticised by the well-known neurologist Adolf von Strumpell, a non-medical reviewer, Alfred von Berger, writing in the *Neue Freie Presse* on 2 February 1896, was appreciative in his analysis. Roy Porter describes the 'shrink' as the 'new priest of the twentieth century' (*Madness*, p. 429).

32 Myers was an early disciple, showing his interest in *Studies on Hysteria* 'in an address of considerable length, first given in 1897' (SE ii, p. xv).

33 For an assessment of their differences as thinkers, see 'Freud and Jung: Contrasts' in C. G. Jung, *Freud and Psychoanalysis* (London, Routledge, 1984).

34 C. G. Jung, *Man and His Symbols* (London, Picador, 1978), p. 92. See also a letter he wrote to Freud in 1910, in which he ponders what can replace '2000 years of Christianity' (Mike Jay and Michael Neve (eds), *1900*, Harmondsworth, Penguin, 1999, p. 326).

35 C. F. G. Masterman, *In Peril of Change* (London, T. Fisher Unwin, 1905), pp. xii–xiii.

36 He also commissioned him to write propaganda (a complex role for Ford) during the war (see Saunders I, pp. 369–71). Trevor Wilson describes Masterman as 'an acute social observer' (*The Myriad Faces of War*, Cambridge, Polity Press, 1988, p. 158).

37 Lucy Masterman, *C. F. G. Masterman: A Biography* (London, Nicholson & Watson, 1939), p. 24.

38 SE vii, p. 257.

39 I am still concerned with his understanding of the 'roots' of his problem. Saunders deduces that he needed analysis, for it was only he who was investigating 'deep within' his nature (Saunders I, p. 186).

40 Adam Phillips, *On Flirtation* (London, Faber & Faber, 1994), p. 69.

41 Hynes, *Edwardian Turn of Mind*, pp. 66, 311.

42 See Wilson, *Myriad Faces of War*, pp. 10–14, 171–82 and the section 'Before Armageddon: Rumours of Total War' in Jay and Neve (eds), *1900* (pp. 283–306) for illustrations of this bellicosity, pre- and during war.

43 Daniel Pick, *War Machine: The Rationalization of Slaughter in the Modern Age* (New Haven, Yale University Press, 1993), p. 121.

44 Peter Gay, *The Bourgeois Experience: Victoria to Freud*, Vol. I, *The Education of the Senses* (Oxford, Oxford University Press, 1984), p. 107.

45 Cate Haste, *Rules of Desire: Sex in Britain World War I to the Present* (London, Pimlico, 1992), p. 28.

46 Jay and Neve (eds) *1900*, p. 118.

47 Samuel Hynes, *A War Imagined: The First World War and English Culture* (London, Pimlico, 1992), p. 5.

48 Geoff Dyer, *The Missing of The Somme* (London, Hamish Hamilton, 1994), p. 6.

49 Ford Madox Ford, *Between St Dennis and St George: A Sketch of Three Civilisations* (London, Hodder & Stoughton, 1915), p. 42.

50 George Dangerfield, *The Strange Death of Liberal England* (London, Constable & Co., 1936), p. 380.

51 It also occurred in 1906 (see David Cannadine, *The Decline and Fall of the British Aristocracy*, London, Macmillan, 1996, p. 47).

52 Wilson, *Myriad Faces of War*, p. 10.

53 Haste, *Rules of Desire*, p. 16.

54 Dangerfield, *Strange Death of Liberal England*, pp. 91, 177, 135.

55 Anthony Elliott, *Psychoanalytic Theory: An Introduction* (Oxford, Blackwell, 1994), p. 41; SE xvi, p. 285.

56 See my previous discussion of the relationship between psychoanalysis and literature. Harold Bloom attests to the significance of Freud's writerly skills: 'Freud as a writer will survive the death of psychoanalysis', *The Western Canon* (London, Macmillan, 1995), p. 376. So does Roy Porter, see *Madness*, p. 407.

57 Marcus, *Freud and the Culture of Psychoanalysis*, p. 2.

58 Niall Ferguson writes that 65,000 British ex-soldiers drew their pensions due to 'neuraesthenia' post-war (*The Pity of War*, Harmondsworth, Penguin, 1998, p. 341). Trudi Tate puts the total figure of sufferers much higher, at 200,000, but suggests the real figure is more serious still (*Modernism, History and the First World War*, Manchester, Manchester University Press, 1998, p. 96).

59 Dyer, *Missing of the Somme*, p. 35.

60 Jay Winter, *Sites of Memory, Sites of Mourning: The Great War in European Cultural History* (Cambridge, Cambridge University Press, 2000), p. 1; Allyson Booth, *Postcards from the Trenches: Negotiating the Space Between Modernism and the First World War* (Oxford, Oxford University Press, 1996), pp. 26–7.

61 Ambrose Gordon writes on this subject of the 'sudden emergence [of war] as the outward and visible sign of an inward and spiritual disgrace: the social, or cultural, disarray that such [of Ford's] novels as *A Call* or *Mr. Fleight* were already, if fumblingly, trying to express'. The war made this disarray explicit; it also gave Ford the perspective, Gordon argues, by which fully to develop his cultural critique. Ambrose Gordon, Jr., *The Invisible Tent: The War Novels of Ford Madox Ford* (Austin: University of Texas Press, 1964), p. 18.

62 Quoted in Hynes, *Edwardian Turn of Mind*, p. 356.

63 Ford Madox Ford, *It Was the Nightingale* (1934) (New York, Ecco, 1984), p. 64.

64 Dangerfield asserts, however, that the Tory Rebellion, the Workers' Rebellion, and the Women's Rebellion only collapsed as the war began. Without that war, he suggests, civil war might have broken out in Ireland (*Strange Death of Liberal England*, p. 394). Wilson flatly contradicts this opinion (*Myriad Faces of War*, p. 9). For a discussion of the significance of maps, and of topography in war generally – for 'the war was too big to see from a distance . . ., too confusing to see from up close' – see Booth, *Postcards from the Trenches*, pp. 87–95. I discuss the visualisation of war in Chapter 4.

65 *It Was the Nightingale*, p. 80.

66 Gay, *Education of the Senses*, p. 280.

67 Ford Madox Ford, *Parade's End* (Harmondsworth, Penguin, 1988), p. 54.

68 SE xiii, p. 161.

69 Ford used the concept 'Hamlet' adjectivally on many occasions. It symbol-
    ised incapacity, inactivity, opposing forces. On the subject of sex pre-war,
    Cate Haste writes that 'scientific studies by sex psychologists [e.g.
    Havelock Ellis and Freud] round the turn of the century were beginning to
    infiltrate the culture and sex had begun to be detached from the divine'.
    Though the war 'accelerated the break with past conventions' she finds no
    evidence for a 'dramatic breakdown in codes of sexual behaviour' (*Rules of
    Desire*, pp. 4–5, p. 26). She admits, however, that other commentators have
    found to the contrary.

70 Paul Fussell, *The Great War and Modern Memory* (Oxford, Oxford
    University Press, 1975), p. 271.

71 Frederic Manning, *The Middle Parts of Fortune* (Harmondsworth,
    Penguin, 1990), p. 40. Pat Barker has talked of the juxtaposition of sex and
    death in Wilfred Owen's letters; she has also called his language concern-
    ing going over the top 'erotic', especially his feeling that he was 'exposing
    himself openly' (Radio 4, *Kaleidoscope*, 12 September 1995).

72 Manning, *Middle Parts of Fortune*, p. 215.

73 SE xiv, p. 291; Winter, *Sites of Memory*, p. 195.

74 Fussell, *Great War and Modern Memory*, p. 192.

75 SE xiv, p. 295.

76 Manning, *Middle Parts of Fortune*, p. 40.

77 Henri Barbusse, *Le Feu* [*Under Fire*] (1916), tr. W. Fitzwater Wray
    (London, Dent, 1988), p. 40; Conrad, *Modern Times*, p. 217; Ferguson, *Pity
    of War*, p. 357.

78 Pick, *War Machine*, p. 2.

79 Dyer, *Missing of the Somme*, p. 122.

80 The sight of the war-wounded would be set against a civilised backdrop.
    And that of a war memorial could not fully attest to the carnage of a battle-
    field.

81 *It Was the Nightingale*, pp. 63–4. According to Barbusse, you needed to be
    mad to see the visions of the truth of war, *Le Feu*, pp. 2–4.

82 Booth, *Postcards from the Trenches*, p. 22.

83 Issues of the *Lancet* in 1917 and 1918 detailed – and provided photographs
    of – some of these injuries. Also see Vera Brittain's description of wounded
    soldiers in *Testament of Youth* (New York, Macmilllan, 1933), p. 339; Peter
    Conrad's commentary on Remarque's novels in this respect (*Modern Times*,
    p. 215); and Wilfred Owen's poem 'Disabled' for a less violent portrayal.

84 Barbusse, *Le Feu*, p. 100.

85 Patricia Dunker, *Hallucinating Foucault* (London, Serpent's Tail, 1996),
    p. 124.

2

Novel perspectives

D. H. Lawrence's essay 'Why the Novel Matters',[1] focuses on issues of communication and plurality as displayed by the effective novel. Christopher Gillie cites this important essay at the beginning of his book on English literature from 1900 to 1940; he uses it to help create the relevant context for the modernist revolution.[2] The ideas in it echo those found in Chapter 1 of this book: the fight for communication that the novel represents; the ability of writing to stretch and extend human experience; the novelistic provision, in tune with modernism, of multiple truths; the primacy of change. The relationship between Ford and Lawrence at times was close, and at times was difficult. It began when Ford first published Lawrence in the *English Review* and 'introduced him to literary London'.[3] Later Ford remembered reading 'Odour of Chrysanthemums' and discovering 'another genius', and, though he didn't want to publish *The White Peacock* (Lawrence's first novel) in the *Review*, he sent it with a recommendation to Heinemann, who published it in 1911.[4] Here, Lawrence's thoughts are a useful way into Ford, his prose and his beliefs concerning that prose. Lawrence wants to be affected by a novel – 'I do ask that the whole of me shall tremble in its wholeness, some time or other' (p. 105). He doesn't specify the sort of connection for which he is looking, although it seems spiritual, and it is based on communication. What is communicated in Ford's novels, and how?

Ford's thoughts on the capabilities of the novel are impressive in their scale. They can be divided into two categories: the emotional or psychological; and the more intellectual or theoretical. The former is expounded in a review of Lewis's *Dodsworth* in the *Bookman* in 1929:

The fact is, if you go to look at a landscape, or to observe a country you won't much do so, your impressions being too self-conscious; whereas, if you live and are your normal self and, above all, suffer in any given environment, that environment will eat itself into your mind and come back to you in moments of emotion and you will be part of that environment and you will know it. It is because Mr. Dodsworth suffers and endures in odd places all over the European and semi-European world that both he, as a person, and the settings in which he suffers, as settings, seem to me to be very real. When you have finished the book you, too, will have suffered and had your own emotions in the rue de la Paix.[5]

In order to really know one's fictional – and actual – surroundings, one must be made to suffer by them (perhaps this is why Dowell needs to return to places and parts of his story in *The Good Soldier* – his ignorance protects him from suffering). Suffering renders the relationship Lawrence would desire: the trembling of emotion in the response of the reader to the text. In the properly reflexive relationship between book and reader a system for communication is made possible, one that moves, extends, probes and unsettles. Lawrence stresses the physicality of this communication; in Ford's and Conrad's modernist methodology of impressionism, the communication would be based primarily on what that novel would 'make you see'.[6]

Ford establishes his theoretical stance in writing the four novels that became *Parade's End*.[7] He expresses it in his autobiography: 'The work that at that time – and now – I wanted to see done was something on an immense scale, a little cloudy in immediate attack, but with the salient points and the final impression extraordinarily clear. I wanted the Novelist in fact to appear in his really proud position as historian of his own time'.[8] This is an ambitious aim. It describes the attempt to capture and to report the pluralities of a whole (and complex) age. In her description of him as 'a historian of our culture' who understood the 'great historical shift' from the nineteenth century to the twentieth, Sondra Stang suggests that Ford fulfils that role.[9] But what sort of an historian, what sort of a chronicler, would Ford wish to be? An impressionist one. This would mean living, suffering and writing in, creating many pictures of, 'his own time'.

Like Lawrence (who writes in his essay, 'we should ask for no absolutes'), Ford holds back from the idea of a literature with one prescriptive purpose. Ford does not simply stimulate growth, or life, in one direction alone. In addition, Ford's novelist is not a moral arbiter ('he sought to point no moral'; 'he desired neither to comment nor to explain' he writes of himself as novelist in his epilogue to *A Call*[10]). The novel provokes suffering, then, and is also pluralistic and unpredictable in the livid truths that it contains. It works as the kaleidoscope works (see the Introduction), with its author manipulating light and perspective. The rest of this chapter will be concerned with Ford's practical application of these theories, considering them from the internal world of some of his novels. Concentration will be less on context and more on content, on the 'how' and the 'why' of multiplicity in Ford's fiction. I will conclude by offering an explanatory framework for Ford's approach.

Time, knowledge and the dramatic perspective

The Good Soldier: plot

John Dowell, the American narrator of the text (in a nice pun, he, 'Do well', is from Philadelphia), has Puritan roots. With his wife, Florence, who suffers from a heart condition, he meets an English couple, Edward and Leonora Ashburnham, whilst taking the waters in continental Europe. The two couples are at Nauheim when they meet in 1904; Ashburnham impresses Dowell with his physical presence, his 'county family' air, his wealth, and his soldierly credentials. He is the 'Good Soldier' of the title. They are friends for nine years, during which time – unbeknownst to Dowell – Florence and Edward have an affair with each other, and take numerous other lovers too. Leonora tries to apprise Dowell of the state of things soon after they meet, on a joint trip to Marburg, scene of Luther's 'Protest'. Dowell, due to excessive naivety, thinks that her distress is caused solely by the fact that she is a Catholic in a Protestant stronghold, being taunted by Florence. Dowell does eventually discover Florence's duplicity; she does not have 'a heart' at all, but merely uses their separate bedrooms as an excuse to take other men into hers. On the night she sees herself as discovered by her husband, the same night that she sees herself as replaced in Ashburnham's affections by Nancy Rufford, Florence commits suicide. Nancy Rufford is the Ashburnhams' ward, and, towards the end of the chronological development of the tale, Edward does indeed conceive a passion for her. Rufford is a devout Catholic, and is devoted to her guardians, and to her faith. She, too, is ignorant as to the truths of human sexual behaviour that seethe through this text, to the extent that when she sees that truth, she loses her mind. She is sent away from Bramshaw Teleragh, the Ashburnhams' Hampshire house; Dowell accompanies her and Edward to the train station, and, shortly afterwards, Edward cuts his own throat. As the novel concludes, the hypocrisy of the upper-class 'game' of sexual infidelity has been exposed. Edward and Florence are dead as a result; Nancy is mad.

Dowell compares the destruction with the 'sack of the city' or the 'falling to pieces of a people'. Even to the attentive reader, it is only clear why when the last page is turned.

Ford adopts a method of 'supporting' many of his apparently oppositional characters, perhaps most visibly so in *The Good Soldier*. This novel is driven by knowledge and understanding, by issues of communication, not preconceived ideas of good and bad. Its character patterns are unpredictable, changing as one level of knowledge is placed upon, or ranged against, another. Here, Dowell thinks back to his moment of vision of his wife's hidden (only to him) character:

> No, I remember no emotion of any sort, but just the clear feeling that one has from time to time when one hears that some Mrs. So-and-So is *au mieux* with a certain gentleman. It made things plainer, suddenly, to my curiosity. It was as if I thought, at that moment, of a windy November evening, that, when I came to think it over afterwards, a dozen unexplained things would fit themselves into place. But I wasn't thinking things over then.[11]

Viewed in isolation, the lack of response in this passage seems pathological. Dowell stereotypes his feeling as akin to that of a society murmur. He relates no anguish, no pain, no disappointment, no anger: he attempts to incorporate it into his experiential history, without ever experiencing it. And this point is one of the clues to the novel as a whole. Nietzsche says of human existence that it is 'an imperfect tense that never becomes a present'[12] – as is precisely the case in the majority of this text. The imperfect tense dominates in Dowell's story because it is designed to short-circuit habitual responses. Dowell cannot be in complete control (for 'control' read 'sight/knowledge') of his present, for he is not in complete control of his past. He simply 'goes on'. Ford seems to be more interested in the confused impulses of Dowell's brain at this point, and in their relationship with its later impulses, than in the production of a state of mind that is, in whatever way, certain.[13]

In *The Good Soldier* Ford follows, he renders or alludes to, the deepest, perhaps secret motivations as characters relate to each other. He is not a hospitable novelist, but a demanding one: confusion and struggle with one's own memory of the narrative ('*Have* I read about this already?') are the most frequent states of mind for the reader of this text. The apparent incompleteness of the narrative has been discussed:

Dowell tells it in 'spots of colour'; his narrative has been read as an analysand's tale.[14] However, Ford has ways of suggesting what it is that Dowell doesn't, or cannot, say. Ford is busy communicating – as below Leonora is busy communicating, although they both adopt unorthodox means.

The following extract comes from towards the beginning of the novel, and doesn't make sense until near its end. Then it assumes its rightful linear position as the beginning of the end: 'Her eyes were enormously distended; her face was exactly that of a person looking into the pit of hell and seeing horrors there. And then suddenly she stopped. She was most amazingly, just Mrs. Ashburnham again' (p. 38). Leonora sees horrors that Dowell cannot – the fact that her husband intends to have sex with his wife (and, contrary to most analysis which focuses on the touch, it is Edward's *look* answering Florence's touch that convinces her[15]). Although Dowell is convinced by her excuse for her distress – she is a Catholic at Marburg – the reader senses that this is not the whole truth. Dowell, however, does not. His status as an innocent is often signalled by his visual, and thus dramatic, exclusion; Leonora's first look *at* him is like that of a lighthouse – she sees him completely, from every angle, dazzling him as she discovers the extent of his asexuality (she, then, should be the cubist narrator) (p. 29). Ever afterwards, to her, he is an 'invalid', not a man. His wife also has 'the seeing eye' (p. 16), and whilst it doesn't protect her from the late shock, which she gets 'in the face', of the 'beacon' of Edward's love for Nancy, it shows her that Dowell is a man who will willingly remain outside her bedroom door (pp. 76–7). The narrative levels thus expand, fragmented and differentiated, as are the characters, by sight or its lack in these instances, and Ford articulates the presence of that which is awful, incompletely. Perhaps he wants the reader to see self-inflicted horrors in Leonora's face, to guess at others, but perhaps he also simply wants him or her to wait, with Dowell, in that imperfect tense, delaying certainty.

In *Parade's End* (summarised later in this chapter), Ford's war tetralogy, sight fragments the narrative/cognitive levels, sometimes more completely. When Valentine sees Edith Duchemin 'mad before her', an explanation follows: Edith wants to know about abortion. With this sexual shock Valentine's fantasy of 'bright colonies of beings, chaste, beautiful in thought', surrounding Edith and her set, is destroyed; sex has intervened.[16] Her experience is like Nancy's, who reads the divorce report in the newspaper near the climax to *The Good Soldier*, and learns

something terrible about the truth of human sexual relationships from
what she sees (it leads to her madness). Dowell's wranglings with such
knowledge are more protracted.

A resultant effect of novelistic formations of this kind is a powerful
sense of drama. A series of events unfolds, sometimes excruciatingly
slowly, with emphasis on each link in the chain, and one must watch
carefully to try and ascertain the whole (cubist) picture. Indicative of
great attention to the psychological and sexual revelations of *The Good
Soldier* as each in turn rears its disturbed, disturbing head, it is these
aspects of the main characters that regale the reader's own consciousness: 'It was as if his passion for her hadn't existed; as if the very words
that he spoke, without knowing that he spoke them, created the passion
as they went along. Before he spoke, there was nothing; afterwards, it
was the integral part of his life' (p. 80). Surprised by his unconscious,
Edward Ashburnham is the living embodiment of the pluralistic power
of sexuality.[17] His response is involuntary and he follows the anterior
calling of his unconscious need: he knows not what he says. It is left to
Dowell to relate the shape of Edward's desire for Nancy, whom until
then he had regarded 'exactly as he would have regarded a daughter' (p.
77). Confused (incestuous) and conflicting emotional and sexual needs
are precipitated out of the convolutions of the text and then resub-
merged, to appear in other forms. Motivational understanding comes
much later; the unrelenting dramatic technique is paramount.

This technique is prefigured, in part, by Ford's trilogy *The Fifth
Queen* (1906–8), named for Catherine Howard (spelled 'Katharine' by
Ford), the fifth of Henry VIII's wives. This is, as a spectacular display,
a 'virtuoso performance – the first of Ford's great shows' in the opinion
of William Gass.[18] Less mature in this work, the drama is expressed by
Ford not in the tortuousness of human sexuality and despair, but in the
wealth of strong, and confrontational, characters; in the extent of visual
effect; in questions raised by belief. Politics and theology, in the time of
Henry VIII, were the big questions that shook the times and those who
inhabited them: these were the matters for debate. Ford's early novelistic mind interpreted and used these issues in the way that his later
novelistic mind interpreted and used sexuality. The vibrancy in the
historical novels is not that of emotion, but of the livid pregnancy of
detail. Gass warns of the need to watch closely, for '*The Fifth Queen*
[...] is like Eisenstein's *Ivan*: slow, intense, pictorial, and operatic.
Plot is both its subject and its method. Execution is its upshot and its
art. *The Fifth Queen* is like Verdi's *Otello*: made of miscalculation,

mismaneuver [*sic*], and mistake. Motive is a metaphor with its meaning sheathed like a dagger'. The need for such warning is exemplified in the following scene, in the menace implicit in King Henry's approach:

> The Duke, hearing behind him the swish pad of heavy soft shoes, as if a bear were coming over the pavement, faced the King.
>
> 'This is my brother's child,' he said. 'She is sore hurt. I would not leave her like a dog,' and he asked the King's pardon.
>
> 'Why, God forbid,' the King said. 'Your Grace shall succour her.'
>
> Culpepper had his back to them, caring nothing for either in his passion.
>
> Henry said: 'Aye, take good care for her,' and passed on with Privy Seal on his arm.
>
> The Duke heaved a sigh of relief. But he remembered again that Anne of Cleves was coming, and his black anger that Cromwell should thus once again have the King thrown back to him, came out in his haughty and forbidding tone to Culpepper:
>
> 'Take thou my niece to the water-gate. I shall send women to her.' He hastened frostily up the path to be gone before Henry should return again.[19]

Character, personality: neither of these more subtle tools are crucial here. The language is primitive – the scene takes place adjacent to the Thames – basic, sensual. The only reference to passion is made because Culpepper turns his back upon the main action, that of power and politics, as propagated by Henry VIII, and the Duke of Norfolk, Katharine's uncle.[20] Katharine's foray into the heart of her uncle is foreshortened by Norfolk's remembrance of the real issue at hand, that of the renewed power of Thomas Cromwell with the coming of Anne of Cleves. Ford's inhospitable novelistic behaviour makes an earlier appearance; the exploration of the brutal side of human sexuality in *The Good Soldier* resonates instead in the politically and visibly tormented protagonists of Tudor England.

For H. Robert Huntley, Ford's belief that 'successive historical ages produce different and dominant psychological types' is realised fictionally for the first time in the *Fifth Queen* trilogy.[21] It is in these novels that Ford begins to express fictionally a relationship between the systems of the time and those who live in them: Magister Udal is sly, greedy and predatory; it is only the elderly printer (unafraid for his life) who can afford to bemoan that 'in my day we could pray to St Leonard for a fair wind' (p. 7). Potential self-destruction lurks in any careless

act, and Ford investigates the external manifestations of political and
theological adherence to which he can later add the complications and
more internal tensions of sexual morality (sex does figure here, of
course, however). It is as though Ford has had to become the historian
of another time in order to learn more fully how to become a better,
more thorough, historian of his own time. The classifications pertaining to this period are comparatively clear: one risks death by the faith
one holds. Faith is thus of ultimate strength. The singular choice is
clear, visible; by the time of Dowell it has become plural, embedded
and complex.

The Fifth Queen is dedicated in some senses to discovering how
people experience their belief or faith, how they respond to what they
perceive as being larger and infinitely more permanent than themselves: their king and their God. Ford appears to revel in influential
ideologies, and in the shadows that they throw. There is room for an
author to move amidst such a tapestry of strongly and violently held
opinion. The times carry the plot. The semantic and physical environment is one of near-hysteria due to the power wielded by a religious
and paranoid king, a fact rendered dramatically so that its full
contrastive energies are felt – 'Katharine fell upon her knees before this
holy man' (p. 91). Similarly, she goes to her death 'slowly down over
the flags of the great hall. Her figure in black velvet was like a small
shadow, dark and liquid, amongst shadows that fell softly and like
draperies from the roof' (*Fifth Queen Crowned*, p. 313). The action
must be watched, for this is about the way in which people behave in
the face of situations; it is about how the light of favour falls.[22]
Katharine herself pays the ultimate price, hence Ford's interest in her,
for she will not repent.

The devotion of the human being, in droves, to a particular faith,
belief or pattern of behaviour is a source of inspiration and motivation
to Ford in the writing of this trilogy. Why?

> Of course [Lewis's] characters do indulge themselves in a great number of
> expository disquisitions but Mr. Lewis makes it sufficiently clear that he
> backs neither set of views when they do discourse. Thus, things remain
> very much as they were at the beginning and the final impression is one
> of a sort of solidarity of mankind from Altoona to the Adriatic and back.[23]

Ford admires Lewis for providing what amounts to a forum for debate
on human truths (see Chapter 7 for a discussion of this in relation to
Ford's autobiography and opinion of the novel as genre). It is a

dramatic, multiplicitous, exploration. Lewis does not need to make his personal feelings clear, and Ford, too, 'supports' all sides (as he usually does), relating the historical fact of the popular swing towards Katharine Howard and thus Catholicism and then away from her as she goes to the scaffold. Both faiths, indeed, are 'murdered'; things ultimately 'remain very much as they were at the beginning', as they do for Dowell.[24] The reader has been witnessing an exploration into what people need to believe, how they express it, what they will sacrifice for it, and how the power thus caused shifts and divides.

As is to be expected, Katharine Howard's story ends in her execution. By not renouncing her beliefs when pragmatism dictates, she sentences herself to death. The psycho-political geography of Ford's writing is thus confirmed in its period of relative certainty, especially when compared with the suicides of Edward and Florence in *The Good Soldier*, and the suicide of Tietjens's father in *Parade's End*. These later novels are distinguishable from the *Fifth Queen* trilogy primarily due to their more complex interweaving of levels.

Parade's End

Parade's End: plot

The four novels that make up this tetralogy follow Christopher Tietjens through his domestic, emotional, political and moral crises – crises that are held to be typical of the age. Arthur Mizener writes that 'the focus of our attention is on the slow, tortured process by which Christopher becomes consciously aware that the conventional life of Edwardian society no longer embodies the principles that it professes and that he has tried with such heroic literalness to live by' (p. 499). The text opens on Tietjens, on a train with his great friend Macmaster, as they travel to Rye to play golf. Things change very quickly, not least when suffragettes interrupt their round. Tietjens fights in the First World War – he is an officer, and suffers shell-shock, but this experience causes him arguably less pain than the cuckolding by his wife, Sylvia, and its concomitant, excessive, cruelty. He has a prospective lover, Valentine, but remains unable to make love to her for most of the tetralogy; he has friends who rely on him more than he can on them; his Tory, feudal attitude to his land, at Groby, is relentlessly challenged by the modern world. The narrative is told from a variety of perspectives, and shifts its geographical location regularly. The time shift is almost, but not quite, as pronounced as it is in *The Good Soldier*.

Roger Sale has claimed that 'Ford needs Sylvia just as he needs Valentine, as major alternative sources of energy and complication to set off against Tietjens'.[25] Ford thus arranges three textual interests as a typical paradigm. These interests are sexually connected, and although Tietjens finds himself at war, he expresses the main difficulties of his existence as those forced upon him by the question of sex. 'My problem will remain the same whether I'm here or not', says Tietjens to General Campion, of his presence at the front in France, 'For it's insoluble. It's the whole problem of the relations of the sexes' (p. 491). He doesn't even know that Campion is himself sexually linked with the most rabid protagonist in the sex paradigm, his own wife, Sylvia. The contemporary political and cultural 'trouble with women' was discussed in the Introduction. The war, according to some commentators, exacerbated it: 'the war had demolished the myth of female sexual apathy, since there had been so much evidence, and fear, of women's sexual activity'.[26] Cate Haste refers here to the 'fear', amongst certain men, of the 'new woman', and her threat to the status quo. It is hard to imagine a more sexually active woman in fiction than Sylvia Tietjens: sadist, serial adulteress, voyeur. It is also crucial that Tietjens's problem is 'the relation between the sexes'; what constituted the connection between masculinity and femininity was one of the most hotly debated sexological questions of the time – as I discuss later in this chapter.

It is the battlefield that best signifies Tietjens's movement through the novels, but it is a field that is established for the wrangles of domestic and sexual existence as well as of military power. Again, the language of physical geography is used as an effective analogy for the contemporary extending map of personal geography.[27] Sylvia, deprived of the object of her sadistic evisceration and driven by her sexual frustration, travels to France, augmenting the terror of the front with the terror of the sexual predator:

> Not one line of Tietjens's face had moved when he had received back his card. It had been then that Sylvia had sworn that she would yet make his wooden face wince...
>
> His face was intolerable. Heavy; fixed. Not insolent, but simply gazing over the heads of all things and created beings, into a world too distant for them to enter... And yet it seemed to her, since he was so clumsy and worn out, almost not sporting to persecute him. It was like whipping a dying bulldog... (p. 381)

The violence of the last image survives, despite the 'concessionary' attitude of which it is the product. The continuation dots propagate its life: Sylvia will institute it. The first continuation dots are also effective (and such a preferred technique) for they serve to symbolise the non-effectiveness of language in reaching and describing the levels of imagined suffering.

Graham Greene examines this multiplication of the zones of personal suffering: 'While a novel like *All Quiet on the Western Front* confined its horror to the physical, to the terrors of the trenches, so that it is even possible to think of such physical terrors as an escape for some characters from the burden of thought and mental pain, Ford turned the screw. Here there was no escape from the private life'.[28] Ford 'turned the screw', and wrote of the misery of two worlds instead of one. Tietjens is wrong when he simplifies this into one 'problem', of the 'relationship between the sexes'; the weight of the work is derived from the meticulous attention to both, and, more importantly, to the psychological interplay between them. The manifestation of fragmenting systems, the opening out of existential levels and the exhibition of the movement between them, the analysis of plural 'interests' as they make themselves known, are essential to Ford's fiction. The dramatic technique is pursued by him into the internal dynamic of a man's mind (think here of the discussion of fragmentation in Chapter 1):

> Back in his room under the rafters, Tietjens fell, nevertheless, at once a prey to real agitation. For a long time he pounded from wall to wall and, since he could not shake off the train of thought, he got out at last his patience cards, and devoted himself seriously to thinking out the conditions of his life with Sylvia. He wanted to stop scandal if he could; he wanted them to live within his income; he wanted to subtract that child from the influence of its mother. These were all definite but difficult things... Then one half of his mind lost itself in the rearrangement of schedules, and on his brilliant table his hands set queens on kings and checked their recurrences.
>
> In that way the sudden entrance of Macmaster gave him a really terrible physical shock. He nearly vomited: his brain reeled and the room fell about. He drank a great quantity of whisky in front of Macmaster's goggling eyes; but even at that he couldn't talk, and he dropped into his bed faintly aware of his friend's efforts to loosen his clothes. He had, he knew, carried the suppression of thought in his conscious mind so far that his unconscious self had taken command and had, for the time, paralysed both his body and his mind. (pp. 79–80)

This is the description of a nervous breakdown. W. H. R. Rivers wrote in 1920 that 'mental health depends on the presence of a state of equilibrium between instinctive tendencies and the forces by which they are controlled',[29] and in the psychoanalytic model of the mind a continual system of negotiations between the *id*, *ego* and *superego* is in operation. In Tietjens, balances have ceased to work. In the first line, the word 'nevertheless', between two commas, clearly decides the issue of self-control; Tietjens has lost it, for that word also signifies the concept 'despite himself'. Concentrated physical activity cannot restore his equilibrium and so he looks to planning his future life with Sylvia to escape his mental agitation. He decides what he wants, but the threefold repetition of that word seems to lessen its power; he can articulate the wants, but fears impotence in bringing them to fruition – 'These were all definite but difficult things ...'. He reaches an impasse.

And so he returns to his cards, and because his mind can achieve great things, one half of it dedicates itself to the brilliance of the table. The other half of it, for now, is unmentioned in order for the full irony of Macmaster's entrance to become apparent. When Macmaster does come in, the enormity of the effort it has taken to keep that other half silent shows itself in the physicality of the shock caused. Tietjens has been hovering on the edge of collapse, and in the presence of this catalyst he succumbs to it. Ford relates this collapse in quintessential manner, for, in the language he chooses, Tietjens seems almost to exceed normal human existence, rather than become less than it. Ford expands upon the expanding levels of the man. Tietjens's mind is working too fast for him to be able to talk, to control himself: even an enormous amount of tranquilliser in the form of whisky does not work. He is beyond talking, he is somehow above Macmaster's efforts to loosen his clothes, and the part of him that can now vaguely think is undergoing something like an out of body experience. The final sentence quoted splits him up into many parts – 'he had' is the experiential Tietjens, the living one; 'he knew' is the part of him that understands and comprehends the present paralysis.[30] This part sees the suppression of thought in his conscious mind, things being so 'difficult' and, more importantly, it sees the necessary and self-protective action of the unconscious in stepping forward and trying to shut everything down. To all intents and purposes, it succeeds: only one part remains functional, that which watches, cognitively – and that part seems to be beyond any feelings at all. Ford's shattering of the man into his constituent parts (using grammatical tools) mirrors the dissolution of the system of marriage that is its catalyst.[31]

Fifty pages earlier in the novel, Ford has related the above incident in a very different fashion, one that helps to give such weight and depth to the account above. At the point in question, Ford is a novelist merely describing a scene. Macmaster is seen to give Tietjens a start, but they manage a small conversation and there is no way of divining the extent of Tietjens's mental anguish. The external vision is ordinary; what is extraordinary is the technique of regressively pursuing the incident to a much more profound level. Ford's adoptive style is that of deepening the reader's understanding, making it more complex, rather than progressing it; he constructs parallel lines of narrative. These lines correspond to differing levels of consciousness, differing levels of communication, and perfectly complement the subject matter. The latter introduction of the deeper level of communication is similarly appropriate, for as Tietjens's unconscious moves forward to take control, so the reader is embedded more effectively, more complicatedly, in the tale.

The reader of *Parade's End* has been granted access to Tietjens's unbalanced mind. Ford reveals the inner workings of the human subject. *The Good Soldier* could be interpreted as an earlier version of this novelistic task.

In 1934 Ford claimed to 'sit frequently and dream of writing an immense novel in which all the characters should be great masses of people – or interests. You would have Interest A, remorselessly and under the stress of blind necessities, slowly or cataclysmically overwhelming Interest Z, without the attraction of sympathy for a picturesque or upright individual' (*It Was the Nightingale*, p. 215). I think he had already written this novel, though not in exactly the form he imagines here. In *The Good Soldier* the 'great masses of people' are absent, but the 'interests' are there; the interests may relate to characters, but they could map onto the psychic components of *id*, *ego* and *superego*. Interest A, compelled by destiny and blind, erotic necessity, is the *id*; Interest Z is the *ego*, negotiating (and fighting a losing battle) with the *id*; finally there is the forgotten *superego*, abandoned in its moral compunction in the primitiveness of the fight. As we know, conceptions of right and wrong have no place in this text; its *superego* is as yet fairly undeveloped. Instead the reader witnesses varieties of the *id* rampant (in Florence and Edward), with the *ego* just, at times, holding on to its coat-tails, its reality principle thrown into disarray by the libido's unfeasible strength. (Dowell offers a peculiar manifestation of this principle: he guards Florence's locked bedroom, enabling her to take as many lovers as she chooses. Leonora's manifestation of the reality principle poses more of a challenge.) Perhaps, though, the more effective reading pays attention to the characters' distinct and discrete contributions to what has become, in this text, a psycho-sexual debate.

Sex roles

Ford's reply to John Lane, his publisher, on hearing of a complaint against the subject matter of *The Good Soldier*, supports a reading of the novel as an indication of the plurality of the sex drive; 'that work', Ford explains, 'is as serious an analysis of the polygamous desires that underlie all men [...] as 'When Blood is their Argument' is an analysis of Prussian Culture' (Saunders I, p. 403). A current Ford would add 'and women' to that statement of intent (Florence, after all, enjoys many sexual encounters, Dowell none), one that reveals his professional dedication to his subject matter: it is serious, academic, investigative, and it seeks to portray the contemporary chaos caused by the sex debate in all its polymorphous glory.

The fight for understanding is terrible in *The Good Soldier*, fuelled by a force that it shares with sexuality: matter for understanding always has to do with sex. Dowell here struggles with two manifestations of the sex instinct:

> If poor Edward was dangerous because of the chastity of his expressions – and they say that is always the hall-mark of a libertine – what about myself? For I solemnly avow that not only have I never so much as hinted at an impropriety in my conversation in the whole of my days; and more than that, I will vouch for the cleanness of my thoughts and the absolute chastity of my life. At what, then, does it all work out? Is the whole thing a folly and a mockery? Am I no better than a eunuch or is the proper man – the man with the right to existence – a raging stallion forever neighing after his neighbour's womankind? (p. 15)

This is a pathetic struggle. Dowell embraces an intellectual approach, yet he evokes a Lawrentian image of primitive sexuality, rendered all the more desireable in this expression by a man inappropriate to its demands. Dowell feels its strength, or, rather, the metaphorical strength of its expression, and simultaneously cannot feel it: he is one stage removed. His pitiable need for self-justification renders him in awe of the power to which he can only allude. This patterning of allusion and reflection evokes *his* vision of *Leonora's* vision of 'the pit of hell'. Dowell flounders then, as he flounders now, equipped only to watch open mouthed as sexual terror is wrought through another, whether it be the metaphorical stallion or the tortured and impotent woman. In the proliferations of fecundity, in the maelstrom of deception and desire, sexual knowledge, naivety and excruciating sexual cruelty, a question is found; it is not which man has the right to existence, but which projection, which human manifestation, of the sex drive.

'In the nineteenth century', writes Joseph Bristow, 'the idea that the sexes were polar opposites magnetically attracted to each another had a tight ideological grip on the culture'. He suggests that even such 'sex radicals' as Karl Heinrich Ulrichs and Edward Carpenter conceived of the distinctions between the sexes in 'strikingly orthodox terms'.[32] However, in 1903 Otto Weininger produced a (more populist) work on the subject. *Sex and Character* sold extremely well, and contributed to what has been called Weininger's 'cult' status in Austro-German intellectual life, as well as having a much wider cultural impact.[33] In this book, as part of a thesis concerning the supposed decline of modern civilisation, Weininger suggests that the sexes are not, in fact, polar opposites, but are rather like 'two substances combined in different proportions'.[34] Ford read Weininger's text.[35] In *The Good Soldier* he provides examples of differently mixed proportions of masculinity and femininity: all four protagonists manifest a singular (though changeable) combination, equating them with either a 'eunuch' or a 'raging stallion' or their female equivalents.

Ford has animated his characters with proportions of masculinity and femininity, of libidinous capacity, that will cause a massive implosion once all is known. Until that time, when suicide curtails the battle, the shifting systems of psychological and sexual knowledge and control can be likened to the display of Tietjens's fragmented mind, when one elemental force wrestles with its 'neighbour' – back to the psychological imaging. Dowell is like the side of Tietjens's brain that seeks ignorance in the card game whilst Florence, Leonora and Edward whirl around one another, advocating varying levels of sexual expression, from cold and punitive abstention to the suggestion of enjoying one another in secret. Ford is not advocating free love; he has no moral stance, but he is attempting to show how life is – in this respect concerning himself with the reality of 'polygamous desire'. Foucault was cited in Chapter 1 to show that fragmentation comes out of repression lifting: with an increase in questioning comes a multiplication of possibilities and a collapse of what can be taken for granted. Dowell is the foil for the non-repression of the other three, for he doesn't know about sex, and takes Florence's chastity for granted, validating the 'game' – as she takes numerous lovers behind her locked door. When he can no longer ignore how it is, so the whole hypocritical edifice collapses.

Tietjens undergoes a similar discovery, much to Macmaster's discomfort, and advocates honesty instead of hypocrisy: 'it would be better [for a fellow] just to boast about his conquests in a straightforward and exultant way' he exhorts (p. 18). He has no illusions as to the effect this would have on the upper-class 'game',[36] or system, as understood, and relied upon, by Macmaster, by Edward and Florence, and by Leonora: it would destroy it, and in the apprehension of this destruction Macmaster is reduced to an inarticulate and spluttering rage. Tietjens is not playing the game when he challenges Macmaster thus:

> 'It's like you polygamists with women. There aren't enough women in the world to go round to satisfy your insatiable appetites. And there aren't enough men in the world to give each woman one. And most women want several. So you have divorce cases. I suppose you won't say that because you're so circumspect and right there shall be no more divorce? Well, war is as inevitable as divorce...' (p. 21)[37]

Macmaster, unable to take any more, has caused those ellipses. He escapes, interrupting the psychological battering he is receiving from Tietjens by putting his head out of the carriage window to call for a porter. One might equally interpret this as a call for help from Macmaster's view of the status quo. Yet war, and divorce, are come to fragment it.

Pre-war, the challenge to the polygamists is rarely so vocal and certain, and, due in part to the narrative style, the levels of intimacy created between the four protagonists of *The Good Soldier* undermine the differences between them. This intimacy is of an incestuous strength. As Leonora turns her lighthouse stare upon Dowell he writes that it was 'the look of a mother to her son, of a sister to her brother. It implied trust; it implied the want of any necessity for barriers' (p. 29). Leonora thus merges the love of mother for a son, the love of a sister for a brother – although Dowell may simply not recognise the difference. This incestuous sense translates into the sexual relations between the four figures. Leonora and Dowell do not copulate, true – and nor do Dowell and Ashburnham. And yet Dowell says of Edward, in terms reminiscent of Cathy's transgressional love for Heathcliff, 'For I can't conceal from myself the fact that I loved Edward Ashburnham – and that I loved him because he was just myself' (p. 161).[38]

Such intimacy shortens the perspective; it exacerbates the narrative chaos. Even Dowell understands that sex has an impact on the human subject, musing that 'a love affair, a love for any definite woman – is something in the nature of a widening of the experience ... there appears to come a broadening of the outlook, or, if you like, an acquiring of new territory' (p. 79). With each sexual experience comes a concomitant development in the character, an increase of knowledge. What Dowell doesn't, and cannot, completely understand, is how devastating the acquisition of this new territory can be.

Ford's framework

In his book *Beginnings: Intention and Method*, Edward Said draws Freud into the history of the novel and regards his function primarily as a writer (see Chapter 1). Said says of Freud that 'for "dreams" we can easily imagine substituting the word "fiction", for "distortion" the "point of view", for "regression" and "condensation" the term "biography", for "parents" the novelistic "family" and so on'.[39] In Said's view (and in the view of many others) the writing of fiction can be linked to the interpretation of the unconscious. To prove his point, he conflates the independent languages associated with the two disciplines and shows that, in certain cases, they are interchangeable. Said, using Freud, introduces the idea of interpreting the patterns of fiction as though they were the symbol of something deeper. Within the text of *The Good Soldier* Ford pays attention, employing delaying tactics, to the nature of his characters as they perform, ignore, are jealous and frantic about, repress, sex. In the battle just witnessed in *Parade's End*, Macmaster's conscious systems of will, and 'proper' behaviour, have been challenged by Tietjens's attention to the less conscious systems of desire. In *Parade's End* the issue is clear; in *The Good Soldier* it rarely is so. Why? 'A way of breaking through the barrier is to be found', Said might suggest,

> in Freud's interpretation of the Oedipus story – specifically, in a footnote that he added in 1914 and that was apparently the section of his text that provoked the most controversy [...]. Once again Freud draws attention to a type of knowledge so devastating as to be unbearable in one's sight,

and only slightly more bearable as a subject of psychological interpretation. In essence, this knowledge is of incest, which can be very correctly
described as a tangling of the family sequence [...]. What overwhelms
Oedipus is the burden of plural identities incapable of coexisting within
one person. (pp. 169–70)

The 'barrier' Said refers to in the first line describes a 'tangle' which
resists interpretation. In Freud's work, this usually presents itself in
the form of a dream, or part of a dream, which stubbornly remains
obscure (Dowell dreams of course), but it can be translated into
fictional terms, using Said's model, as representing secrets of motivation and what is yet deeper, sexual desire. In *The Good Soldier* the
narrative structure both occludes, and alludes to, desire and sex. At
its heart is the possibility of incest (see Saunders I, pp. 420–7). If the
subject matter of the novel were examined without the protective
barriers provided by the text – the novelistic (modernist) technique
of time-shift that delays the true impact of each revelation; the narrator's predominant calm which softens each blow; and the general
refusal of the characters to discuss what is going on – it would emerge
as singularly Freudian in its distastefulness. As it eventually does. Is
Ford attempting to contain the barest and most basic forces that he
sees at work within humanity by placing them within story, and
within this kind of story, in this way? Is he attempting to render them
more cunningly than if they were overt, stark, and thus more easily
dismissable? Perhaps. But he is also being true to the nature of his
exploration, for the levels amongst which he explores are those of the
normally functioning, repressive and expressive human mind. As
Saunders writes, 'Ford's description of [*The Good Soldier*'s] "intricate
tangle of references and cross-references" cannot be bettered for its
tangling together of terms of technique and psychological bafflement'
(Saunders I, p. 402). The subject matter requires a certain style, and
it is the 'tangle' that resists interpretation that it requires.

Despite the view of the *New Statesman* in 1923 that 'we are all
psycho-analysts now. That is to say that it is as difficult for an educated
person to neglect the theories of Freud and his rivals as it would have
been for his father to ignore the theories of Darwin',[40] there was fierce
public resistance to much of what Freud was trying to say (see Chapter
1). The classical story of Oedipus shaped Freud's thought in an
example of adroit design; the design of *The Good Soldier* is similarly
adroit, created to avoid a too swift denial of the force of the subject, and
to lodge it in the less conscious minds of its readers in the battle with

its tangles. But despite these attempts, if attempts they were, both to be truthful to the nature of the material, and to assure the longevity of his worrying hypotheses, Ford also met much opposition to the substance of his work. People often did not like what they read. Three contemporary reviews of *The Good Soldier* follow, reviews that emanated from both sides of the Atlantic:

> The novel may be called 'realistic' – with all the limitations of the term. This realism and consistency are the sole virtues of the story. The portrayal of marital infidelity is dangerous enough even when delicately handled, and for the written page to linger upon the indelicacies of intrigue [...] there is no excuse whatever.[41]

> Its plot is most unsavoury [...] whereas Mr. James concerns himself with the minds and motives of his characters, Mr. Hueffer is concerned with their actions, deducing their psychology from what they do rather than from what they think.[42]

> We can well imagine that the work will prove of some value to the specialist in pathology.[43]

Though these reviews do not constitute the complete critical response to Ford's novel, what is interesting is that they all concern themselves with the morality of the text. The reviewers all adopt a moral position from which they judge Ford's vision of current life. Ford is providing what could be described as an unwelcome challenge that unsettles; he is taking the novel to a new place in its relation to society. All three reviewers are condemnatory of behaviour that defies restrictions and breaks boundaries, of action as opposed to the relative safety of cerebral emphasis. Ford is telling it as it is, not as it should be; thus he puts his belief in the novel and its relation to society, discussed at the outset of this chapter, into practice.

Said states that the Oedipus story is not simply about the factual horror of what he does (although this is enough to make him put out his eyes); it also displays 'the burden of plural identities incapable of coexisting within one person'. Ford's story also represents the different manifestations of a man, and indicates the unimaginable pain caused by their dislocation and totalitarian action. There are implications of incest in *The Good Soldier*; the characters could be said each to represent part of the same psyche; death, madness and suicide crown the tale. Finally, in a stunning allusion to the matter, if not the exact occurrence,[44] of Sophocles's text, Dowell muses, once he can reveal all: 'I think that it would have been better in the eyes of God if they had all

attempted to gouge out each other's eyes with carving knives' (p. 158).
'Better' it would have been, maybe, but also impossible; for they had no
'God' to show them how it would go. Instead, they are left, in a phrase
that Dowell repeats, 'under four eyes' – of judgement, of their better
selves, or, ultimately, for those who avoid death or madness, of
memory.

Saunders has examined the links between Ford's thought and that of
Freud, concluding that 'there is no record of Ford's having read Freud'
(Saunders I, p. 425). However, Freud's influence on the thought
processes of Tietjens's son, as he thinks about his mother and about
sex, is pronounced: 'The dominion of women over those of the opposite sex was a terrible thing. He had seen the General wimper like a
whipped dog and mumble in his poor white moustache... Mother was
splendid. But wasn't sex a terrible thing... His breath came short' (p.
713). The boy both sees and condones his mother's sexual cruelty, a
cruelty that has been evoked in exactly the same words when applied to
her treatment of his father. His sexually triumphant mother is splendid, and she excites him, 'his breath came short'. Sylvia would approve
of this; after all, she has said herself, '"I prefer to pin my faith to Mrs.
Vanderdecken. And, of course, Freud"' (p. 37). In this world of collaps-
ing faiths, Sylvia has found hers. As discussed in Chapter 1, this is an
intially fragmenting faith, based on communication and on narrative.
As such, it is peculiarly resonant in *The Good Soldier*, due to the sheer
irredeemable scale of tragedy, the confusion and repression and
manipulation of sexual identities, and the obscurantist nature and the
dualistic technique of the text.

The tragedy of *The Good Soldier* is indeed irredeemable; the design of
the text is such that it resists, in the dynamic between knowledge and
ignorance, revelation and implication, 'easy' incorporation by the
reader. This is partly out of a dedication on Ford's part to expressing
the true, multiple nature of his subject. But Allen Tate suggests that
'*The Good Soldier* falls short of tragic action', because 'it is Ford's great
theme that tragic action must be incomplete in a world that does not
allow the hero to take the full Oedipean responsibility for the evil that
he did not intend but that he has nevertheless done'.[45] Not only is the
reader encouraged to keep the subject matter alive, therefore, and
effective, but the characters are similarly encouraged. Unable to take
responsibility, and to atone, for their sins (unable to put a symbolic end
to what they have seen), they guarantee incompleteness. The matter
of the book holds onto its animated existence. It cannot be put away.

This stubborn non-closure takes the end of this chapter back to its beginning. Ford has found the perfect way to make his novels live, and be fragmentingly true, in modernist fashion, to the 'whole man alive'.[46] In Robert Grimshaw of *A Call*, the subject of my next chapter, the fragmenting systems of Edwardian society are used to communicate an alternative version of this novelistic task. The extent of the threat posed by women is explored, and the individual battle with sexual identity is further explained.

Notes

1 D. H. Lawrence, 'Why the Novel Matters' in Anthony Beale (ed.), *Selected Literary Criticism D. H. Lawrence* (London, Heinemann, 1967). This essay was published posthumously in 1936.

2 Christopher Gillie, *Movements in English Literature 1900–1940* (Cambridge, Cambridge University Press, 1975), p. 11.

3 Alan Judd, *Ford Madox Ford* (London, HarperCollins, 1990), p. 169.

4 See Saunders I, pp. 247–8, 297–8.

5 Ford Madox Ford, review in *Bookman* 69, April 1929, p. 191.

6 Ford Madox Ford, *Joseph Conrad: A Personal Remembrance* (New York, Ecco, 1989), p. 178.

7 These four novels are: *Some Do Not...* (London, Duckworth, 1924); *No More Parades* (London, Duckworth, 1925); *A Man Could Stand Up-* (London, Duckworth, 1926); *Last Post* (London, Duckworth, 1928).

8 Ford Madox Ford, *It Was the Nightingale* (1934) (New York, Ecco, 1984), p. 199.

9 Sondra Stang (ed.), *The Presence of Ford Madox Ford* (Pennsylvania, University of Pennsylvania Press, 1981), p. xxvi.

10 Ford Madox Ford, *A Call* (1910) (Manchester, Carcanet, 1984), epistolary epilogue.

11 Ford Madox Ford, *The Good Soldier* (1915), Martin Stannard (ed.) (New York and London, Norton, 1995), p. 73.

12 Friedrich Nietzsche, 'The Use and Abuse of History' in Oscar Levy (ed.), *Complete Works of Friedrich Nietzsche*, Vol. 5, ii, *Thoughts Out of Season* (Edinburgh, T. N. Foulis, 1909), p. 7.

13 No, he is not interested in certainty, and neither was the literary tradition to which he had come. Think of the framing of *Heart of Darkness*, of the train-enabled town and country conflict in *Howards End*, of the multiple viewpoints of *Dubliners* (which appeared as *The Good Soldier* was being written, in June 1914).

14 See Peter Childs, *Modernism* (London, Routledge, 2000), p. 52; Saunders I, p. 456; and the Introduction here.

15 'And then – smash – it all went. It went to pieces at the moment when Florence laid her hand upon Edward's wrist. Or rather, it went when she noticed the look in Edward's eyes as he gazed back into Florence's. She knew that look' (p. 123).

16 Ford Madox Ford, *Parade's End* (Harmondsworth, Penguin, 1988), pp. 229–31.

17 The text is linked in this way, as Saunders avers, to the controversial work of sexologists Edward Carpenter and Havelock Ellis (I, p. 427).

18 William Gass, 'The Neglect of the Fifth Queen' in Stang (ed.), *Presence of Ford Madox Ford*, p. 35.

19 Ford Madox Ford, *The Fifth Queen: and How She Came to Court* (London, Alston Rivers, 1906), p. 49. This is the first volume of the trilogy. Volume 2 (*Privy Seal*) was published in 1907, Volume 3 (*The Fifth Queen Crowned*) was published in 1908.

20 Whereas *A Call* had the subtitle *The Tale of Two Passions*, and *The Good Soldier* that of *A Tale of Passion*.

21 H. Robert Huntley, 'Ford, Holbein and Dürer', *South Atlantic Bulletin* 30: 4–6, May 1965.

22 When Katharine comes to confess, she halts at 'the edge of the sunlight'; when Henry tries to persuade her to retract, 'she confronted him, being in the shadow' (*Fifth Queen Crowned*, pp. 302, 305). On Katharine's final exit, Ford concentrates on the sound of her departure (p. 314).

23 *Bookman* review, pp. 191–2.

24 'Here I am', Dowell says, at the end of the novel, 'very much where I started thirteen years ago' (p. 151).

25 Stang (ed.), *Presence of Ford Madox Ford*, p. 75.

26 Cate Haste, *Rules of Desire: Sex in Britain World War I to the Present* (London, Pimlico, 1992), p. 56.

27 I refer the reader to chapter 4 ('Maps') of Allyson Booth's *Postcards from the Trenches: Negotiating the Space Between Modernism and the First World War* (Oxford, Oxford University Press, 1996). Her analysis includes metaphorical and symbolic uses of maps at war and in fiction; she also adopts a more historical approach.

28 Stang (ed.), *Presence of Ford Madox Ford*, p. 10.

29 W. H. R. Rivers, *Instinct and the Unconscious: A Contribution to a Biological Theory of the Psycho-Neuroses*, 2nd edn (Cambridge, Cambridge University Press, 1922, p. 119. In *The Problem of Nervous Breakdown* (London, Mills and Boon, 1919), Edwin Ash calls the chapter on cure 'Redressing the Balance' (p. 173).

30 In an emulation of this narrative structure, which reveals the different parts of a man's mind, Ford pushes Tietjens into battle with the possibility of sexual union with Valentine, 'She loved him, he knew, with a deep, an unshakeable passion' (p. 214). That 'he knew' displays his continued

fragmentation, his mental delay and moral debate, for he is still unable, and remains unable for hundreds of pages of the book, to make love to her.

31 In 1912 Ford wrote on the subject of marriage that 'on the one hand, it is appalling that any two incompatible beings should be tied together; on the other, it is abhorrent that any two beings joined together by the Lord should be severed by mortal means. The State should render divorce as easy as possible. The Churches should continue to punish with the threat of Hell any of their communicants who infringe their marriage laws. Society should go along doing what it does – ignoring, as far as possible, the decrees of Church and State' ('Church, State, and Divorce' in *The Bystander*, 24 January 1912, pp. 188–9).

32 Ulrichs produced a detailed typology of sexual variation between 1864 and 1879 (including male homosexuality); Carpenter published three pamphlets in 1894 that were concerned with sex and sexual behaviour. See Joseph Bristow, *Sexuality* (London, Routledge, 1997), pp. 19–25.

33 Editors' introduction to extract from *Sex and Character* in Charles Harrison and Paul Wood (eds), *Art in Theory: 1900–1990* (Oxford and Cambridge, MA, Blackwell, 1995), p. 34. The editors also term the work 'violently misogynistic and anti-Semitic'.

34 Otto Weininger, *Sex and Character* (New York, AMS Press, 1975), p. 8. 'Thanks to *Sex and Character*', celebrates Gunnar Brandell, 'the name of Freud and something of his theories for the first time reached a broad and interested public' (*Freud: A Man of His Century*, Brighton, Harvester Press, 1979, p. 27).

35 See his disparaging mention of it in *Women and Men* (Paris, Three Mountains Press, 1923, p. 32), a work that also addresses stereotypical male and female behaviour; refer also Saunders I, p. 336.

36 Of her inability to take a lover adulterously, Leonora says 'That certainly wasn't playing the game was it now?' (*The Good Soldier*, p. 13). This 'game' is the collective noun for what Dowell calls a 'whole collection of rules' applying to class structure, behaviour and that which one can take for granted about one's fellow man. The rules are no longer clear or dependable in the world that he sees.

37 I want to extract two further points from this quotation: the first is the mention of the polygamy of women, ten years on from Ford's letter to John Lane; the second is the fact that the war has appeared in their discussion. In the same way that Macmaster cannot accept the end of the sex game as he knows it, and the resultant necessity for divorce, he also cannot accept the thought of war.

38 'He shall never know how I love him', cries Cathy, 'and that [...] because he's more myself than I am'. Emily Brontë, *Wuthering Heights* (Harmondsworth, Penguin, 1961), p. 80.

39 Edward Said, *Beginnings: Intentions and Method* (Columbia, Columbia University Press, 1985), pp. 161–2.
40 Quoted in Samuel Hynes, *A War Imagined: The First World War and English Culture* (London, Pimlico, 1992), p. 366.
41 *Boston Transcript*, 17 March 1915.
42 *Outlook* (London) XXXV, 17 April 1915.
43 *Bookman* (London) XLVIII, 117, July 1915.
44 Allen Tate discusses why this inexactitude is deliberate on the part of the author, but nonetheless intentionally evocative of Sophocles's text (see p. 60). John Meixner's reading of the novel foregrounds its 'visceral intensity', an intensity that is 'completely unknown to James – one we are more likely to associate with the Greeks'. John A. Meixner, 'The Saddest Story' in Richard Cassell (ed.), *Ford Madox Ford: Modern Judgements* (London, Macmillan, 1972), p. 70.
45 Stang (ed.), *Presence of Ford Madox Ford*, p. 13.
46 Lawrence, 'Why the Novel Matters', p. 105.

3

Personal perspectives

A Call: The Tale of Two Passions, was published in 1910, and declares its interest in the plurality of passion in its title. A splintered image of the protagonist emerges early on: Grimshaw's father was English, his mother Greek; orphaned at 3, he was adopted by relations who also died; Greek Orthodox until public-school age, he assumed the mantle of the Church of England on entering Winchester; when older, close friendships with women confuse further an inability to decide which of them he desires – and whether he can legitimately pursue them. Grimshaw's ideas of civilised society, of received opinion, offer him safety from knowing his own fragmentation. But *A Call* ejects him from this safety zone. As it does so it evokes previously addressed issues in a concentrated context: the levels of narrative that reflect the plural truths of existence; the role of female sexuality in provoking them; the fragmenting qualities of sight in Ford's modern world – particularly when related to psychology. Arthur Mizener claims that *A Call* 'conveys feeling with a Jamesian minimum of dramatic gesture, the faintest of smiles, the simplest of words, the slightest gesture', and whilst the comparison with James is well-judged, Mizener misses the edge to this text, one that raises its game and enables comparison of its drama with that of *The Good Soldier* and *Parade's End*.[1]

Freud has much to say of the active implications of 'civilized society'. This society is one that

> demands good conduct and does not trouble itself about the instinctual basis of this conduct, [and] has thus won over to obedience a great many people who are not in this following their own natures. Encouraged by this success, society has allowed itself to be misled into tightening the moral standard to the tightest possible degree, and it has thus forced its members into a yet greater estrangement from their instinctual disposition.[2]

Freud draws attention in his famous essay to the possible human cost of the gradual restriction of individual natures. In this chapter I focus on one of Ford's fictional creations that plays out this problem. Sondra Stang says of Ford's novels that

> during the same years Freudianism came to dominate our psychology – Ford gave us some of the most powerful delineations we have of repressed feeling, and the questions he raised about the cost of civilization to the individual personality were questions raised by Freud after *The Good Soldier* was written [and therefore long after the publication of *A Call*] and made more familiar to us from our reading of 'Civilization and Its Discontents'.[3]

She suggests that, as a novelist, he foraged for material alongside (and ahead of) Freud. Part of Ford's achievement in *The Good Soldier* involves tracing to its logical, violent conclusions a hypocritical pattern of existence where 'good people' (society people, civilised people) also follow their instincts. *A Call* similarly investigates the repression of instincts, mental breakdown, and, in greater detail than *The Good Soldier*, the new threat of the 'New Woman'.[4] Karl Kraus referred to the new twentieth century as the 'vaginal century';[5] *A Call* suggests some reasons as to why. It goes about its work in a less embedded and convoluted style than *The Good Soldier* – though Ford does employ time shift to reflect accurately the way in which the characters come to knowledge. And in this text, more than in others so far examined, it is possible to look closely at the fragmentation that occurs as repression is confronted. Dowell has had 'eye-openers enough' on the day he is married; when Florence is taken ill on ship, doctors suggest he shouldn't exert his marital privileges. Fearful of sex, Dowell is positively eager to comply.[6] Grimshaw is also terrified by the instinctual self he is forced to face in Ford's text; yet there is no ship's doctor, no 'get-out clause', for him.

Blind but august destiny

Although Ford takes care to point out that his job as impressionist novelist of *A Call* is to render, not to 'comment nor to explain', he is being disingenuous.[7] He does believe in intent, and shows how in his critical, some would say adulatory, work on Henry James. In confident and generous style, Ford describes 'Mr. James' as having

> never committed the sin of writing what he 'wanted' to write. If you ever chance to make, to an English novelist, any objections to parts of his work

– he will, your English friend, reply that he 'wanted' to write it; as who should say he wanted to get it off his chest. That of course is a very reliev-ing process for the novelist; as for the individual may be the practice of expectoration in public places. To the community, as to literature, it is death. The novelist is not there to write what he 'wants' but what he *has*, at the bidding of blind but august Destiny to set down. Not what he wants but what he *can*, finally and consummately, put on paper is the final duty of the writer.[8]

Ford does not seem to be as clearly on one side of this equation as the level of his rhetoric implies. He is trying to range his concept of autho-rial integrity against that of 'wanting' to construct a text, but the two components become indistinct. A post-Freudian reading of 'blind but august Destiny' would identify the unconscious as the 'writer' – this is a phrase Ford often repeats. And yet he criticises the possibility of writing providing relief through the liberation of the unconscious: to write to 'get it off the chest' is no way to write. There is an explanation for this apparent paradox.

In the final discussion in Chapter 2, Ford was seen to aim for the location of his material at an unconscious level in his readers, where it would worry, and fester, and not easily be dismissed. The concept of relief in this instance is not, in Ford's mind, to do with the liberation of the writer's unconscious: for Ford words should continue to affect their readers. What he is saying, therefore, is that conscious digressions, added to a text for no other reason than a predilection for the topic on the part of the writer, have no place in the novel. They would weaken its overall effect, being easily assimilated by the reader and then, presumably, forgotten. Ford is looking for writing that is driven at the behest of 'blind but august Destiny', not the dictates of conscious intent. This is the rationale behind the distinction between 'want' and 'can'. He is advocating, then, in his own language, writing that emerges from the unconscious.

Ford is thus talking about rules: rules for the construction of a text – 'Destiny', not conscious wants, should dictate writing – and rules as they pertain to the unconscious. His statement can be added to those discussing the novel in Chapter 2: the novelist (particularly the modernist, impressionist novelist) must maintain an allegiance to the depths, rather than to the surfaces, of human psychology and experi-ence. Ford does have an aim: to listen to, and to communicate, the bidding of destiny. In *A Call*, as he manifests that aim, he also places himself in the tradition of the modernist writer as expressed by Unger:

modernism puts received conceptions of personality and society to the
test, forcing us to purge them of arbitrarily restrictive assumptions about
the limits of personal and social experience or about the ways that we may
moderate the conflict between the enabling circumstances of self-assertion [...]. We advance in self-understanding and goodness by opening
ourselves up to the whole life of personal encounter.[9]

Ford experiments with the truly naked, fragmented, man.

A Call

At the beginning of the novel, Robert Grimshaw presides over the
wedding, one that he has precipitated, of Dudley Leicester and Pauline
Lucas, his best friend and the woman that he loves. Shortly afterwards
he goes to the railway station to see them off on their honeymoon. Both
are deeply traumatic circumstances for him, but he does not recognise
the trauma. This task is left to Ellida Langham, sister to another
woman, Katya, with whom Grimshaw shares 'a history':

> It is not to be imagined that Ellida did anything so unsubtle as to put
> these feelings of hers, even to herself, into words. They found vent only in
> the way her eyes, compassionate and maternal, rested on his brooding
> face. Indeed, the only words she uttered, either to herself or to him, were,
> with deep concern – he had taken off his hat to ease the pressure of blood
> in his brows – as she ran her fingers gently through his hair: 'Poor old
> Toto!'
>
> He remained lost in his abstraction, until they were almost at her door.
> Then he squared his shoulders and resumed his hat.
>
> 'Yet I'm sure I was right,' he said. 'Just consider what it was up to me
> to do... I want to see to it that Pauline has a good time, and I want to see
> her having it.'
>
> 'How can she have it if you've given her Dudley Leicester when she
> wants you?'
>
> 'My dear child', he answered, and he had become again calm, strong,
> and infinitely lofty. 'Don't you understand that's how Society has to go
> on? It's the sort of thing that's got to happen to make us the civilised
> people that we are.' (pp. 22–3)

In this passage Ford aggravates the patterning of gendered themes. The
exchange between the two characters occurs in passages and words that
echo one another in naturally opposite ringing formalisations: she
advocates emotion, he rationalisation; she is maternal, he self-
absorbed; she talks of wants, he of society. The stereotype of the

male–female divide is powerfully drawn – we could almost be faced with a regurgitated *Lancet* article that cited the female as 'an animal in which the evolutionary process has been arrested or, more accurately, diverted from the general to the particular'.[10] He generalises, she does not; he abstracts, she feels instead. Speech finds its equally significant partner in silence, for Grimshaw only speaks when he has reached the relative safety of her door, where she will leave him: rationalism and passion each have their ordered place. And yet, despite the stereotypical gender-specifics of their debate, his need for a patronising, public and blustering unselfconscious stance seems to pale beside her measured self-sufficiency. She is calm with her emotion, he passionate as he rejects feeling. The existential picture of this text, as it begins to emerge, is a complex one. It is a picture that develops fastest when female characters are part of the scene.

Grimshaw, for a time, allows himself to need comfort after he has carried out his crucial decision to encourage this marriage. Ellida, wisely, says almost nothing to him; she comforts him, holding him with her eyes, validating his experience only by witnessing it.[11] It is unlike Robert Grimshaw to brood. The fact that he is quiet for a time now is testimony to the difficulty of the scene that he has just witnessed. Watching Pauline and Leicester pull away together into a future that he could have had for himself proves a blow strong enough to make him physically react. He removes his hat – signifier of society (he is an expert on dress codes) – to ease the thumping pressure of the blood in his temples, the signifier of his instinctual life. Grimshaw has only been seen by Ellida to be feeling and suffering like this because he is 'lost in his abstraction', unaware of how he is displaying himself. Only in time of uncontrolled mental activity is such feeling expressed. 'The unconscious is what we know about when defences break down', claims Adam Phillips,[12] and Ford indicates Grimshaw's unconscious in this Jamesian, understated way; later it will make a much more dramatic appearance. In the collecting action with which he replaces his hat and simultaneously his rationality, he begins to talk once more, asserting the impeccable correctness of his behaviour. In the eyes of 'Society' he is beyond reproach – 'Yet I'm sure I was right', he states.

Ellida does begin to question him; her daring suggestion that his actions are less than explicable provokes a swell to such enormous proportions of patronising energy that he almost fulfils the projected grandeur of his statement: 'My dear child. Don't you understand that's how Society has to go on? It's the sort of thing that's got to happen to make us the civilised people that we are.' Her muted opposition spurs him on to redefine and rediscover his public existence: governed behaviour, in Grimshaw's eyes, is and should be expertly constraining – it is Freud's 'civilized society'. Should he ever find himself in doubt as to the strength of 'Society', Ford grants him an additional religious role to bolster his resistance to instinct.

'Religious ideas have arisen', Freud tells us, 'from the same need as have all the other achievements of civilization: from the necessity of defending oneself against the crushingly superior force of nature.'[13] Though in one moving episode Grimshaw encounters the faith of his childhood in the form of an Orthodox priest, it is really Grimshaw himself who tries to function as God in this text. Not only is he a character who manipulates, who decides, who directs action; he is also described as 'Sultan father-confessor', 'father protector' and 'God Almighty' himself (pp. 94–6). *Mr Fleight*, a slightly later novel, contains the fearsome Mr Blood, here described by Fleight: '"Of course, you are a most wonderful man! It's astounding how things fall out as you predict"'.[14] Predictions are also one of Grimshaw's particular talents: 'His eyes wandered over the form of a lady who passed them in earnest conversation with a porter. "That woman's going to drop her purse out of her muff," he said' (p. 21). And so, though characters find themselves to some extent 'without God' in this text and in this time,[15] Grimshaw is carefully provided with, and in turn provides, substitute protections against the basic instinctual, wilful freedoms that Sartre predicts for God's absence[16] – and that Freud does too. This rationale seems to work, until the 'crushingly superior force of nature' makes its claim.

In relishing the supportive strength of the status quo, Grimshaw revivifies an abstraction concerning form: in his vision of society lies the notion of comfort within preordained boundaries of morality or intent. This is a prefabricated abstraction for which Ford has expressed disdain as a novelist. 'Society', capitalised, provides Robert Grimshaw with his apparent rescue, his apparent solidity after the slough of emotion with which he has just had to contend. Grimshaw says – 'It's the sort of thing [not wishing to be too humiliatingly specific] that's got to happen to make us the civilised people that we are'. His action, his sacrifice, must lend itself to the preservation of 'Society'; he must help to cement the image. His blustering betrays panic – despite his religious bolstering – at the alternative that Ford, as a self-conscious, impressionist novelist of his time, must provide. This alternative survives Grimshaw's rationality, his godliness, his replacement of his hat, and his projection of his sex instinct into his Dachshund (of whom more later). It is found in Ford's multi-formed vision of femininity (Freud's 'nature'), one that stands impressively ranged against 'Society', in positive way as well as in startlingly negative ways.[17] Ellida and other women in this text will come to be understood as its high priestesses, celebrants at a shrine of self-knowledge and sexual expression. How is this status confirmed? Often by what the women alone can *see*.[18]

What women see

In the encounter between Grimshaw and Ellida, eyes are significant; it is her eyes that show what she is thinking of the 'masculine madness' of his action, despite her silence, yet they rest unquestioningly and undemandingly upon his face as he 'broods'. Whilst he is vulnerable it is only her eyes that speak – they could speak volumes (about desire) were he only to regard her. When his rationality returns, she gently questions him, and he is then able to reject her approach. Perhaps Ellida is unwilling to probe his behavioural systems too forcefully. Her sister Katya does not share her circumspection.

Katya Lascarides is a psychotherapist, one of the earliest depictions in literature of a female professional of this kind. Financially independent, she travels the country diagnosing obscure cases of nervous disease. Her knowledge is hard-won: she herself suffered a breakdown, the implied cause of which (in addition to her later split with Grimshaw) was an 'hysterical devotion' to her mother (pp. 17–18). Mothers are credited with, amongst other things in Ford, teaching their daughters about sex (*The Good Soldier*, p. 14). Perhaps Ford intends his reader to infer that too much knowledge about sex, combined with a devotion to the mother, is what creates a female psychotherapist. It is Katya's eyes that betray the multiple strands of her professional awareness in time and space, 'her eyes changed colour by imperceptible shades, ranging from blue to the slaty-blue colour of the sea itself, express[ing] tender reminiscences' (p. 60).

Katya's mother has taught her to strive for sexual relationships based on trust, on equality, rather than the state's sanction – she didn't marry Katya's and Ellida's father. Katya and Grimshaw are no longer together because she sought the same foundation for their relationship: she asked Grimshaw to sacrifice 'Society' for sex with her. A legacy of her mother's teaching may also be the psychotherapist's sight with which she diagnoses her own Electra complex, through her professional work with Ellida's daughter, her six-year-old niece Kitty.[19] Reading back over a letter on the subject of Kitty's coming treatment she feels she may be about to diagnose 'her own case'. Though she doesn't realise how until that treatment starts, reading her letter she begins to reclaim a psychological truth about herself as a character (thus evoking the ideas of the personal narrative as discussed in Chapter 1). The time delay is crucial (she wrote it days before), and signifies the possibility of fundamental realignment. Transformation of the kind that comes to Katya (and to Kitty) is beyond the reach of Grimshaw; though taken apart, he is not put back together again.

Away from 'Society', in rural retreat next to the sea, where jewel-like Pre-Raphaelite colours signify Paradise regained, aunt and niece live in silence for the cure (Kitty presents with the fact that she cannot speak):

> In the shadow of a huge mulberry-tree, upon whose finger-like branches already the very light green leaves were beginning to form a veil, Katya Lascarides was sitting in a deck-chair. The expression upon her face was one of serenity and resigned contentment. She was looking at the farm-house; she was knitting a silk necktie, a strip of vivid green that fell across her light grey skirt. With a little quizzical and jolly expression, her hands thrust deep into the pockets of cream-coloured overalls, Kitty Langham looked sideways for approval at her aunt. She had just succeeded in driving a black cat out of the garden. [Soon afterwards Kitty struggles with her pet lamb, clenching her white teeth, falling into yellow crocuses.] (p. 65)

Peace is in this place. It is radiated by the content, but by the form as well (the lull of the imperfect, the number of hyphens). The female sex is alone and transcendent: both Kitty and her aunt have power. The pleasure of both women is expressed by sight; Katya's face registers an internal pleasurable response to her surroundings, Kitty's is flashed at her aunt. In the farmhouse at which Katya gazes lives a childless farmer's wife, one who has compensated for her barrenness by popu-lating the farm with motherless animals. Rivalry has no place in this family romance. But these calming, unthreatening sights are soon ruptured by violent versions. When Robert Grimshaw arrives at the garden, coming into 'the shadow of a huge mulberry-tree', soon after the scene is described, this atypical family order is broken; with him comes jealousy instead. The image of the farmer's wife recedes, and the three newly configured characters establish an Oedipal pattern. Kitty sees Grimshaw embrace Katya; she witnesses their passion. She is precipitated into speech by her visualised, dramatic, exclusion, 'interrupted by sobs and the grinding of minute teeth, there rose up in the child's voice the words: "Nobody must be loved but me. Nobody must be loved but me".' She is 'cured'.

Tears of pity and of identification come to Katya's eyes, for here 'she recognised the torture of her own passion' (pp. 65–7). Seeing Kitty's rage and grief completes the self-analysis begun as she read back over the letter to her sister. Freud's Oedipal theory had been developed as long ago as 1897, and the idea of 'rivalry in love' as experienced by children was obviously common enough currency by 1910 for Ford to produce this intensely powerful scene (see Chapters 1 and 2 for discussions of Ford's knowledge of Freud). It is a scene in which the sight of a psychotherapist is augmented by the sight of a precocious and suffering child (which produces speech and an expression of unconscious needs). This is only for the women though: the male instigator of the conflict is left to catch up with how things are by looking into Katya's eyes. The transformation scene climaxes (a tautology, it has climaxed earlier) in Robert Grimshaw reaffirming that there must still be a marriage if he and Katya are to converge once more. For him, 'Society' remains in the ascendant.

What men see

When the male characters in this text open their eyes, assuming that they can, which isn't always the case, they see something very different from that which confronts Kitty (essentially, symbolically, father with mother). Trauma is also the result, but it is one that, differently orchestrated by Ford, is more disturbing. Mid-way through the text, Dudley Leicester finds himself at a dinner party. Though his wife, Pauline, is away, staying with her sick mother (signifying family tangles again), he experiences a 'comparative tranquillity in his soul' (p. 33). The reign of tranquillity is ended when he looks at his neighbour at the table: 'at the dinner-table he had at his side red-lipped, deep-voiced, black-haired, large, warm, scented, and utterly uncontrollable Etta Stackpole. She had three dark red roses in her hair' (p. 33). It would be hard to imagine a more conclusive embodiment of the Lawrentian sex instinct. The list of adjectives is an erotic pulse that begins to beat, emanating from his fantastical description of the woman: this is how Leicester sees and senses her. Each unqualified mini-clause embeds him more completely in her sensuality, and from her red mouth to her foreign and exotic appearance she fragments tranquillity, she fragments order. She comes to wreak havoc. Wielding the knowledge men cannot make explicit of their unconscious minds, of their secrets, women in these texts also seem to know about sex. Ellida counsels expression of desire. In the above instance, Etta embodies its subversive power.[20]

Leicester accompanies Stackpole home after dinner; taking advantage of his wifeless state, she entices him into her house, 'pulling him into the inner [symbolically vaginal] darkness' where he 'can see nothing' (p. 45). He is out of his depth. At this point in the text, Ford adds to his more common technique of using sight to signify fragmentation or multiplicity, by using sound too. In true modernist style, he is aided by technology: in this instance, the telephone.[21] The telephone posed interesting challenges to theories of time and space (and still does: where exactly is the person to whom you are speaking?; when are they speaking, especially if from different time zones abroad?).[22] Modernist writers employed it to make some of these challenges. Men and women could be close together, at night, through sound if not through sight and touch. In A Call this version of the challenge proves disastrous for the mental health of at least one protagonist.[23]

In A Call, as Etta and Leicester hover together, he certainly unsure as to what happens next, the telephone rings. In the confusing darkness Etta tells him to answer it, pretending to be a footman. She has begun to walk upstairs. Grimshaw is on the other end of the line, and though he recognises Leicester's voice, and asks if it is him, Leicester has no idea to whom he is speaking. He hangs up, not knowing who can place him at Etta's house in the dead of night. His neurosis, which leads to his nervous breakdown, begins at this moment. Ford's use of the telephone, and its tendency to cast reality into doubt (the phone as it was then would not have reproduced voices terribly clearly), as the instrument of this collapse bears out Nordau's view that technology is represented in this text as being responsible for the modern malaise. The effect of the call on Grimshaw is equally dramatic:

> Lying in his white bed, the sheets up to his chin, his face dark in the blaze of light from above his head – the only dark object, indeed, in a room that was all monastically white – his tongue was so dry that he was unable to moisten his lips with it. He lay perfectly still, gazing at Peter's silver collar that, taken off for the night, hung from the hook on the back of the white door. His lips muttered fragments of words with which his mind had nothing to do. They bubbled up from within him as if from the depths of

his soul, and at that moment Robert Grimshaw knew himself. He was revealed to himself for the first time by words over which he had no control. In this agony and this prickly sweat the traditions – traditions that are so infectious – of his English public-school training, of his all-smooth and suppressed contacts in English social life, all the easy amenities and all the facile sense of honour that is adapted only to the life of no strain, of no passions; all these habits were long gone at this touch of torture. (p. 153)

Hitherto Grimshaw has known where he stands, supported by a collective habit of humanity that legislates against instinct. But owing to what he has heard on the telephone, and now sees in his mind's eye, he is acutely, desperately, unsure. Emotion is no longer controlled, it has broken free, and it independently assaults him. Ford illustrates stunningly the gradual breaking apart of his protections. He paints an only partly ironic picture of monastic purity as Grimshaw lies on his white bed. There is nothing sexual about the mouth Ford now describes; it is instead the mouth of abject terror, unable to know or to control the stream of words that issue from deep inside of him. 'At that moment Robert Grimshaw knew himself'; in fear, in lack of security, in nakedness, in the enforced removal of habitual niceties, lies a truth. Grimshaw then knew himself, inarticulately, as Ellida had proved she always knew him.

The mention of Peter in this passage is instructive, as is the fact that Grimshaw gazes at his collar, for Peter is a projection of Robert's latent sexuality. It is hard to avoid the obvious, post-Freudian, interpretation of the fact that Peter is a sausage dog, a Dachshund, and, moreover, one that enjoys a liberation that is peculiar to him in this text. He spends much of his time roaming, with licence, and investigating 'with a minute attention' the skirts of ladies present at social gatherings. Indeed he does so at Pauline's and Leicester's wedding, when Grimshaw is intent only on self-transcendence. Furthermore, when Grimshaw calls 'upon a lady at tea-time' he tends to 'set the dog upon the floor between his legs' where he remains, 'as motionless and as erect as a fire-dog' (p. 7). Ford seems to be indicating that Grimshaw is terribly conscientious where his dog is concerned, but overly watchful. The extent of his watchfulness prevents him from internalising the symbolic qualities attached to this creature, and consequently he cannot experience his own sex drive.

Coming back to the passage above, at night even Peter's collar is removed, and Robert's gaze is transfixed by the symbol of his freedom as it hangs in what had, up until this point, been a sexually unconscious zone. It is no longer that: 'The light shone down on him beside the bed. At the foot Peter slept, coiled up and motionless. At the head the telephone instrument, like a gleaming metal flower, with its nickel corolla and black bell, shone with reflected light' (p. 155). Although Peter and his collar, or lack of it, are significant, it is the telephone that has induced this trauma. Its depiction as a sinister instrument in the above quotation, gleaming and mysterious and smug, is entirely appropriate. He knows because of it that Dudley Leicester, already married to the woman Robert loves, is now, to his horror, and, worse, to his new-found and primitive sexual jealousy, experiencing a consciously pleasurable sexual freedom (at least in his fantasy). Grimshaw's agony is unsurprising.[24] Awful though this knowledge is, the method by which Ford transmits it is the cruellest part of the blow. What Grimshaw has heard allows his imagination to configure a relationship in his mind's eye in which he is *almost* a third party. He has *almost* found himself with Dudley and Etta, late at night, but feels his exclusion all the more because of that temporarily and partially induced proximity (Kitty's experience of the mother/father embrace and her sense of her own exclusion was similar) during the call. If he had been there in person, seeing the situation, he would have known Leicester had no intention of sleeping with Etta; his imagination creates very different pictures, fuelled by the voice he has recognised being in the place that he knows/fears/desires. Forster's epigraph to *Howards End*, published in the same year as *A Call*, and a novel which also gives attention to problems of sex and marriage in a technologically driven, mad world, was 'Only connect'.[25] When a connection is formed by that quintessentially modernist instrument, the telephone, it seems to be one that causes confusion, fragmentation and a sense of a divided self.[26]

A fully conscious recognition by Grimshaw of what it is that he is experiencing would result, perhaps, in the vocalisation of a want or desire, something upon which he might act. But he has not arrived at the necessary position of stability for self-expression. Until now coherent language has been a firm part of his public and reliable stance; now all at once he is a novice, and he is terrified. He is held down as Ford drags him through the list of his vanishing protections; Ford shows us the process (again the interest in the change in a man) as he strips him bare and leaves him speechless.

Man against woman

Ford obviously admires Ellida, though he despises her sister.[27] Grimshaw parades only with an 'air of tranquil wisdom' (p. 23), scant covering for his psychological naivety, but Ellida, the woman, has wisdom within her. And it is Ellida that Ford uses to express the perpetual dichotomies which lie at the centre of this text: the public as it stands against the private; the known against the unknown; the external against the internal, and, finally, the man against the woman. Ellida muses to herself:

> There they are, these men of ours. We see them altogether affable, smiling, gentle, composed. And we women have to make believe to their faces and to each other that they're towers of strength and all-wise, as they like to make out that they are. We see them taking action that they think is strong; and forcible, and masculine, and that we know is utterly mad; and we have to pretend to them and to each other that we agree in placid confidence; and then we go home, each one of us with our husbands or our brothers, and the strong masculine creature breaks down, groans and drags us after him hither and thither in his crisis, when he has to pay for his folly. (p. 22)

This stream of thought exists only in silence, but there is power in the lines. Ellida positions the pretence between women as well as between women and men: loyalty to the myth in public, as Ford sees it, is complete and final. Public stands and public displays, public wisdom and public action gain expressional superiority over the private, and feminine, knowledge of the other existence, the crisis, the fear and the weakness. Ellida recognises the dichotomy. She has said 'I never saw such misery' (p. 21) as Pauline was driven away. She gives Grimshaw the chance to be different, and he rejects it, for the fear of the unknown is far greater than the sadness at Pauline's loss.

A Call is not a realistic novel. It is a fantasy novel, dedicated to pursuing a series of dramatic, what Arnold Bennett called 'fairy-tale',[28] scenes, in which characters stage their traumas and their moments of vision. In addition, the social scene it depicts is narrow in the extreme – a close relation, in fact, of the one that Ford identifies as James's 'hunting grounds': the 'West End and the country house, [hardly] east of Temple Bar or lower than Fourteenth Street'.[29] In Ford, according to C. H. Sisson, this social restriction is 'absurd'.[30] Despite these assessments, and despite the fact that the portrayal of sexual morality becomes more realistic in *The Good Soldier* (though Etta is shown to be

the envy of society women for managing her love affairs so easily), Ford
does raise important questions here. The text highlights contemporary
fears about women, and contemporary sexological debates, in unique
ways. Some differences between men and women are presented in a
benign fashion (the form Ellida's rather gentle thoughts about men
take, for example), others less so. What is always true is that male experience of women, if not traumatic, is either infantilising or
emasculating.

   Women 'have everything' in this fairy-tale. They are professionals:
Kitty is not Katya's only successful treatment in the novel; she cures
Dudley Leicester too when her male peers fail (there is something
godlike about her then).[31] Women are also sexually confident, and
predatory. They are spiritually developed: 'the window, being of
stained glass, showed the story of St George. Little, and as it were
golden, Pauline stood motionless in the middle of the room; she looked
upon the floor and appeared lost in reflection' (p. 112). Finally, and
perhaps most surprisingly, they also maintain their ability to mother:
'she appeared to look downwards upon Dudley, not as if she were
expecting him to answer, but with a tender expression of a mother
looking at a child many months before it can talk' (p. 82). In a text
where losing the ability to speak is central to traumatic experience (in
Kitty and Grimshaw) Pauline's ability to articulate felt needs, which
seems to be Ford's implication, is a powerful one. When related to an
adult man, it is also disturbing – as is Grimshaw's response when Katya
expresses her continuing desire for him: 'I am not the motherless boy
that I was' (p. 72). He misses the point rather catastrophically in this
totally inappropriate, exultant, reply.

   What is left for masculinity amidst these multiple illustrations of
Kraus's 'vaginal century'? To Dudley Leicester, pre-breakdown, 'a man
was a man and a woman a woman' (p. 30); they were polar opposites.
His breakdown is instigated by a woman who 'out-sexes' him; he is
cured by a woman; he recuperates with a wife who is also like his
mother. What is a man, then, now? Earlier in this chapter I suggested
that Weininger's theories (to do with the transitional nature of sexual
forms, the fact that there are only to be found the 'intermediate stages
between absolute males and females' in human beings[32]), theories that
Ford knew, find a fictional outlet in this text. Here, though, the intermediate, fragmented stages seem to belong to the males, forced into
compromise by the Platonic absolutes of the females that face them:
Katya is blessed with 'the aspect of a divinity like Diana' (p. 131).

Bristow's analysis of sexual theory in the twentieth century traces a chain of thought from Weininger's populist sexological treatise to Camille Paglia's *Sexual Personae: Art and Decadence from Nerfertiti to Emily Dickinson*, published in 1990.[33] In *Sexual Personae* Paglia undertakes an interpretative journey into historical and philosophical representations of men and women. Dealing in polarities, the one with which she is most concerned is that of nature and culture; culture, in the form of society and the things it builds, is the masculine standing in direct opposition to that of which it lives in constant fear: nature, the feminine. Grimshaw's experience is invoked by her maxim that 'Individualism, the self unconstrained by Society, leads to the coarser servitude of self by nature'.[34] Grimshaw's protection from the rawness, the coarseness, of his desire for Pauline has come in the form of the 'we' of society as opposed to the 'I' of individualism. But Grimshaw also grudgingly admits the primitive power of instinct:

> I suppose what I really want is both Katya and Pauline. That sort of thing is probably in our blood – yours and mine – and no doubt in the great days of our race I should have had both of them, but I've got to sacrifice physical possession of one of them to the amenities of a civilisation that's pleasant enough, and that's taken thousands of years to put together. (p. 23)

In this admission, which is polygamous, the plurality of the sex drive becomes paramount, as it does later in *The Good Soldier* (Grimshaw sounds sadly like Dowell in his polygamy speech). But in this desperate attempt at self-assertion Grimshaw completes the circle of irony waiting for him. His mealy-mouthed concession is not enough. He does not achieve 'possession' of either woman – what woman would have him after this statement of terms?

Grimshaw is finally destroyed by a twist of the knife in Katya Lascarides's hands. Spurned by Pauline, in the final pages, he returns to his allegiance to Katya, and agrees to live with her as her lover, rather than as her husband – thus privileging sex and simultaneously rejecting 'Society'. And she refuses, saying that instead they will marry, casting him into a confusion from which he will not recover. She fully sounds the void that is within him, stripping him of the final attempt he makes to control his destiny. Grimshaw thus prostrates himself before the strength of this new woman, the intellectual who does not arouse his desire. In the final words of the novel, Grimshaw owns this double destruction: '"So that you get me both ways", Robert Grimshaw said; and his hands fell desolately open at his side. "Every way and altogether", she answered' (p. 158).

Ford has shown Grimshaw a complex, sensationalised picture (one that seems to owe much to Nordau and to Kraus), a picture that includes representations of women as intellectual, as threatening, as beautiful, as wise, as maternal, as sexual. There is little room for him in this picture, and although his instincts are awoken they are not satisfied. He gives himself up to Katya, dependent on her mercy and deprived of catharsis. She gets him 'both ways', managing to stymie the articulation of his need for society, and the need for sex, at once. Grimshaw, exposed, vulnerable and fragmented would, I think, given the choice by Ford, have clung to his conception of society. The world as Ford shows it in *A Call* means this option is removed.

The codes of behaviour and the personal perspectives (of sex and society) that Ford takes as his subject matter in *A Call* were further and more conclusively fragmented by the sustained bombardment that was the First World War. How did this international event extend already mutating literary techniques? How does the writing it provoked express and augment the fragmented nature of existence at the beginning of the twentieth century? Is sight still so significant to this fictional struggle? These questions, amongst others, will be addressed in the chapter that follows.

Notes

1 Arthur Mizener, *The Saddest Story: A Biography of Ford Madox Ford* (New York, Carroll & Graf, 1985), p. 478.

2 SE xiv, p. 284.

3 Sondra Stang (ed.), *The Presence of Ford Madox Ford* (Pennsylvania, University of Pennsylvania Press, 1981), p. xxvi.

4 Cate Haste dates the regular appearance of the 'New Woman' in fiction to Ibsen's *The Doll's House* (1879) (*Rules of Desire: Sex in Britain World War I to the Present* (London, Pimlico, 1992), p. 16); see also Joseph Bristow, *Sexuality* (London, Routledge, 1997), p. 101.

5 Quoted by Mike Jay and Michael Neve (eds) in *1900* (Harmondsworth, Penguin, 1999), p. 223.

6 Ford Madox Ford, *The Good Soldier* (New York, Norton, 1995), pp. 62–3.

7 See his epistolary epilogue, published with the novel in 1910, and in recent editions, *A Call: The Tale of Two Passions* (Manchester, Carcanet, 1984).

8 Ford Madox Ford, *Henry James: A Critical Study* (London, Martin Secker, 1918), p. 121.

9 R. M. Unger, *Passion: An Essay on Personality* (New York, The Free Press, 1984), p. 23.

10 'The "Can" and "Shall" of Woman Culture', *Lancet*, 1886 (quoted in Jay and Neve (eds), *1900*, p. 238). Even in 1920, Virginia Woolf was contemplating a 'counterblast' to Arnold Bennett's 'Our Women', a collection of essays in which women are depicted as the intellectual, and creative, inferiors of men (*The Diary of Virginia Woolf*, ed. Anne Olivier Bell, vol. 2, 1920–24, Harmondsworth, Penguin, 1981, p. 69).

11 Thus acting very much like May Bartram in Marcher's similar existential struggle in Henry James's 'The Beast in the Jungle'. For a detailed comparison between these two texts, see my article 'A Question of Knowledge' in the *Henry James Review*, 21: 1, Winter 2000, which concentrates on the gendered nature of epistemology.

12 Adam Phillips, *On Flirtation* (London, Faber & Faber, 1994), p. 22.

13 SE xxi, p. 21.

14 Ford Madox Ford, *Mr Fleight* (London, Howard Latimer, 1913), p. 76.

15 Gunnar Brandell writes of Darwin's challenge to religious beliefs as the necessary precursor to Freud's (*Freud: A Man of His Century*, Brighton, Harvester Press, 1979, p. 59). Freud would probably have included that of Copernicus too.

16 I am thinking of his classic statement that 'everything is permitted if God does not exist' in *Existentialism and Humanism* (London, Methuen, 1984), p. 33.

17 Ideas gleaned from Otto Weininger's *Sex and Character* ((1903) New York, AMS Press, 1975; refer to Chapter 2 for a discussion of this text), as well as from contemporary portrayals of the 'New Woman' (Katya is a driven, sexless professional), and from Pre-Raphaelite 'beauties', appear in the way in which some female characters use their sexuality. In Chapter 5 I debate more fully Ford's typification of womanhood for more regenerative ends.

18 In this way they prefigure Florence Dowell, who has 'the seeing eye', rather than her narrator-husband, who 'had not a glimpse that anything was wrong' until Florence, Maisie and Edward are all dead (p. 52).

19 Even being aware of Freud's theories on incestuous desire would not have given Katya this description of it: Freud didn't develop his thinking about the father/daughter pattern until 1933. As will be seen, however, Ford's symbolic family situation works like a Freudian case study. As a novelist he forces this family through a quasi-analysis in which the unconscious is revealed.

20 In *The Portrait of a Lady* (1881) James introduces the character of Henrietta Stackpole. This American friend of Isabel is described as one who 'doesn't care a straw what men think of her'; Ralph certainly does not like the idea of this 'reporter in petticoats' (Harmondsworth, Penguin,

1970, p. 83). She was a Jamesian trope of subversiveness, this Etta Stackpole, before she became a Fordian one.

21 The telephone was first demonstrated in public by its inventor, Alexander Graham Bell, in 1876 in Philadelphia. Great Britain was seriously behind the United States in introducing and developing telephone systems; partly as a result of this sluggishness, the telephone was still capable of causing excitement emotionally, technologically and literally in 1910. See Herbert N. Casson, *The History of the Telephone* (Chicago, A. C. McClurg & Co., 1910), p. v.

22 As such it is not surprising that at first it was suspected that the telephone could spread disease between users (speakers on the phone, not just those who shared handsets). See Chapter 1 for a discussion of similar fears caused by the plans for a Channel tunnel.

23 Ford thus runs the risk of displaying thought processes more akin to Max Nordau's than those of other, forward-looking modernist contemporaries. In *Degeneration* (London, Heinemann, 1895) Nordau develops a notorious thesis that technology is causing late-nineteenth-century degeneration and hysteria in the human race (see the Introduction).

24 Julia Kristeva writes of the relationship between pleasure and fear, between the potential of sexual fulfilment and the terror which it brings: 'We have lost the relative strength and security that the old moral codes guaranteed our loves either by forbidding them or by determining their limits [...]. Expectancy makes me painfully sensitive to my incompleteness, of which I was not aware before [...]. The call, its call, overwhelms me with a flow [...]. Would the symptoms of love be the symptoms of fear? Both a fear and a need of no longer being limited, held back, but going beyond. Dread of transgressing not only proprieties or taboos, but also, and above all, fear of crossing and desire to cross, the boundaries of the self' (*Tales of Love*, New York, Columbia University Press, 1987, pp. 5–6). Grimshaw finds himself on just such a threshold, at the boundary which divides his sense of society from his sense of himself and his needs. Ford is forcing him to know and to confront it.

25 E. M. Forster, *Howards End* (Harmondsworth, Penguin, 1989).

26 In Chapter 4 I discuss Ford's use of the telephone in *Parade's End*.

27 He writes of her in the epistolary epilogue as someone whom 'personally I extremely dislike' (p. 162).

28 See Saunders's discussion of the novel in Saunders I, pp. 300–4. He considers it from primarily an autobiographical perspective.

29 Ford, *Henry James*, p. 47.

30 See his afterword to the text.

31 Leicester has a breakdown when he remains unable to work out who called Stackpole that night. At its worst, he takes to asking complete strangers if they 'rang up 4259 Mayfair?' (p. 80).

32 Quotation taken from *Sex and Character*, in Jay and Neve (eds), *1900*, p. 239.
33 Bristow, *Sexuality*, p. 44.
34 Camille Paglia, *Sexual Personae: Art and Decadence from Nerfertiti to Emily Dickinson* (Harmondsworth, Penguin, 1991), p. 14.

4

In sight of war

'Just imagine it,' murmured Bazarov, 'what a word can mean! You've found it, said it, the word "crisis" – and you're happy! It's astonishing how a man can still believe in words.'[1]

I don't know that the large words Courage, Loyalty, God and the rest had, before the war, been of frequent occurrence in London conversations. But one had had the conviction they were somewhere in the city's subconsciousness... Now they were gone.[2]

Ford admired Turgenev, so it is not surprising that one comes across ideas borrowed, perhaps, from him in the later writer's work. In this case, though, there is a development at work; a development precipitated by the First World War. Turgenev's self-confessed nihilist Bazarov expresses amazement at the tenacity of human belief in words – words that, in his example, can diminish and deaden a feeling of catastrophe. Were he to find himself instead in the volumes of *Parade's End* (or one of a number of other war novels), Bazarov's amazement would be tempered. Ford, post-war, has lost belief in words. He has lost belief in the power of words to induce comfort and happiness, to describe large concepts. It is the big words that have 'gone'.

The 'big words'

This expression of a wartime linguistic fragmentation is one for which I can find no etymological evidence (I have checked the *Oxford English Dictionary* and etymological dictionaries). And yet, it is one that is ubiquitous in certain kinds of writing of the First World War. Ezra Pound wrote in 1915, in structuralist vein, that 'when words cease to cling close to things, kingdoms fall, empires wane and diminish' (seemingly transposing cause and effect).[3] Symbolising his character as a soldier of a previous order, Edward Ashburnham still holds to his profession as 'full of the big words courage, loyalty, honour, constancy' (though God is missing).[4] Ernest Hemingway's protagonist can no longer do so in *A Farewell to Arms* because 'abstract words such as glory, honor, courage were obscene beside the concrete names of villages'.[5] French novelist Henri Barbusse knew that marshalling against French nationalism from a soldier/writer's perspective would mean attacking its tendency to 'gather to itself all prejudice and all the "Big Words"' – he cannot speak that language any more.[6] In both Paul Fussell's and Samuel Hynes's work on the war, the notion of the death of the 'big words' figures prominently; Jay Winter relates the 'big words' to the 'lies' of an older generation (p. 2).[7]

Allyson Booth evokes Hemingway's expression of this notion when she calls it a 'tension between capitalized abstractions like Heroism and the concrete details of trench warfare'.[8] Her explanation of the abstract coming into semantic conflict with the concrete makes far more sense of it than Peter Conrad when he suggests simply that 'the war gave language a dressing down'.[9] This linguistic crisis is not about language, but about how words are understood and why, about how they can be used to communicate. In this chapter, I discuss why and how the abstract was fragmented by the concrete in the First World War, as expressed in the fiction that it produced. Attention to presenting the detailed, the concrete, is one aspect of the modernist tradition to which Ford was allied. Despite the way in which he often spoke about the war, his writing about it displayed an increasing and continuing allegiance to his impressionist poetics.[10]

Ford is sensitive to the texture of words. Previous discussions of his narrative technique have concentrated on his tendency to explore among, and represent, the plural levels of human consciousness. He chooses how best to do this not just by way of narrative technique, but by way of the building blocks, the raw material that he uses (think of the basic linguistic sensuousness of *The Fifth Queen*). Graham Greene draws attention to his craftsman's ability when he writes that 'he was not only a designer; he was a carpenter: you feel in his work the love of the tools and the love of the material'.[11] When it comes to Ford's writing of the war, this aspect of his strength is notable – because of the perceived absence of the 'big words' and what he does with the resulting gap.

Ford's apprehension of a pre-1914/post-1918 linguistic dualism is signified, visibly, in the quotation from his post-war autobiography at the head of this chapter.[12] The homogenising, codifying words are capitalised, privileged, and were accorded cognitive supremacy (pre-1914). In characters such as Macmaster, due to his ignorance of the new realities (post-1918), they still are: '"What is loathsome"', Tietjens spits, '"is all your fumbling in placket holes and polysyllabic Justification by Love [...]. That's all right if you can get your club to change its rules"'.[13] The process by which the 'big words' lose status is also made visible to the readers of his fiction – because it can be attributed in part to what has been *seen*, at war, 'beneath Ordered Life' (*It Was the Nightingale*, p. 64). Following the concentration of previous chapters, then, my discussion of war focuses (though not exclusively so) on the role of sight in the writing of this event that fragmented language.

Before leaving the discussion of language behind, however, it is important to note that as Ford expresses his anxiety he relates it to the (quasi) Freudian map of the mind: 'One had the conviction that [large words] were somewhere in the city's subconsciousness.... Now they were gone'.[14] Unconscious understanding of linguistically signified codes, by which one lived, has been made conscious by the newly discovered lack of it. Thus language that connected one to a definable code of conduct is to be replaced by something else, a more diverse and disjunctive system of communication, connected in its turn to more diverse behaviour. So there is a similarity here between Grimshaw's conception of 'Society', restraining his instinct, as discussed in Chapter 3, and Ford's conception of the 'big words' (Courage, Loyalty, God) – perhaps also restraining his instinct (refer back to the discussion of the liberation of war in Chapter 1). Both are fragmented. Ford's dedication to multiplicity continues; he discovers that in other ways, too, language can point towards, or visually allude to, the existence of the unconscious.

Ford is often unsatisfied with the capacity of language to express the totality of thought or experience; speech constantly 'gives out', to be replaced by his most characteristic grammatical tool: ellipsis.[15] Tietjens's consistent inability to find the exact words for a feeling or a thought creates visible proofs of, amongst other things, the difference of Macmaster's conceptual position, in which the latter is protected from the doubting, fearful multiplicities of human existence by a repressed hold on capitalised comfort. Conversely, Ford pushes Tietjens into battle after battle with his own language, in ways that test its limitations and extend its boundaries, whilst simultaneously indicating the continuing existence of things he *cannot* say:

> Because what the devil did he want of Valentine Wannop? Why could he not stall off the thought of her? He could stall off the thought of his wife... or his not-wife. But Valentine Wannop came wriggling in. At all hours of the day and night. It was an obsession. A madness... what those fools called 'a complex'!... Due, no doubt, to something your nurse had done, or your parents said to you. At birth... A strong passion... or no doubt not strong enough. Otherwise he, too, would have gone absent. At any rate, from Sylvia... Which he hadn't done. Or had he? There was no saying.... (p. 338)

Tietjens is right, there is no 'saying' but there are many sayings; there are many contradictory and exploratory ways of attempting to express the complexities of his feelings at this time. His prolonged need for codes is being disturbed by his desire for Valentine. But desire he now almost knows it is. His conscious control of himself is being challenged by his presence at the front and the fragmenting effects of that existence. It is also being challenged by a defensive and grudging acknowledgement of the psychological developments of the time (it is undoubtedly significant here that his wife, Sylvia, pinned her 'faith' to Freud (p. 37)); he is indirectly rethinking his history, and his psychological history at that.[16] Learning, visibly, he is being pushed to give tentative, linguistic life to concepts that make him uncomfortable. The still dark areas are represented by ellipses; these are the points where his brain proves it is ill-equipped for the broadening of knowledge.[17] To use Freudian terminology, as does Tietjens, these are indicative of his repression. This repression is mostly sexual. Yet Tietjens has made a tortured progression in the allusion to, if not direct expression of, desire in his speech.

Tietjens's speech fragments as it attempts to incorporate his desire; he approaches and reapproaches the feeling he has, but cannot do other than affirm the fragmentation of himself as subject as he linguistically wrestles with his sexual existence. Tietjens is at war with himself, signified by his speech, and he is also in France, at war. Whilst there, as I have suggested, his sense of fragmentation is keenly known and expressed through the medium of sight.

In sight of war: the kaleidoscope

When Ford's Englishman 'looked at the World' in 1915, in the first book of war propaganda he was commissioned to write by his friend C. F. G. Masterman, he saw 'kaleidoscopic days'. Ford was outlining 'British psychology' of the time, and he chose an intensely visual image – one discussed in the Introduction – with which to do so.[18] (As Allyson Booth points out, 'men and women enter into war with the same perceptual equipment that they rely on to understand and articulate any other experience': Ford's choice of imagery is not surprising.[19]) The kaleidoscope is an optical device, invented c. 1815, consisting of mirrors that reflect bits of coloured glass in a design that may be changed endlessly (by rotating the section that contains the fragments of glass). In Ford's imagistic use of it, the kaleidoscope signifies the complex multiplicity of British wartime psychology, one that depended partly on how the light (of experience, of understanding, or of narrative) was thrown. It can be related to Ford's impressionist ethos, where he uses the reflective properties of light and glass to illustrate how the past co-exists with the present in ever-changing combinations (see his 1914 essay, 'On Impressionism).[20] It is important to bear it in mind as I proceed.

Two quotations provide a framework for this exploration into how and why sight functions in the fragmentation of war. They have been chosen because of the way in which they illustrate, and provoke discussion of, the notion of the abstract versus the concrete. I discuss both of them, and the quintessential ideas that they raise, in detail.

The face of battle

The first is from John Keegan's book, *The Face of Battle*, and it concerns officer training (Ford himself was an officer, enlisting at the end of July 1915, despite being 41[21]). At this point in his analysis, Keegan is describing the 'rote-learning and repetitive form and the categorical, reductive quality' of the capabilities necessary to the activity of war. During war, forming and shaping and categorising are essential aspects of soldierly behaviour. They are designed to promote the ability of the fighting man (including officers), 'to avert the onset of fear or, worse, of panic and to perceive a *face of battle* which, if not familiar, and certainly not friendly, need not, in the event, prove wholly petrifying [my italics]'.[22] It is the ability to repress fear by swathing it in a particular linguistic shape, by giving it a 'repetitive form', to which Keegan refers. (Bazarov's amazement could be inferred.) It will mean that, in Keegan's vivid image, the face of battle turned towards the combatant will be interpreted professionally, in the abstract, not personally.

As he writes of the First World War, Trevor Wilson suggests that it was not simply fear that had to be repressed in order to avoid the personal face of battle; training was (and presumably still is) about conditioning the individual soldier to avoid many instinctive responses. The army, as he points out, required human material that 'had been rendered proof' against such urgings as flight.[23] Instincts must be bypassed, then, repressed, if the face of battle is not to prove petrifying. Sassoon knew this, writing that, at war, 'the instinct of self-preservation automatically sank below all arguments put forward by one's "higher self"', meaning, perhaps, by 'higher self', the moral and professional self, the *super ego* to one's instinctive *id*.[24] W. H. R. Rivers, Sassoon's wartime doctor after his breakdown, would agree, and suggests in his clinical writings that training was intended 'to free the soldier' from the collapse that terror would induce and from the 'flight of panic';[25] he would be freed in order to do his work. So: freedom from the personal face of battle comes with training that categorises and reduces, that shapes and orders instincts and behaviours. From such training emerges a man who has been 'rendered proof' against instinctive urgings (one wonders what this human would be like); such a man would be united with his comrades in a singular abstract vision of a professional war.

However, in a text that has been called 'the finest and noblest book of men in war', and 'one of the greatest books about soldiers in the whole of western literature', Frederic Manning has something very different to say about that face of battle (and this is the second framework quotation).[26] His novel, *The Middle Parts of Fortune*, which is about the experience of being a fighting man, contains the absolute assurance that 'a man might rave against war' but 'war, from among its myriad faces, could always turn towards him one, which was his own'.[27] War possesses not one but a myriad faces, then, including one for every man who fights, one for every man who trains in order to avoid just that experience of a concrete and identifiable face.

Keegan's 'fighting man' does not look closely enough at war to pick up the elements of his own face; he does not trace its impact upon him as he goes about his soldierly work. Manning's fighting man does not have a choice, for eventually he will be forced to pick himself out, made by war 'to face a fact as naked and inexorable as himself' (p. 40). This chapter concentrates on the disintegration of the former, idealised, behavioural and psychological position, one that is not just tied to the discussion of war but can be related to many contemporary concerns. Grimshaw was forced to abandon abstract, coded 'Society' and to know his individual soul, and Manning's multi-faceted image also evokes the discussion of modernism from the Introduction and Chapter 1.

Ford was of a social class that would automatically have entitled him to officership. For his major novelistic character who lives and fights through the First World War, Christopher Tietjens, he chose a background of a family of 'landed proprietors'. Tietjens comes from old money, then, old influence. Ford calls his kind 'Good People', using capitals again (*It Was the Nightingale*, p. 219); he is one of 'God's elect'.[28] Ford also makes him 'an officer of sufficient authority to make reports that would get through at times to the higher commands' (*It Was the Nightingale*, p. 218). He wanted him, then, to be of two worlds instead of one (see Chapter 2 and its discussion of *Parade's End*). Tietjens can communicate with higher commands, perhaps about logistical decisions, but must also attempt to turn towards his men a face of war that does not prove to be 'wholly petrifying': initially, he manifests the abstract, visually and linguistically, in his approach to the war.

Most importantly, he must enable his men to fight, and to continue to fight. He himself recognises this when as close to the front as he is ever stationed, 'It had occurred to him that it was a military duty to bother himself about the mental equilibrium of this member of the lower classes. So he talked ... any old talk' (p. 305). The apparent nonchalance, and arrogance, of his thought is designed to signify his class and concomitant authority, which bestow upon him this quasi-feudal responsibility for the men in his care. At the same time, it must be noted, he believes the army to be cursed by an 'imbecile national belief that the game is more than the player'. (He details some of the rules of this game: if the quartermaster refuses to give him tin hats for his men, 'That's the Game!' – capitalised; if any of his men are killed, he is expected to grin and invoke the national belief (pp. 305–6).)

Tietjens adopts a code signified by those capital letters that later become obsolete: Military Duty. He provides the aura of distance between his men and the war that will prevent them from being petrified; he protects their minds, if it is possible, from the truth of that which they must face. This perspective continues into the fashion in which Tietjens translates to himself that which goes on around him. In the following extract he avoids his own face, though idiosyncratically, and the experience does not petrify:

> In the bright light it was as if a whole pail of scarlet paint had been dashed against the man's face on the left and his chest. It glistened in the firelight – just like fresh paint, moving! The runner from the Rhondda, pinned down by the body across his knees, sat down with his jaw fallen, resembling one girl that should be combing the hair of another recumbent before her. The red viscousness welled across the floor; you sometimes so see fresh water bubbling up in the sand. (p. 307)

Here, the overwriting of that which *is* happening by that which is *not* happening is uncanny. It points, I think, towards two conclusions in particular. The first concerns the tendency of Tietjens's brain to work in the abstract manner in which he is supposed to be instructive regarding his men; the second relates to the peculiar priority which the passage grants to that which is *not* happening whilst it also relates that which is. His speech to himself is divided between two conceptual levels (Allyson Booth writes that 'dead bodies at the Front were simultaneously understood as both animate subjects and inanimate objects'[29]) in the attempt at avoiding petrification. He sees O Nine Morgan's dying face, but transposed on it is another very different reality. Tietjens is *really* seeing that which he experientially knows, a sight from his past, not that which is in front of his eyes, and in this case it looks like the impressionist painting by Degas: 'A Maid Combing a Woman's Hair'. (Susan Greenfield provides a fascinating physiological account of why this should be: a significant part of the brain's interpretation of what the eye sees has its roots in the subject's memory.[30])

The Degas painting is dominated by a swathe of red paint, which draws the gaze from the bottom left corner across the canvas, but the scene it depicts is one of ideal, domestic, harmony and trust (note too the ordered socio-political construction of the title). One woman reclines toward the other as her hair is brushed – the fact that women are the subjects heightens the sense of abstraction in relation to the war. There is an atmosphere of seductive peace created by this action that can be nothing like the scene, with its dead male body, that confronts Tietjens. It is what he needs to know, however, as an abstract rescue from the concrete; thus it is what he sees. At this point this is how he can translate it to himself. The exclamation mark placed at the

close of the phrase 'just like fresh paint, moving!', would be callous
were the tone of the paragraph different, and more in tune with the
actual reality. And yet it is not, because Tietjens is seeing, not a man
dying in front of him, but a man covered in recently thrown paint.

The process of mental assimilation of the face continues: 'It was
extraordinary how defined the peaked nose and the serrated teeth were
in that mess.... The eye looked jauntily at the peak of the canvas hut-
roof.... Gone with a grin. Singular the fellow should have spoken!
After he was dead' (p. 309). Tietjens now seems fully acclimatized to
the factual nature of the horror that he has seen. He knows now that the
man is dead, and the lack of humanitarian interest is stunning if the
reader considers the stark reality of the mangled body. Within the
writing itself, however, his journey into art has managed to deaden and
soften the response of the reader as well as his own. Tietjens then
divests the man of his humanity, rendering him as though he were a
cubist painting, splitting him up into his component but dislocated
parts: the nose, the teeth, the eye, the mouth, his speech. The peak of
the nose mirrors the inanimate peak of the canvas roof above them –
merely as a point of scenic interest. There is no grief. Why not? Partly
because of the internal acrobatics that Tietjens has performed, and
partly because it is essential that he should not show any. It would not
be possible for him to attempt the continual reflection of a face of battle
that was not that of each one of his men whilst beset by emotional loss.
It would render the attempt invalid, and Tietjens incapable of doing his
job. Tietjens is thus shown to exist, for the time, in a state of supremacy
for the coded, abstract, behaviour pattern.

O Nine Morgan's death has occurred as though it were something
else, and Nietzsche's maxim that 'forgetfulness is a property of all
action' is percipient in this context[31] (as is much of the opening of Jay
Winter's *Sites of Memory, Sites of Mourning*[32]). Keegan draws attention
to a related cognitive problem, caused by the necessity of persuading
the men to fight, again, and to risk their lives, again. He says of the
nature of battle that there is 'an anterior and yet more important
psychological trick to be played before a breakthrough can occur – one
which, as we have seen, has to be pulled off in both armies, the attacking and defending: that of getting their soldiers to stand' (*The Face of
Battle*, p. 296). The third of Ford's novels in his tetralogy – *A Man
Could Stand Up- –* is partially dedicated to the critical, and conditional,
moment of leaving the trenches. The extent of the officer's responsibility in this role is revealed when Tietjens becomes almost inadvertently

caught in the action. His general exclaims that, '"A fellow like you has no right to be where he can be wounded"' (p. 643). He has the right, rather, to be where he can make his men into effective fighting machines; he must give names to things and to actions, names like 'Loyalty' and 'Courage', and he must help them to forget, painting pictures of another reality. Duly, then, volume 2, *No More Parades*, begins with a description of the hut that will soon be the site of O Nine Morgan's demise (I choose the word carefully). It is 'shaped like the house a child draws', not the scene of a murder: language and picture indicate here the men *must* be safe (p. 291).[33]

Abstract versus concrete

As well as possessing a function within the action and the development of the novel, theories of picture-making and capitalising figure in Ford's non-fictional writing on the subject of the war. In 1916 he was wrestling with what he then deemed to be an insurmountable problem: how to write about what surrounded him. He states that 'as for explanation I hadn't any: as for significant or valuable pronouncement of a psychological kind I could not make any – nor any generalisation. There we were: those million men, forlorn, upon a raft in space. But as to what had assembled us upon that landscape: I had just to fall back upon the formula: it is the Will of God'.[34] He uses capitals still at this point – 'The Will of God' – in the formula he finds to arrest a conceptual fall (structuralism again). It represents solidity amidst chaos, just as the superimposed likeness of the house a child would draw over the army bunker is the way to a small psychological refuge. His fictional, autobiographical alter ego, Gringoire in *No Enemy*, articulates another version of the same task: 'But coming back [from the war] or not, Gringoire was certainly going back to it and, in its desperate and fleeting atmosphere, the idea of Lord Kitchener was the one solid thing onto which our poor poet could catch'.[35] Those minds that constructed the advertising posters for Kitchener's army gave their potential recruits a face that was not their own to encourage them to war. Kitchener's face would encourage a man to 'stand up'. Whether or not 'the idea of Lord Kitchener' as expressed in the poster campaign by his face was the reason, it was a successful campaign.[36]

Ford, of course, being a modernist and an impressionist (think of the kaleidoscope), never believed in the singular perspective of 'one solid thing', expressed by Gringoire, and aimed at by the writers of training

manuals, though he recognised the need for it. In *Parade's End*, it is ultimately the shock of humanity with which Tietjens must deal; it is the
flash of recognition that his troops are individual men as well as soldiers
– and deserve to be treated differently in each role – that triggers his
cognitive move away from the surface comfort of abstract codes. And
when the shelling burst that ultimately kills Morgan begins this is
signalled: 'An enormous crashing sound said things of an intolerable
intimacy to each of those men, and to all of them as a body. After its
mortal vomiting all the other sounds appeared a rushing silence, painful
to ears in which the blood audibly coursed' (p. 293). The beautifully
counterpoised 'intolerable intimacy' evokes the mutual exclusivity of
the states of soldier and man in its uneasy alliance. Intimacy is not the
word of a soldier who cannot see his own face in the death that is around
him. Such concrete, bodily intimacy is intolerable because to maintain
awareness of the shared tenuousness of the hold on life might be enough
to send one mad.[37] Tietjens does know this, and this he can speak about
(one is reminded of Ford's writing to Conrad of the unbearable effects of
the sounds of battle[38]) as can be seen in a conversation with Mackenzie
when he becomes impatient: '"Look here, pull yourself together. Are
you mad? Stark, staring?... Or only just play-acting? [...] If you let yourself go, you may let yourself go a tidy sight further than you want to"' (p.
302). To 'let yourself go', as figured in the ellipses, means to relax one's
hold upon one's emotions, to lose language, to forgo self-control. It
means acknowledging the individual face of battle.

When such an acknowledgement comes it represents a creative, as
well as a cognitive, leap: Keowan, asleep under the bloody overcoat of
a dead French dragoon, was disturbed by 'the shrieks of the dying and
the agitation of our minds, for the waves will roll high, after the storm
has ceased, and as much of the fight recurred to me as I had time to
dream of'.[39] Keegan encourages his reader through Keowan to begin to
imagine the 'living' of the battle of Waterloo in its sensational
extremes. Likewise, Ford demands kindred recognition via intimacy:
the 'body' of men has been birthed into a new reality, in which they
hear their own and others' blood (as does the reader in the prose) and
know everything has changed. Keowan and Ford are each exposing in
their words the painful dynamic of mental existence and experience in
war.[40] The revelation of a new and extended reality comes out of the
silence and space these soldiers sense after the high tides of battle, after
which one can never be the same.[41] In this extended reality, intolerable
sights are seen for what they are.

The house that the child draws then mutates into art of a quite different order:

> You may say that everyone who took part in the war was then mad. No
> one could have come through that shattering experience and still view life
> and mankind with any normal vision. In those days you saw objects that
> the earlier mind labelled as *houses*. They had been used to seem cubic and
> solid permanences. But we had seen Ploegsteert where it had been
> revealed that men's dwellings were thin shells that could be crushed as
> walnuts are crushed. (*It Was the Nightingale*, pp. 63–4)

Sight splinters, followed by language: a House (or *house*, he uses italics
here) is now just a house that can be crushed like a walnut. The abstract
has become concrete, and the concrete cannot last. What one sees, in
instances like this, can indeed make one mad. I don't believe Ford's
contention to be that every former soldier was certifiable. What he is
saying is that they were shattered human beings, shattered by the
assault on the conceptual mechanism that deprived them of a vision of
the world (defined by Ford as fundamental) where houses were seen
and known as *houses*.[42] They have 'seen' (past tense) Ploegsteert: they
are mad. This isn't just to do with the sight of inanimate objects; it is to
do with the sight of the human body, bodies like O Nine Morgan's.
'Like Cubism', writes Peter Conrad, 'the war redesigned the human
body.' 'Remarque's novels', he continues

> are specific about the metamorphoses. Soldiers whose feet have been shot
> off hop towards shell-holes on splintered stumps. One man turns up to
> have his wounds dressed, clasping his spilled intestines with his hands.
> One casualty is 'light to carry, because almost half of him is missing'. A
> stretcher bearer has been minced. Another veteran has one eye interred
> beneath scar tissue, while its partner is made of dull glass. A patch
> conceals the cavity where his nose was. His mouth, sliced in half, has
> grown back together askew.[43]

Here are other 'fictional' versions of cubist canvasses, more brutal and
more concrete than Ford's example.

Sight and madness

The fragmentary relationship between sight and madness in *The Good
Soldier* is of critical interest to Max Saunders (see my discussion in
Chapter 2): 'Leonora is fighting to suppress that maddening vision of
the truth [...]. When inexperienced Nancy sees what is happening,
she does go mad'.[44] Nancy 'sees' figuratively due to what she 'sees'

literally, the story of the Brand divorce and adultery in the newspaper (*The Good Soldier*, p. 140). For Florence, sight means a different kind of death (she 'got it in the face' (p. 77), Ford writes aggressively, of her night-time vision of Edward and Nancy together). Having seen Edward and Nancy, she then sees her husband with Bagshawe: her part in the 'game' is up and she kills herself. 'Prose', quintessentially and shockingly, for Ford and for his characters, is 'a matter of looking things in the face'.[45]

War creates similarly mortal, fragmenting patterns of sight; Ford develops this technique from the earlier text, and others use it too. Indeed in (the writing of) war, such sights seem almost omnipresent, either metaphorically or literally. Though Tietjens looks at the 'trench face' at the front, made from flint and soil and pebbles, and finds it friendly, it costs to extend this kind of sympathy to the animate (p. 553): 'one sees such things', thinks Bourne, 'and one suffers vicariously. The mind is averted as well as the eyes. It reassures itself after that first despairing cry: "It is I!" "No, it is not I. I shall not be like that"' (*The Middle Parts of Fortune*, p. 11). The metaphor of the face is often stretched by war into an overt relationship with life-threatening behaviour: if one looks and sees oneself, one may not be able to fight, one may go mad, or die. (Siegfried Sassoon associates his mental breakdown with an ability to see with the near-focused eyes of his troops, but not with the abstract vision of his employers.[46]) Many soldiers seem to have maintained a splintered perception of reality, the fragmenting pendulum of which swung between the carapace suggested by Keegan and the real terror of the apprehension of one's own face in war. Each new sight increased its parabola. When Bourne steps over the dead version of himself, from which he manages to dissociate ('"It is I! No, it is not I"'), he knows too that the sight, that 'I', will return, if only in sleep.

Pat Barker's novel *The Eye in the Door* uses the metaphorical and the actual functions of sight to precipitate the breakdown of her working-class officer protagonist, Billy Prior (much of Barker's research for her famous trilogy was based on W. H. R. Rivers's wartime work[47]). The eye of the title refers to that which was often painted on the inside of the prison cell door of conscientious objectors, designed to promote continual unease and the permanent effect of being watched; it also precipitated mental problems, or compounded them, of a much more serious nature. For Billy, the eye, seen in prison, serves to bring back to him unbidden the worst experience of his war career: the realisation, after an explosion, that he holds in his hand the eyeball of Towers, one of his men. He is sent to consult a fictional/factual Rivers. The real Rivers was one of the pioneers in the reappraisal of madness made necessary by the 'shell-shock' of the First World War[48] (although he was not exactly radical, as Elaine Showalter points out, he 'also saw male hysteria as an inferior kind of psychic response to conflict'[49]).

In the course of Prior's therapy, Barker's fictional Rivers fathoms the link between the eye and the conscience of the officer. Prior has dreamt that he was stabbing the eye in the door after visiting a conscientious objector in prison.[50] His guilt after the visit is allied in his unconscious to his responsibility for Towers's eye. The image of the eye in the door and of himself, standing, holding an eye, merge and culminate in a dreamtime attack on his externalised conscience in an attempt to destroy it: 'eye was stabbing myself in the "I"'. Using similar language to Bourne ('It is I. No it is not I'), Prior tries to avoid recognition of a painful and fragmenting part of the self. But in the analytical encounter this link between sight and guilt becomes plain, and Prior is typically scathing as he achieves clarity. Ford's war fiction also displays a consciousness of this link (though the repeated phrase, 'under four eyes', from *The Good Soldier*, is relevant too[51]).

In Ford's exploration of this topic, the class considerations driving Prior's breakdown are replaced by the complexities of gender at war: it is Tietjens's struggle with his role of officer that renders the abstract concrete. The case of a boy losing his eye is what Tietjens isolates, in conversation with Valentine's mother, from the whole of his war experience. It has made him mad:

> 'It's that that's desperate. I'll tell you. I'll give you an instance. I was carrying a boy. Under rifle-fire. His eye got knocked out. If I had left him where he was his eye would not have been knocked out. I thought at the time that he might have been drowned, but I ascertained afterwards that the water never rose high enough. So I am responsible for the loss of his eye. It's a sort of monomania. You see, I am talking of it now. It recurs. Continuously.' (p. 659)

Just previously, 'the boy', Aranjuez, has admitted to Tietjens that 'it would be awful to have anything happen to your eyes' because 'your girl would naturally not look at you' (p. 599). Although this remembered conversation, in its portentousness, helps to reinforce Tietjens's feeling of madness, it does not instigate it. The instigation is provided by his concomitant emasculation. Aranjuez, pre-battle, 'had clung

to Tietjens as a child clings to an omnipotent father'; this is because
Tietjens, 'all-wise, could direct the awful courses of war and decree
safety for the frightened!' (pp. 598–9). Aranjuez worshipped him –
which was what was supposed to happen in successful army units,
in which the 'rank and file' would come 'to identify with the units in
which their whole lives were now immersed'.[52] Then the battle begins.
In the midst of prose that evokes brilliantly the stuttering time and
shock, the confusion and brief moments of vision, caused by shelling,
the reader is offered glimpses of Tietjens looking down on Aranjuez.
He has the advantage, being an officer (like Prior), being omnipotent;
he has 'a considerable view'. Aranjuez is then buried by flying mud.
Only his face, 'brown, with immense black eyes in bluish whites' can be
seen (p. 637). He looks at Tietjens; all words are lost in the noise. In
these chaotic seconds what is transmitted between the two faces is the
knowledge that Tietjens is not omnipotent. He has failed his charge,
one who looked to him as a father (just as he may have failed his real
son, who he has recently learned may have been fathered by Sylvia's
lover instead of by him). Thus he is impotent; the all-powerful, all-
seeing officer cannot even protect his own.

    In the later conversation with Valentine's mother, sight has come to
represent Tietjens's conscience. Sight is knowledge is responsibility.
War has proved this relationship without guaranteeing the ability for
an officer to act accordingly (seeing a Degas doesn't work in battle).
The fragmenting impact on his sense of self can be seen by the number
of differently functioning 'I's in the quotation. Tietjens's primary need,
later, is to try to talk; he seeks to fill an acquiescent, caring, female
vessel with the torments that until now have remained internal.[53] The
shortness of the first five sentences reveals his relief at speaking to her,
inclusive of disbelief that he now actually has someone to tell. His
mind's eye provides the links between the sentences, the details, the
reality, because there he can still see the horror – there it 'recurs' (also
Keowan's word for what happens in the lull after battle). Afterwards, it
is Tietjens's vision of his responsibility that causes the monomania,
which works like a repetitive self-punishment. Each short sentence is a
blow against himself, a slow, unstoppable lambasting. As he talks, he
also remembers; when he can no longer bear it, his words cease. His
words struggle with showing what it is his mind has been doing to him;
this experience feels like madness. It is crucial, of course, that Tietjens
speaks not to Valentine herself at this point, but to her mother, on the
telephone. Valentine overhears their conversation. Emphasising the

fragmentation of his sense of self, Ford has Tietjens talk not directly to his beloved, but to her via the telephone (that instrument of displacement and disguise – see Chapter 3) and her mother.

Masculinity at war

Issues of physical (enforced) passivity, of impotence, issues that become very complex, are raised by this incident in Ford's tetralogy. Such passivity or impotence, linked in this case with Tietjens's sight, stands as another explanation of why Keegan's projected ideal of the fighting man disintegrated in the face of war. It helped to prevent men from holding on to a vision of Kitchener's face, of themselves as masculine 'Soldier'. Pat Barker here elaborates upon it:

> The Great Adventure. They'd been mobilized into holes in the ground so constricted they could hardly move. And the Great Adventure – the real life equivalent of all the adventure stories they'd devoured as boys – consisted of crouching in a dugout, waiting to be killed. The war that had promised so much in the way of 'manly' activity had actually delivered 'feminine' passivity, and on a scale their mothers and sisters had hardly known. No wonder they broke down.[54]

At the beginning of this chapter, I suggested that soldiers are trained to suppress some instincts (flight, and disordered retaliation, for example). Whilst this is true, they have also been trained to release, and to reclaim, others. Trevor Wilson writes simply of the number of men who signed up for military service that 'war stirred feelings deeper than many men were able to articulate', his language implying that such feelings had a long way to travel before they could be expressed.[55] Training could capitalise on such stirrings. Tietjens himself considers it to be a condemnation of *civilisation* that he should never have had to use his significant physical strength (p. 638).

Niall Ferguson analyses the question of instinct in detail, finding a variety of literary evidence – in Wyndham Lewis, Robert Graves, Ernst Jünger and W. S. Littlejohn, amongst others – to support Freud's theory in 'Thoughts for the Times on War and Death' that the war signified the reassertion of primitive instincts.[56] In his assessment of a wartime letter by Wilfred Owen, Alvarez finds no simple 'reassertion' has taken place, but identifies 'two forces', 'each pulling in the opposite direction: nurture and nature, training and instinct'.[57] 'Manly' instincts may be released, then, if incompletely, but in the waiting of the trenches, or in the failure to safeguard one's men, they cannot be used. Barker's resulting picture is bleak: the tension, the marked absence of glorious activity, led to the men breaking down; men could be 'feminised' by war.[58] Though Edwin Ash doesn't talk of men in this position as feminised, he suggests that periods of time at the front, where men 'are frequently kept in a state of nervous tension for days at a time', deplete men of energy. Consequently their grip on sanity is compromised: 'hunger, exposure, fatigue, and want of sleep all tend to sap the nervous energy whilst strong emotional waves disturb mental calm'.[59] Lyn Macdonald's history of the war presents an image of such men, waiting, at the battle of le Cateau (26 August 1914): 'In the path of the shockwaves, hunched close to the trembling earth, ears ringing, teeth rattling, nerves screaming with every explosion, they could do nothing to retaliate and nothing to avert disaster'.[60] Their training has given them the controlled ability to liberate and activate their most violent and destructive instincts. Having been taught to kill and maim, behaviours that tore through all previous civilised codes of conduct (Rivers attributes war neurosis in part to the new call made on instinctive tendencies[61]), they must now rein in those ideas and wait. It is no wonder that Macdonald imagines that their nerves were screaming. The reader is placed high above them, looking down upon those who are like animals – 'hunched close to the trembling earth' – trapped. They are split, as Tietjens has split a dead soldier, into parts: ears, teeth and nerves. But these men are living, and it is the word 'nothing' that Macdonald chooses to repeat, they can do nothing. Of this impotence Barker states 'No wonder they broke down'.

The breakdown is a hysterical one, as Juliet Mitchell argues. As such, it forced a redefinition of one of the major tenets of contemporary psychological thought:

> The First World War leads Freud to a complete reformulation of the main thesis of psychoanalysis [...]. During the First World War what happened was that, instead of the typical 'Victorian' woman hysteric, shell-shocked soldiers displayed hysterical symptoms [...]. The literature of the war period and the descriptions of hysteria are fascinating because exactly the same symptoms were being produced by the men as had been produced by the women in an illness that was still associated with femininity.[62]

The rules of psychology must be extended to incorporate a new phenomenon, as the writing of the time must expand to give witness to its truth. And Ford rises to the occasion, proving in his fiction an intense absorption in the task. Ford states that Tietjens remained closer to the lines than he was instructed to do; he took his position desperately seriously: 'If I had left him where he was his eye would have not have been knocked out. . . . So I am responsible for the loss of his eye.' Tietjens also becomes intensely affected by the 'femininity' historically associated with 'passivity' and with the hysteric. In an extraordinary way, though, Tietjens's madness is caused by femininity that becomes more than passive; it is actively portrayed by Ford. Aranjuez has been buried, as we have seen. But Tietjens, and then two colleagues, pull him out of the viscous mud to safety: 'Cockshott and the corporal pulled Aranjuez out of the slime. He came out reluctantly, like a lugworm out of sand. He could not stand. His legs gave way' (pp. 638–9). Aranjuez is reborn, with Tietjens presiding as midwife. How much more concrete can the abstract become? Having let him down as omnipotent father, Tietjens becomes a mother, 'he felt tender, like a mother, and enormous', as he carries the boy (p. 639). Seconds later, snipers' bullets destroy Aranjuez's eye.

Tietjens has divested himself of the protections of officer-language and officer-distance. Ceasing in the attempt to blind both himself and his men to reality, he has fully become that most difficult of things (harder even than an officer who acts like a father, see note 52): an officer who cares for his men like a mother. As Trudi Tate has suggested, the differences between types of masculinity in this period are in many ways more interesting than those between women and men.[63] Tietjens abandons the carapace and allows his feelings to show; he fragments the organised mechanism of the 'big words'. This response is 'realistic' in the strongest sense of the word, and it is deeply, psychologically astute of Ford to reconstruct it.

The carefully constructed image of the fighting man is shattered by Ford; the image of the officer swiftly follows suit. Tietjens picks up Aranjuez, and carries him like the baby he is shown he has become. When he cannot protect him in this role as his mother, when his impotence is proved twofold, he loses his mind.

Madness comes too to Manning's fighting man, due to the return of the repressed to the visual imagination:

> One had lived instantaneously during that timeless interval, for in the shock and violence of the attack, the perilous instant, on which he perched so precariously, was all that the half-stunned consciousness of man could grasp; and if he lost his grip on it he fell back among the grotesque terrors and nightmare creatures of his own mind. Afterwards,

> when the strain had been finally released, in the physical exhaustion
> which followed, there was a collapse, in which one's emotional nature was
> no longer under control. (p. 3)

In the attack, there is simply no possibility of thought. Manning cites
two reasons for this. The first is that man's consciousness is 'half-
stunned'; it is not working to its full interrogative capacity (one
wonders about the role of the obligatory rum ration in this; Ferguson
states that 'without alcohol the First World War could not have been
fought' (p. 351)); it cannot think about what is being done. The second
reason comes out of the realisation that the mind cannot afford to
question or to analyse. If it did, a man would 'fall back among the
grotesque terrors of his own mind'; he needs to be protected from
himself. Once a man is committed, once he will 'stand up', time
appears to work to support him in this protection from himself. It
moves instantaneously, a self-perpetuating cycle of movement that
simply repeats itself, complicit with the survival instinct and with the
need not to think. The truncated consciousness of man is accommo-
dated perfectly by time in this sense. The instinct of self-preservation
can be buried in this flickering cine film where the black split-seconds
are the ignored possibilities of knowing exactly what is being risked.
Film 'language' can be allied with Ford's modernist quest in other
important ways.[64]

But Manning refers to a 'collapse'. The consequences of the subli-
mation make themselves stunningly felt in the time 'afterwards' when
the sights and feelings return; in Keowan's 'low tide'; in Ford's time of
'intolerable intimacy'; in Barker's 'feminine passivity'. According to
Edwin Ash (still writing in a dated way of shell-shock in 1919) there is
a time lag between the shell-explosion and the collapse of the neurotic
soldier. In this time lag, the sufferer is got to safety by the intensity of
self-preservation. Then, 'left to his own conscious control', he collapses
(p. 275). To Manning, once physical exhaustion has intruded upon the
possibility for continuing action, one's 'emotional nature' takes over
and gains absolute control. One pays for the continual neglect of how
one feels in repeated small breakdowns. Ash observes that 'dreadful
sights of mutilation and slaughter' play their part in the collapse
(p. 270).

'Shell-shock'

'The army eventually reconciled itself to the inescapable fact of the breakdown of so many of its soldiers', writes John Keegan, 'by inventing the notion of "shell-shock" which suggested for it a single physical cause' (p. 328). Ferguson, disagreeing, states that this term was used to describe 'a variety of mental disorders resulting from combat stress' (p. 341). Numbers of cases cited vary from 50,000[65] to 200,000 or more men suffering from 'mental wounding'.[66] Ford suffered from 'shell-shock' after an incident during the battle of the Somme on 28/29 July 1916. It was during this battle in particular, according to Martin Gilbert, that 'because of the intensification of nervous breakdowns and shell-shock, special centres were opened in each army area for diagnosis and treatment' (p. 276). Ford was taken to the casualty clearing station at Corbie, where he lay having lost his memory (to Rivers, loss of memory was one of the most common features of war-neurosis[67]), with some physical injury too (see Saunders II, pp. 1–4). His experiences become part of Tietjens's war-torn portrayal: Tietjens tells Sylvia that a 'great portion' of his brain, 'in the shape of memory, has gone' (p. 168).

Ford initially attributes his experience of the illness to the physicality of the injuries caused by shells in the attack. He says in a letter to C. F. G. Masterman, 'I was twice knocked down by the percussion from these shells, on the second occasion damaging my mouth & loosening my teeth wh. became very bad, affecting my whole condition'. For the next months – he did not quite recover from this – he spent time trying to avoid his old regiment, the 9th Welch. In December 1916, having heard that he probably would be assigned there, he found himself back in hospital due to his lungs. On this occasion he wrote to Masterman saying 'I lie awake & perceive the ward full of Huns of forbidding aspect ... I am in short rather ill and sometimes doubt my own sanity – indeed, quite frequently I do',[68] revealing that the state of his physical health is causing him less real problem than that of his mental health. His nightmares, and daymares, have become more to the point.

When Ford was originally diagnosed with shell-shock (described in a letter to Masterman on 13 September 1916[69]), he wouldn't go into hospital to be treated for it. Three months later, forced to the Red Cross hospital at Rouen by his 'charred up' lungs, the truth of the Somme begins to emerge. 'I suppose that, really, the Somme was a pretty severe ordeal, though I wasn't conscious of it at the time', he writes to

Masterman, in the subsequent sentence in which he doubts his sanity. In *Parade's End* we only learn the shape of Tietjens's experiences months later, when he is home, talking to Sylvia (blaming a man in hospital for starting his 'tortures'), showing his damaged memory and the sights he does remember.[70] Tietjens's delayed reaction can be equated with those others that have been detailed in fiction, an extended version of the time lag between 'standing up' and mental collapse, between the 'violence of the attack' and the terrors of one's 'own mind'. As Sassoon recovers from shell-shock, in hospital in England, he is aware that all around him men are revisiting the line, at night, in their mind's eye: 'By night, each man was back in his doomed sector of a horror-stricken front line where the panic and the stampede of some ghastly experience was re-enacted among the livid faces of the dead'.[71] In Manning's text, the delay is not so long; he depicts Bourne, surrounded by his sleeping, dreaming companions, hours after the battle, using him to articulate a darkness 'filled with the shudderings of tormented flesh' (p. 6).

Ford sees German soldiers, ready for battle, in his hospital ward. It proves difficult to step back out of the reality he has come to know, that of battle, and appreciate once more the comparatively civilian aspect of a hospital. This difficulty was compounded, and heightened (and very generally felt – see Chapter 1), by the re-entry into civilian life. The sense of difference, between combatant experience and civilian perception, between the 'big words' and the reality, between the abstract and the concrete, is part of what drives Ford into fiction in *Parade's End*. The four volumes that make it up don't begin to appear until 1924, though; there is a time lag here too.

Ford's waking nightmares and the anxiety from which they proceed can be related to the psychological problems that Rivers ascribed to officership.[72] The 'pathological conditions' described, of noise and extreme sensation, and the strain of re-entering civilian life, more than satisfy Rivers's criteria for 'disorders of the nervous system' becoming manifest.[73] But whatever the rank of the men, they were ultimately linked by the problem of the expression of such disorders. Showalter, echoing the discussion of communication in Chapter 1, attributes the final breakdown most of all to this issue of inexpressibility: 'When all signs of physical fear were judged as weakness and where alternatives to combat – pacifism, conscientious objection, desertion, even suicide – were viewed as unmanly, men were silenced and immobilized and forced, like women, to express their conflicts through the body' (p. 171).

They could not say how they felt or what they had seen, because language did not provide them with the words, and because language had changed anyway. Combatant alienation was reinforced when civilians didn't respect this change: a house was no longer a House.[74]

Ford eventually wrote a great deal on the subject of the war, and on its psychological, emotional and linguistic effects; he was committed to his self-perceived responsibility of being historian of his time. He used narrative to explore the many, sometimes conflicting, levels of existence – levels that proliferate in war. He also fought, and experienced mental problems as a direct result. The war provides, then, a crystallised example of systems fragmenting, for all the reasons that have been discussed up to this point in this chapter. And yet Tietjens survives (unlike Bourne, who suffocates on his own blood whilst being carried 'tenderly, like a child', by his pal, p. 246); he not only survives, but is a more complete, aware human being. He is allowed by his author to retire from the front, back to the country. Why? It is to this question that I now wish to turn, as I approach the end of this chapter.

Tietjens

This discussion necessitates at first a further analysis of Ford's narrative technique. Although Ford chose in Tietjens a character through whom he could show the extremes to which war can push a man, much must be inferred by the reader. The 'big words' have gone, and Ford experiments with how to replace them in the text. The language he finds is not explosive or desperately dramatic or even particularly gory or violent. Tietjens's experience of a shell barrage is 'slow, slow, slow ... like a slowed down movie. The earth manoeuvred for an infinite time' (p. 637);[75] it is not frantic or panic-struck. Brains can work like this under stress, revealing the cost of such calm at a later time, as we have seen, but such narrative also represents, perhaps, the stress involved in being unable to say what one thinks or sees because one does not have the words.

Ford thinks he doesn't have the right words, concrete words. He wrote in 1916 that 'when I look at a mere coarse map of the Line, simply to read "Ploegsteert" or "Armentieres" seems to bring up extraordinarily coloured and exact pictures behind my eyeballs... – But, as for putting them – into words! No: the mind stops dead' ('A Day of Battle', pp. 497–8). And so, whilst Samuel Hynes's prosaic account of the war is as 'the most literary and the most poetical war in

English history', there is, nonetheless, a faltering beginning.[76] Ford does find some words, but the reader must work hard with them, for they are representative of something which the reader must articulate; they are impressionistic. Although the need to symbolise repression is perhaps one cause for the profusion of ellipses (and they are a 'tool', as I said at the outset of this chapter) in Ford's work, another is linked to impressionism. These active spaces allow for confusion, for contradiction, and for the uplift of the words that are there:

> ... But, anyhow, these things are official. One can't, if one's scrupulous, even talk about them... And then... You see it means such infinite deaths of men, such an infinite prolongation... all this interference for side-ends!... I seem to see these fellows with clouds of blood over their heads... And then... I'm to carry out their orders because they're my superiors.... But helping them means unnumbered deaths.... (p. 237)

Because of Tietjens's position, secrecy concerning his orders should be absolute. So he acknowledges that he cannot talk about them whilst the necessity that he feels to do so is implied in the following space. Because he must do his duty and follow his orders he does so; yet, in the second space, his mind allows him to consider the consequences. These consequences are deaths, for men in 'infinite' numbers over an 'infinite time'; that which his mind cannot comprehend because of the infinitude is left to the following space to construct. Sharp though he is, Prior states in Barker's *The Eye in the Door* that he 'can't grasp' war though he has 'been there'. 'I can't get my mind round it', he admits, feeling similarly bereft of articulacy (p. 169). But whilst he acknowledges the impossibility and stops, Tietjens carries on through it. He continues, though faltering, embodying the impossibility, besought by the pictures that his brain shows him of the consequences of his actions.

When words fail in Ford, he can resort to pictures. It is his impressionist's eye that overall solves the problem. A fragmented quasi-conversational exchange takes place between Tietjens and General Campion in *No More Parades*. It is the backbone of this volume (2) of the tetralogy. Tortuous, deeply painful, heavy with Tietjens's beleaguered humanity and Campion's bullying, this exchange, which takes many slow and awkward pages, manages to bring to Tietjens's traumatised attention all the aspects of his life that he would rather forget: his unhappy army career, his wife's infidelities, his domestic loneliness, his social inadequacies, his potential status as illegitimate, and his father's suicide. At its climax, Tietjens is quietly desperate. 'I'm sorry, sir', he interjects, 'it's difficult to make myself plain'. The general replies, 'neither of us do. What is language for? What the *hell* is language for? We go round and round' (pp. 468–93). Campion decides their inability to communicate is because he is an 'old fool' who cannot understand Tietjens's 'modern ways'. But of course that's not true, as he then realises, because Tietjens is not modern himself. Tietjens is the product (or at least was the product), in his schooling, in his landed inheritance, in his conception of life, of the 'eighteenth century'. This existence, in its existential clash with the twentieth century (as represented by war, by Sylvia's affairs, and by the circumstances of his father's death), renders him inarticulate, or, in his own understated language, it makes it difficult for him to make himself 'plain'. 'Principles [like the "big words"] are like the skeleton map of a country', Tietjens has said many pages previously. They can show one where to go, behaviourally and morally. Without them, as he is in this twentieth-century world, he must use another map. Ford presents him with one, and simultaneously proves his way of using words impressionistically, to make pictures of fragments when the abstract words have gone and the concrete ones are inadequate:

> Panic came over Tietjens. He knew it would be the last panic of that interview. No brain could stand more. Fragments of scenes of fighting, voices, names, went before his eyes and ears. Elaborate problems... The whole map of the embattled world ran out in front of him – as large as a field. An embossed map in greenish *papier mâché* – a ten-acre field of embossed *papier mâché*, with the blood of O Nine Morgan blurring luminously over it.

This map shows the shape and texture of Tietjens's fragmented struggle. It is a linguistic map. It is a temporal map too, as well as a geographical record of the front, domestic and military. All the sights and sounds of war are there, held in equilibrium by the sea of colour that is before his eyes. Campion recedes, and Ford finds the words to show how it is for this man. The words depict a multi-faceted, kaleidoscopic, image, made of past and present sights and sounds, fed too by his enforced trawl through his life and its decline from the ideal. 'I ask you to believe', Tietjens says to Campion, 'that I have absolutely no relations with that young lady [Valentine Wannop, accused of being his lover]. None! I have no intention of having any. None!' (p. 488). It is not true. He admits the truth, post-war, finding new words on

Armistice Day, and turns this decline from the eighteenth-century abstract ideal into a modern, fragmented, triumph.

Tietjens is opened out, existentially speaking; he is made to be self-aware in his journey through warfare. The man whom Ford was able to describe as having 'an emotional existence' of 'complete taciturnity' at the beginning of the text (p. 6), is made to relinquish, or at least to question, his past. In the most violent and painful fashion imaginable ('Sylvia Tietjens had been excruciatingly unfaithful, in the most painful manner', p. 299), everything has been changed. Groby, his land, his inheritance, is, he believes, to pass into Sylvia's hands. David Cannadine gives an impression of what that loss would have meant: 'Until the 1870s [as usual, Tietjens is slow to catch up] ... land was wealth: the most secure, reliable and permanent asset. Land was status. And land was power: over the locality, the county, and the nation.'[77] Post-war, the 'big words', his preconceptions and safe customs, may have been destroyed. He may have have been tortured by this destruction. But he does learn to admit what he wants.

In sexual terms this means that he will have 'relations' with Valentine: public codes are sublimated to private desires. War has forced him to this point. When Valentine travels to him, her mother attempts to prevent their inevitable union by appealing to the Tietjens who existed before the war:

> Standing at the telephone, Tietjens had recognised at once that this was a mother, pleading with infinite statesmanship for her daughter. There was no doubt about that. How could he continue to... to entertain designs on the daughter of this voice?... But he *did*. He couldn't. He did. He *couldn't*. He did... You may expel Nature by pleading... *tamen usque recur*... She must recline in his arms before midnight... [...] There was nothing to answer to the mother on sentimental lines. He wanted Valentine Wannop enough to take her away. (p. 665)[78]

In comparison with the tortured battle with his desire exposed at the beginning of this chapter, these lines reveal a man who has had to face, and incorporate, his full human existence. His language is still full of difficulty, and is self-contradictory, but there is a new confidence in the unconcealed aspect of his unjustified desire. It becomes a statement of fact. Implicit in this is the relevance of Armistice Day; his sexual union will echo the end of atrocities, proving that some little joy can be salvaged from the suffering undergone. Tietjens's existence has been stretched; he must now show his new, reclaimed, aspects. The repeated 'couldn't' above represents the vestige of pre-war codes of behaviour; his gentlemanly attendance to 'a mother' reminds us of what he would have done. But now he wants Valentine, and there is nothing to prevent him from having her.

As well as discovering the female side of his nature, as has been discussed in his bearing of Aranjuez away from the scene of battle, Tietjens has thus been introduced to the more instinctive and essentially male side of himself. From this base he can experience the desire for sexual pleasure and union with one he loves and wants. 'The war had made a man of him!' he exults. 'What he had been before, God alone knew. A Younger Son? A Perpetual Second-in-Command? Who knew. But to-day the world changed. Feudalism was finished; its last vestiges were gone. It held no place for him' (p. 668). Capitalised words return for what would seem to be the last time, as they are banished from his vocabulary. He can no longer hide in the protection of feudalism, behind the banner of inherited systematised thought. He must adopt the life now demanded of him, which is less defined. I said, as I began this last section of the chapter, that Tietjens is allowed by his narrator to retire from the front back into the country. I now wish to qualify this statement, for although he does indeed move to the country, the last and most significant personal battle takes place here when Sylvia comes to hunt him down. Instead of Christopher, she finds Valentine:

> [Sylvia] bit into a small handkerchief that she had in her hand, concealed. She said:
> 'Damn it, I'm playing pimp to Tietjens of Groby – leaving my husband to you!...'
> Someone again sobbed... [...]
> Marie Leonie said:
> 'C'est lamentable qu'un seul homme puisse inspirer deux passions pareilles dans deux femmes...' (p. 827)

Tietjens may not be there to witness this exchange, but two of the worlds that have at different times claimed him are realigned and brought once more to face each other. The repressive power, of which Sylvia was the prime representative, returns, reminiscent of that diminished 'he couldn't' of the telephone conversation. Perhaps Ford has banished Tietjens from this part of the action because he is aware of a still animate allegiance, somewhere within him, to the time before. Ford will not allow him to retract, and so prevents him from being tested again. It can be intuited from his banishment that the need for

Keegan's carapace, made so obvious by the suffering of war, and equally challenged by the courage of the fighters and writers in their discovery of different truths, is never thoroughly exorcised.

Ford apprehends the destructiveness of war mostly personally, observantly, perhaps encouraged to do so by his life as a writer. He was able to state, of his habitual mental existence just after the war, 'I live in my moment' (*It Was the Nightingale*, p. 112), a moment which is yet multi-faceted and well informed. His experiences of war have solidified and validated this self-awareness. Some things have been gained, at the expense of others. He says of himself at the same time that 'I had no illusions myself' (*It Was the Nightingale*, p. 17) and his 'new' subjects come partly out of this strong sense of disillusionment. Disillusionment out of what he has seen – the mental and physical vulnerability he has suffered and witnessed; disillusionment too comes from the returning home to another world, where communication represents a whole new battle. The 'big words' are no longer in use.

Robert Graves provides a salient post-war observation, one that forms the conceptual partner to Ford's statement that 'everyone who had taken part in the war was then mad'. Graves relates a conversation between himself and Siegfried Sassoon in 1917, when they both had come to adopt an anti-war stance, and Sassoon in particular was suffering severe mental problems: 'I took the line that everyone was mad except ourselves and one or two others, and that no good would come of offering sense to the insane'.[79] Consciousness heightened to the extent of that of fighting men was, in Graves's opinion, the correct, and most sane, system of response to what had occurred. Those who were mad were sane in their vision; Tietjens in his agonised and fragmented self was real. Graves had to appear at the medical board to assess Sassoon, on his behalf. His role was to persuade those examining Sassoon that he was psychologically unfit and therefore not liable for imprisonment for the publication of his 'Soldier's Declaration' which announced his resignation from the British army. Of this meeting Graves states that: 'I had to appear in the role of a patriot distressed by the mental collapse of a brother-in-arms – a collapse directly due to his magnificent exploits in the trenches. I mentioned Siegfried's "halluci-nations" of corpses strewn along Piccadilly. The irony of having to argue to these mad old men that Siegfried was not sane!' (p. 216). Graves thus signifies the presence of a whole generation of men who, to a greater or lesser extent, see reality differently now. A new battle will have to begin, a battle on the grounds of consciousness.

This battle is what has, in part, created Tietjens. His story is one of microcosmic destabilisation. Through the continual battles (personal and international), Tietjens is stripped of one protective convention after another, until he is 'naked', like Bourne (p. 40), and left to face himself: then the face of battle has become his own face. This stripping occurs until Tietjens is aware of himself physically and sexually, until he sleeps with Valentine, until he comes to reject everything he thought was necessary and risks himself.

In Chapter 3 the potential of the Fordian woman as a symbol of containment was tentatively posed in the form of Ellida. Grimshaw, though tested, and reduced completely by Ford, was ultimately prevented from recognising this by the projection of his fear that was Katya. The 'sexual horror' that both Etta and Katya described was triumphant in *A Call*.[80] It meant that Grimshaw, having rejected the protection of society in the form of marriage, also rejected the alternative that was presented by Ford as essentially feminine. In *Parade's End*, despite the horror of Sylvia, Valentine both symbolises and stabilises a new system for existence, one that has emerged from the chaos and fragmentation of war – and yet Tietjens is absent from the scene of its institution. In the chapters that follow, Fordian men will be seen to make the leap of recognition into these alternative worlds more completely. Rather than the nightmare visions of war, it is the sights of fantasy that precipitate them. Multi-faceted though it still is, the fragmenting face of modernism becomes one instead that can be celebrated. The splintering nature of desire and of war is countered by fictional worlds that free and articulate the unconscious entirely, and Ford's protagonists are allowed to be present at their investiture.

Notes

1 Ivan Turgenev, *Fathers and Sons* (Oxford, Oxford University Press, 1991), p. 233.

2 Ford Madox Ford, *It Was the Nightingale* (1934) (New York, Ecco, 1984), p. 80.

3 Ezra Pound, 'Affirmations ...VI. Analysis of this Decade', *New Age*, XVI (11 February 1915), p. 410.

4 Ford Madox Ford, *The Good Soldier* (New York, Norton, 1995), p. 25.

5 Perhaps because, as Peter Conrad suggests, to Hemingway 'the language which offered to give an account of [the war] had given up, or died of shame' (*Modern Times, Modern Places: Life and Art in the Twentieth Century*, London, Thames & Hudson, 1998, p. 213).

6 In *Paroles d'un combattant* (1920), quoted by Jay Winter in *Sites of Memory, Sites of Mourning: The Great War in European Cultural History* (Cambridge, Cambridge University Press, 2000), p. 184.

7 Peter Childs provides a pertinent reminder, however, that for modernists in general language 'was breaking down as it struggled and bent to encompass the world' (*Modernism*, London, Routledge, 2000, p. 62). Kurtz can only say 'The horror!' at the climax to *Heart of Darkness*.

8 See my discussion of Fussell and Hynes in the Introduction here; Allyson Booth, *Postcards from the Trenches: Negotiating the Space Between Modernism and the First World War* (Oxford, Oxford University Press, 1996), p. 6.

9 Conrad, *Modern Times, Modern Places*, p. 207.

10 See Michael Levenson, *A Genealogy of Modernism* (Cambridge, Cambridge University Press, 1984), pp. 140–4, for an interesting discussion of 'the war among the moderns'. Ford's statements about war include that made to his mother: 'I have never felt such an entire peace of mind as I have felt since I wore the King's uniform' (Levenson, p. 144).

11 Graham Greene, 'Ford Madox Ford' (1962) in Philip Stratford (ed.), *The Portable Graham Greene* (Harmondsworth, Penguin, 1985), p. 473.

12 Ford here perhaps provokes brief comparison with Saussure's linguistic models, as I have suggested in my earlier remarks about structuralism. Malcolm Bowie concentrates on the reasons for the capitalisation of the signifier in his analysis ('Jacques Lacan' in John Sturrock (ed.), *Structuralism and Since: from Levi-Strauss to Derrida*, Oxford, Oxford University Press, 1979, p. 128).

13 Ford Madox Ford, *Parade's End* (Harmondsworth, Penguin, 1988), p. 18. As stated in previous references, this text was originally published as four volumes, gathered together by Knopf in 1950 under the title *Parade's End*, Ford's choice for such a project. In the Penguin edition, *Some Do Not...* is pp. 3–288; *No More Parades* pp. 289–500; *A Man Could Stand Up-* pp. 501–674; *Last Post* pp. 675–836.

14 Confusion as to the term 'unconsious' was common. Ford makes a mistake here in using 'subconscious' (refer to Peter Gay, *Freud: A Life For Our Time*, London, J. M. Dent & Sons, 1988, p. 453 for an assessment of this 'common and telling mistake'). Any Freudian would also take Ford on at his suggestion that such concepts as Loyalty, God, etc. would be part of the unconscious framework. Anna Freud puts it well when she writes that 'while our conscious thinking and planning are subject to the rules of reason and logic ... the mode inherent in the unconsious follows its own paths that are directed solely to the pursuit of pleasure' (in her edition of *Sigmund Freud: The Essentials of Psycho-Analysis*, Harmondsworth, Penguin, 1991, p. 77). It is, nonetheless, clear what Ford means here: an underpinning belief in certain concepts has vanished.

15 Where he can, he manipulates that incapacity: in the rules for writing fiction that he designed with Conrad it is decreed that 'no speech of one character should ever answer the speech that goes before it' (*Joseph Conrad: A Personal Remembrance*, New York, Ecco, 1989, p. 200). This is because speech isn't fluent or coherent, but truncated and fragmented.

16 Refer to Chapter 1 for accounts of Ford's experience of mental illness, and of his opinions of the professionals associated with this field.

17 See Allyson Booth's discussion of Wallace Stevens's use of ellipsis in his war writing to suggest 'the radical potential of words to register war's dislocations' (*Postcards from the Trenches*, pp. 15–16); see also Cornelia Cook's discussion of *Last Post*, which includes some assessment of the modernist degeneration of linguistic codes (*Agenda*, 27/8, 1989/90, pp. 23–30).

18 Ford Madox Ford, *Between St Dennis and St George: A Sketch of Three Civilisations* (London, Hodder & Stoughton, 1915), p. 38. He wrote this book for C. F. G. Masterman's Ministry of Information.

19 Booth, *Postcards from the Trenches*, p. 5.

20 This essay is published in full in the Norton edition of *The Good Soldier*. Impressionism is discussed in Chapter 7.

21 After training with the 3rd Battalion of the Welch Regiment at Tenby, he left for France on 17 July 1916, as a second lieutenant.

22 John Keegan, *The Face of Battle* (London, Pimlico, 1993), p. 21.

23 Trevor Wilson, *The Myriad Faces of War* (Cambridge, Polity Press, 1988), p. 248.

24 [Siegfried Sassoon,] *Sherston's Progress* (London, Faber & Faber, 1936), p. 86.

25 See Appendix IV, 'War Neurosis and Military Training', *Instinct and the Unconscious: A Contribution to a Biological Theory of the Psycho-Neuroses* (Cambridge, Cambridge University Press, 1922), p. 210.

26 These opinions are those of Ernest Hemingway, then Michael Howard. They are quoted in Wilson, *Myriad Faces of War*, p. 678.

27 Frederic Manning, *The Middle Parts of Fortune* (Harmondsworth, Penguin, 1990), p. 182. This quotation also gave Trevor Wilson the title for his history of the First World War.

28 David Cannadine, *The Decline and Fall of the British Aristocracy* (London, Macmillan, 1996), p. 2.

29 Booth, *Postcards from the Trenches*, p. 53.

30 See the chapter entitled 'The Mind's Eye' in her book *Brain Story* (London, BBC, 2000).

31 Friedrich Nietzsche, 'The Use and Abuse of History' in Oscar Levy (ed.), *The Complete Works of Friedrich Nietzsche*, Vol. 5, ii, *Thoughts Out of Season* (Edinburgh, T. N. Foulis, 1909), p. 8.

32 Winter writes that, 'to remember the anxiety of 1500 days of war necessarily

entailed how to forget; in the interwar years those who couldn't obliterate the nightmares were locked in asylums throughout Europe' (*Sites of Memory, Sites of Mourning*, p. 2).

33 See Ford's poem 'A House' (in *New Poems*, New York, William Edwin Rudge, 1927), in which the 'permanent' fixtures of the house support a fabric of the changing of fate in its endless cycles. It is a child's construction, under the simplicity of which other truths come alive – and yet that simplicity is not destroyed. The poem can also be found in Max Saunders (ed.), *Ford Madox Ford: Selected Poems* (Manchester, Carcanet, 1997), pp. 126–39.

34 Ford Madox Ford, 'A Day of Battle', *Yale Review*, 78: 4 (Summer 1989), p. 499.

35 Ford Madox Ford, *No Enemy* (1929) (New York, Ecco, 1984), p. 33.

36 Keegan states that Kitchener is still 'accorded respect for his triumphs of army building in 1914–15'; he 'had originally called for a single increment of a hundred thousand men to the strength of the current army. He was, by the spring of 1915, to find himself with six of these "hundred thousands"' (*Face of Battle*, pp. 174, 217). But despite the fact that Wilson discusses Kitchener as a 'symbol of the Government's determination to prosecute the war to victory', he thinks the famous poster did little in the way of persuading men to enlist (*Myriad Faces of War*, pp. 243, 409–10).

37 Hence Ford's sense, as well as his language, is evocative of George Eliot's 'roar which lies on the other side of silence' that she claims one could die of (*Middlemarch*, Harmondsworth, Penguin, 1985, p. 226).

38 He writes typically, in a way that further illustrates the terrible dualities of experiencing war, and being an officer, and attempting to write about it: the real fear comes after the shell-fire. Ford is 'frightened out of his life' by thunder, but does his job as the shells burst; the fear is forced into the 'subconscious' realm, because 'if one of the cooks suddenly opens, with a hammer, a chest close at hand, one jumps in a way one doesn't when the "dirt" is coming over fairly heavily'. Ford Madox Ford, letter to Joseph Conrad, headed Attd. 9/Welch, 19th Div., B. E. F., [September 1916] in Richard Ludwig (ed.), *The Letters of Ford Madox Ford* (Princeton, Princeton University Press, 1965), pp. 71–2.

39 Keegan, *Face of Battle*, p. 196.

40 Like Keegan, Ford pursues the analogy of turbulent water in its relevance to the workings of the mind, 'there it was then: the natural catastrophe! As when, under thunder, a dam breaks. His mind was battling with the waters' (*Parade's End*, p. 477). A force equivalent to a dam-burst of water threatens Tietjens's psychological balance. Using relevant imagery, Jung writes that '[rite and dogma] were dams and walls to keep back the dangers of the unconscious [...]. It is these barriers that collapse when the symbols

become weak with age. Then the waters rise and boundless catastrophes break over mankind'. The 'rite and dogma', the 'big words' and distorted faces, of battle, give way to the watery and possessive storm of the unconscious. Herbert Read (ed.), *The Collected Works of C. J. Jung*, Vol. 9, Part 1, *The Archetypes and the Collective Unconscious* (London, Routledge & Kegan Paul, 1968), p. 18.

41 H. G. Wells wrote that 'in the 1914–18 war [Ford] was a bad case of shell-shock from which he never recovered. The pre-war F. M. H. was tortuous but understandable, the post-war F. M. H. was incurably *crazy*. [His emphasis.]' Wells was not a dispassionate observer, for he and Ford were not on good terms at this time, but the sense of acute change is notable (quoted in Arthur Mizener, *The Saddest Story: A Biography of Ford Madox Ford*, New York, Carroll & Graf, 1985, pp. 292–3).

42 Ford's prosaic quest is thus linked to Remarque's. As Peter Conrad points out, Remarque argued in his novel *Im Westen nichts Neues* (1929), that 'all those who took part in the war were destroyed by it, even if they saved their lives' (*Modern Times, Modern Places*, p. 203).

43 Conrad, *Modern Times, Modern Places*, p. 215.

44 Saunders I, pp. 423–4.

45 *Outlook* 33, 17 January 1914.

46 *Sherston's Progress*, p. 21.

47 The extent of this research, as well as the fact that imagination can't conjure more horrifically than reality can show, is shown when Burns's case, in *Regeneration*, is taken intact (and almost word for word) from one of Rivers's case-studies. (Compare *Regeneration* (Harmondsworth, Penguin, 1992, pp. 18–19) with Appendix III of *Instinct and the Unconscious* (p. 192).)

48 See Richard Slobodin's biography, *W. H. R. Rivers* (Stroud, Sutton Publishing, 1997), pp. 54–7.

49 Elaine Showalter, *The Female Malady: Women, Madness and English Culture, 1830–1980* (London, Virago, 1993), p. 174. Hereafter cited in the text as Showalter.

50 See Pat Barker, *The Eye in the Door* (Harmondsworth, Penguin, 1993), pp. 68–9, 75.

51 *The Good Soldier*, pp. 25, 42. I think the sense of judgement or conscience is implied here (conspicuous by its absence in a way), although what Ford is actually referring to is the unwatched interaction of two characters.

52 Wilson, *Myriad Faces of War*, p. 249. Wilson goes on to quote from Ian Hay's *The First Hundred Thousand* (published as a book in 1915) in a passage that gives an officer the role of strict parent whilst the soldier is depicted as the recalcitrant child. In a (feudal) socio-political echo of this family structure, David Cannadine writes of the aristocracy, 'the warrior class', as men 'who knew how to lead, how to command, and how to look

after the men' (*Decline and Fall of the British Aristocracy*, p. 74). Tietjens is a member of the land-owning class.

53 Tietjens's need to talk revivifies the discussion of analysis as a 'talking cure' (refer to Chapter 1).

54 Barker, *Regeneration*, pp. 107–8.

55 Wilson, *Myriad Faces of War*, p. 244.

56 See Niall Ferguson, *The Pity of War* (London, Penguin, 1998), pp. 357–61. See too the discussion regarding the liberation of war in relation to *The Middle Parts of Fortune* in Chapter 1 of this book.

57 Al Alvarez, *The Savage God: A Study of Suicide* (London, Weidenfeld & Nicolson, 1977), pp. 200–1.

58 This use of language is, in itself, suspect: such behaviour is, of course, neither 'masculine' or 'feminine', contrary to what the psychoanalytic pioneers suspected.

59 Edwin Ash, *The Problem of Nervous Breakdown* (London, Mills & Boon, 1919), p. 270.

60 Lyn Macdonald, *1914* (Harmondsworth, Penguin, 1989), p. 173.

61 Rivers, *Instinct and the Unconscious*, p. 120.

62 Juliet Mitchell, 'Sexuality and Psychoanalysis: Hysteria', *British Journal of Psychotherapy*, 12: 4, 1996.

63 Trudi Tate, *Modernism, History and the First World War* (Manchester, Manchester University Press, 1998), p. 109. Also, both chapters of the second part of this study of the war and modernism debate ideas of masculinity (in terms of sexuality and the feminisation of men).

64 In his study of Ford's war writing, particularly the *Parade's End* tetralogy, Ambrose Gordon states that 'Ford's affinities are more with the movies; his way of building up a scene – out of fragmented details, sudden "cuttings", shifts in "camera angle" closely resembles film montage'. The scene he studies in detail is that of the explosion at the beginning of *No More Parades* which kills O Nine Morgan (*The Invisible Tent: The War Novels of Ford Madox Ford*, Austin, University of Texas Press, 1964, p. 8). See also note 75 here.

65 Martin Gilbert, *The First World War* (London, Weidenfeld & Nicolson, 1994), p. 276.

66 Tate, *Modernism, History and the First World War*, p. 96.

67 *Instinct and the Unconscious*, p. 14.

68 The first letter is quoted by Mizener in *The Saddest Story*, p. 289; the second is in Ludwig (ed.), *Letters of Ford Madox Ford*, pp. 81–3.

69 See Ludwig (ed.), *Letters of Ford Madox Ford*, p. 76.

70 Ford's experiences of a dying man crying 'faith' perpetually, close to him in the hospital, become part of what Tietjens offers up as proof of his damaged mind. See Ford's letter to Conrad, 6 September 1916, in Ludwig (ed.), *Letters of Ford Madox Ford*, pp. 73–4, and *Parade's End*, p. 170.

71 *Sherston's Progress*, p. 88.

72 Samuel Hynes points out that one of Rivers's principal contributions to the subject of war neurosis lies in the fact that he distinguished between the neuroses of enlisted men and those of their officers. Enlisted men tended to suffer from paralysis, mutism and anaesthesia, and their officers from nightmares, obsessions and hysteria (*A War Imagined: The First World War and English Culture*, London, Pimlico, 1992, p. 177).

73 W. H. R. Rivers, 'Why is the "Unconscious" Unconscious?', *British Journal of Psychotherapy*, London, 1918, p. 243.

74 See Booth, *Postcards from the Trenches*, pp. 22–9. She refers the reader to Sassoon's poem 'Blighters' for an example of what civilians don't know about the meaning of words.

75 Childs writes that 'by the 1920s film was having an enormous cultural impact on art and literature' (*Modernism*, p. 123). See also Lyn Macdonald's comment on the 'filmic' nature of war, *1914*, p. 294; refer also to note 64 in this chapter.

76 Hynes, *A War Imagined*, p. 28.

77 *Decline and Fall of the British Aristocracy*, p. 16.

78 Tietjens himself allies the sexual act with a succumbing to 'Nature' and to the woman, in a way reminiscent of the discussion of Freud and Paglia in relation to *A Call*.

79 Robert Graves, *Goodbye to All That* (Harmondsworth, Penguin, 1973), p. 215.

80 Sondra Stang uses this phrase in analysing the relationship between Ford's and James's fiction: 'For Ford as well as for James, concealment and revelation are exercises in seeing how [writing] can best be done, and for both what is revealed is sexual horror' (*The Presence of Ford Madox Ford*, Pennsylvania, University of Pennsylvania Press, 1981, p. xxii).

5
Imaginative visions

In the two previous chapters Ford's major male characters have been seen to be under attack. Their behaviour codes, or vision of how to organise life having been fragmented (by war, by social shift, and by women), they are brought to a self-knowledge leading, particularly, to reflective or compulsive admissions, and to a degree of sexual awareness. War multiplied perspective; it showed Tietjens how to look on his men with love, and how to choose to love Valentine, despite the psychological dangers associated with each case. For Grimshaw, forced to battle of a different kind, the female gaze came to mean intellect along with sexual confidence; both of these undid him in the end: 'she looked up again into Robert Grimshaw's eyes. "I think, my dear", she said slowly, "as a precaution, I think you cannot have me on those terms; I think you had better" – she paused for the fraction of a minute – "marry me"'. Katya 'gets him both ways', and he admits as much to her.[1] Grimshaw's masculinity is partially liberated, and then reincarcerated, in A Call (Tietjens's, by contrast, is heightened and given new life). Ultimately, as the conclusion to these two chapters, the fragmentation endemic to modernism (represented in these cases by the war, by technology and by the contemporary perception of the 'woman problem'), involves multiple perspectives that can destroy one's sense of one's world and one's sense of oneself. But this isn't always the case. Regeneration, of the kind that eventually comes to Tietjens, as the end point of his journey through war, is also in its gift. This chapter traces the roots of this (often atavistic[2]) regenerative possibility in Ford, a possibility that attunes the mind not to the commonly expressed modernist experience of fragmentation, but to its rich and life-giving mirror – multiplicity – instead. The discussion in this chapter, then, will help to disprove Levenson's assertion, in A Genealogy of

Modernism, that Ford 'lapsed towards scepticism' by suggesting that subjectivity and individual consciousness were the only repositories of value in a world racked by the loss of 'comprehensive vision' and 'moral authority'.[3] He does experience this sense of loss acutely, as displayed in the discussion of previous chapters; but this is by no means all that he feels, and nor is his position in the subjectivist (modernist) tradition an unqualified one.

From the vantage point of 1918, Ford wrote in an essay of the events of the Somme that they 'come back to me as some fragments, confused, comic or even pathetic'.[4] Like Gertrude Stein, who talked of the war as having a composition different from that of all previous wars, what she called a 'composition of cubism',[5] Ford makes something out of these fragments. In the same essay, he builds them into a collage that does homage not just to cubism, but to the great impressionist painters too:

> In a corner of this picture is the menu of a sort of restaurant Duval, in Cardiff; 'sweetbread à la financière, fourpence'; and the left eye of a crying woman; and part of Newport station and the large nose of a Colonel; and then, of Waterloo station – the livid light, the canopy, high and banal; and the mothers, and the wives and girlfriends of the Welch officers; and the little brown Tommies, heavily engrossed; and the wives who were carrying pale babies and the tin badges of their husbands. And all laughing and crying and jostling each other... and the alabaster hands shaking behind the 'photographic representative' of the Northcliff papers, who has his head hidden under a black velvet hood, and who exorts us to assume imbecile smiles... Clouds, shadows, pale faces, spirals of violet smoke, out of which loomed the iron columns supporting the station roof – enormous and as it were deathly...

Shattered and fragmented as these images were, Ford's imagination, his literary vision, manages to structure them, to coax them into a shape that bespeaks a new kind of tradition post-war. In this new tradition humour, colour, emotion, tension and class, all supported and framed by the great looming mouth of the railway terminus that sets the light bouncing, are energised and articulated in what seems to become a true moving picture of war.[6] Yes, the cubist perspective is crucial to its construction (the 'left eye of a crying woman'), as is the Turneresque take on the station's structure. Shortly afterwards, though, as Ford develops the collage, by pushing the memory further back (as he so often does), he finds another of its aspects, one that is animated by a more distant part of his imaginative inheritance. The tradition becomes less 'new' and more of a reformation; simultaneously, our

attention becomes focused, as it should be, on the 'Victorian Greats' of
Ford's past. 'And then', Ford writes, 'this cubist picture effaced itself
and gave way to a small canvas [of the kind his grandfather, Ford
Madox Brown, or Rossetti sometimes produced], as who should say
Pre-Raphaelite'; a vision in pink, black, white, green and blue emerges.
The jewelled colours of the pastoral scene become the dominant
scheme for the time, and assert their vibrancy over the bustle of the
station mouth (think back here to the Kitty/Katya scene in *A Call* for
another example of such a scene). It is this Pre-Raphaelite dominance
and inheritance – traced mainly through his grandfather – that will
form the basis of my investigations of the roots of regenerative possibilities in Ford, and the nature and provenance of his imaginative
visions. Lord Leighton judged the duty of visual art to be to 'awaken
those senses directly emotional and indirectly intellectual, which can be
communicated only through the sense of sight'.[7] Ford would agree
with Leighton, but he would stretch his definition to include prose. He
both adopts, and adapts, Pre-Raphaelite techniques and subject matter
in much of his fiction – in *The March of Literature*, published in 1938,
he uses the phrase 'we Pre-Raphaelites'[8] – fiction that will be discussed
here.

In this chapter, then, I will be concentrating on the visions that
inspired, in part, what can perhaps be called Ford's positive fictions.
These fictions possess roots that mean the multiple perspectives central
to modernism often regenerate as well as destroy. Regeneration itself
will be seen to be a potentially painful or fearful process; for Ford – or,
perhaps, for anyone – stimulation in any new or reclaimed emotional
or psychological direction is not unqualifiedly joyous. However, the
mixture of joy and fear is elementary to the process, and the fictional
rewards, of the kind that complemented such texts as *A Call*, are necessary to a complete understanding of Ford's vision of the fragmenting
forces of modernism.

Ancient Lights

The 'Half Moon' (1909), *Ladies Whose Bright Eyes* (1911), *The New
Humpty Dumpty* (1912) and *The Young Lovell* (1913) (the main subject
of the next chapter) are works instructively linked in this exploration
to the publication of Ford's first volume of reminiscences, *Ancient
Lights and Certain New Reflections* (1911). My regenerative reading of
the texts listed above will give particular attention to patterns involving

his treatment of women and sexuality that appear in them; once more, the visual aspects of Ford's imagination and prose will be fore-grounded, and will form further instructive links between the texts. But *Ancient Lights* is also in a category of its own. As I argued in Chapter 1 regarding this text, one of Ford's primary responses to this period of change is to 'go back' to the past story of his life – to reflect, and to reconsider. Emphasis in that chapter lay on the interrelationship between this instinctive narrative technique in *Ancient Lights* and the political and psychological tenor of the time. Focus here will be instead on the role of this text in the regenerative quest; *Ancient Lights* provides complex and sometimes overwhelmingly powerful images of a mind both struggling with, and celebrating, figures deep in its past and deep in its consciousness. The products of that struggle can be witnessed in the fiction that I also discuss in what follows.

Ancient Lights formed part of Ford's narrative response to a chang-ing world (he says in the preface to a later autobiographical volume that the 'only excuse' for writing one's life is to give a 'picture of one's time',[9] perhaps because he believed that 'prose is a matter of looking things in the face'[10]). In a contemporary article in the *Daily News*, he explained the title: '*Ancient Lights* has as its moral the fact that the Pre-Raphaelites were no "great shakes" but they were giant and flaring beacons – ancient lights, in fact, compared with anything today that stands upon any hill tops'.[11] Beacons provide warning of danger; placed on hills, they are used to light the rocks that may otherwise harm unsuspecting sailors. Instead of beacons, Ford sees figures from his familial past on his hills, signalling the way. In *A Call*, published a year before *Ancient Lights*, Ford expressed the existential significance of being able to stand upon a hill. Grimshaw, meeting an Orthodox priest, is granted by this encounter the means to 'stand upon a little hill and look down into the misty "affair" in which he was so deeply engaged'.[12] His fortunate encounter with a crucial yet neglected part of his past (he has Greek Orthodox roots) enables him to see himself with some criti-cal distance, to reflect on his role with a placid eye.[13] In this instance, the ability to be a 'homo duplex', to find oneself in two actual or figu-rative places at one time, often used to connote a Fordian image of hell, is a positive attribute – as it is for the protagonists in this chapter. Is Ford saying that the beacon provided by the Pre-Raphaelites, for whom *Ancient Lights* is named, enabled him to stand on, and to see himself from, a similar existential promontory as the one from the vantage point of which he wrote the text? Perhaps the visual stimulus they provided helped him to construct his picture of this time? We will see. What is certain is that the 'impossible things of the past which assuredly would never come again' in Ford's conception of reality in 1915 do, in his fantasies – his positive fictions – and that the 'polished armour, shining swords, fortresses, conflagrations' and impressive women (all common Pre-Raphaelite props) are joined by mental forays that produce magnificent archetypes and felt reminiscences that invigorate his prose.[14]

Ford dedicates *Ancient Lights* in the preface to his two daughters, Christina and Katharine (named, I suggest, after Christina Rossetti and Catherine Howard). After an initial paragraph, quoted and discussed in the Introduction to this book, he writes the following:

> The earliest thing that I can remember is this, and the odd thing is that, as I remember it, I seem to be looking at myself from outside. I see myself a very tiny child in a long, blue pinafore, looking into the breeding box of some Barbary ring-doves that my grandmother kept in the window of the huge studio in Fitzroy Square. The window itself appears to me to be as high as a house, and I myself to be as small as a doorstep, so that I stand on tiptoe and just manage to get my eyes and nose over the edge of the box, while my long curls fall forward and tickle my nose. And then I perceive greyish and almost shapeless objects, with, upon them, little speckles like the very short spines of hedgehogs, and I stand with the first surprise of my life and with the first wonder of my life. I ask myself, can these be doves – these unrecognisable, panting morsels of flesh? And then, very soon, my grandmother comes in and is angry. She tells me that if the mother dove is disturbed she will eat her young. This, I believe, is quite incorrect. Nevertheless, I know quite well that for many days afterward I thought I had destroyed life, and that I was exceedingly sinful [...]. [I]t was my misfortune to have from this gentle personality my first conviction – and this, my first conviction, was one of great sin, of a deep criminality.[15]

Despite the obvious significance of this passage (Thomas Moser quotes it in full in his autobiographical study of Ford's fiction, *The Life in the Fiction of Ford Madox Ford*, as do Sondra Stang in her *Reader* and Max Saunders in his biography), especially to those of psychoanalytic intent, there seems to be very little in Ford's description of his sight that can be described as regenerative, or as anything other than fundamentally disturbing. I will move to discuss the Pre-Raphaelite connections that frame the incident shortly, but for now I want to concentrate on the stunning memory which has as its locus the squirming box of Barbary doves. Ford is using the adjective 'Barbary' most obviously geographically (as well as scientifically): it refers to the countries along Africa's northern coast. And yet, other connotations attached to the definition of this word must also be used to analyse this memory (see the *OED*). These are connotations of foreignness, of heathen and uncultivated behaviour, of the primacy of nature over civilisation.[16] The primacy of nature over civilisation seems to include in Ford's Oedipally revolutionary vision the devouring primacy of the female over the male. We have been here before.

In Chapter 3 I quoted from Camille Paglia's somewhat sensationalist trawl through literary and philosophical history, in which she constructs, as gendered polarities, nature versus civilisation. She could herself have been extrapolating from Freud's study of civilisation, society and religion, which declaims as follows:

> We have spoken of the hostility to civilization which is produced by the pressure that civilization exercises, the renunciations of instinct which it demands. If one imagines its prohibitions lifted – if, then, one may take any woman one pleases as a sexual object, if one may without hesitation kill one's rival for her love or anyone else who stands in one's way, if, too, one could carry off any of the other man's belongings without asking leave – splendid, what a string of satisfactions life would be! [...]
>
> But how ungrateful, how short-sighted after all, to strive for the abolition of civilization! What would then remain would be a state of nature, and that would be far harder to bear. It is true that nature would not demand any restrictions of instinct from us, she would let us do as she liked; but she has her own particularly effective method of restricting us. She destroys us – coldly, cruelly, relentlessly, as it seems to us, and possibly through the very things which occasioned our satisfaction. It was precisely because of these dangers with which nature threatens us that we came together and created civilization. (SE xxi, p. 15)

Freud projects a feminine gender onto 'nature', as does Paglia (and as Ford has seemed to – see Chapter 3), and he uses the present tense, warning of the continuing 'dangers' with which surrendering to her threatens us (so is he advocating repressing desire?) in society. Thinking about it further, it appears, somewhat bizarrely, that women have no place in this vision of society: Freud seems to address males only as the protagonists in the collective civilisation massed against the female subversive that must be excluded. Sexology with which Ford would become familiar (years after the Barbary doves event occurred, as a writing adult) would have suggested the same pattern of analysis: Weininger, as Joseph Bristow points out, concludes that woman 'is sexuality itself', and man must protect himself accordingly.[17] Ford, though perhaps proving himself in 1911 to be imaginatively aware of these deeply felt opinions, by evoking them in expressing his childhood memory, does not see himself as protected in this way.

As Ford reflects on the memory of the doves, rather, he finds himself to be vulnerable in his situation. Despite the barriers with which his memory furnishes him – the box, and the window, and the doorstep – these seem to exacerbate, rather than to contain, the sight. In fact, the size of the window focuses the attention along with its light and warmth on the alliterative, fecund, 'breeding box'. Ford, small and frail, peeks over the top of the box which conceals, and then, worse, reveals, the wonder of sex and procreation that is suddenly and permanently rendered co-existent with death. The dove, which in Judeo-Christian symbolism represents purity and simplicity, stands for something very different here.[18] It provides Ford with an image in which the female is not only omnipotent, but is voracious, and comes at him from two different (though then united) directions, as the procreative and the murderous mother. Seemingly, Ford's presence in the imposing house of his grandfather is forgotten at his point; the female is in the ascendant.[19] Despite, or perhaps because of, his vulnerability, he is evidently fascinated, enthralled. His curiosity in this incident is unsurprising; Freud argues, as Bristow puts it, 'that when children first examine their social worlds, they are pre-occupied with only one question: where do babies come from?'.[20] What is of note is the fact that he chooses to revisit this powerful and female-oriented memory in such vivid form, and places it at the start of his autobiography, in the dedication to his female offspring. Ford isn't simply displaying an interest in origins here, though placed as it is in the preface, this rich scene could be described as the source of the text; it is more to do with a fascinated recognition of female power over those origins. Here we can begin to spy the regenerative roots of the memory, especially as they are revisited in other, fictional, soon to be encountered, scenes.

Ford's memory of the above occurrence is detailed in the extreme; it is hard to believe that he has ever 'forgotten' this aspect of his past – his ostensible explanation for the writing of the memoir. He shifts from the past tense into the present almost imperceptibly as the comparatively weak constraints of the intervening years fall away. The Oedipal influences present in the picture that he paints concentrate the attention on the sexual identity of the young doves and the wrath of his grandmother. Ford sees himself as the young innocent, curls falling about his face, surprised simultaneously by the sexual nature of the scene before him and by the resultant fury of the 'disturbed female', whom he confuses and conflates with his grandmother acting *in loco parentis*. The part of this passage that stands out over and above any other is, perhaps, the question, formed in the present tense, 'I ask myself, can these be doves – these unrecognisable, panting morsels of flesh?' Here the 38-year-old writer articulates his remembered and still experienced enthralled anxiety as to identity, as to sexuality, and as to the power of the female figure. Compelling though this scene is, it cannot be fully appreciated until the forces it generates are traced into the fictions that emerged at the same time; particularly resonant in this instance will be the imagery Ford employs in *The New Humpty-Dumpty*, published the year after *Ancient Lights*.

The Pre-Raphaelites and Ford

In addition to the story behind the title of the text, reference to the Pre-Raphaelites both frames and punctuates this memory that is placed by Ford at Fitzroy Square, Ford Madox Brown's London house and studio from 1865. (Though on the fringes of the Brotherhood, Brown knew most of its members well, and shared some of their artistic aims.) The occasion of Ford's remembrance is introduced by the phrase, 'I seem to be looking at myself from outside', perhaps indicating his attainment of some small hill from which to view the scene.[21] The necessary space for such a view is certainly formed by those words, a critical distance is thereby established, but it is more complicated than that. In the first edition of *Ancient Lights*, the dedication is preceded by a portrait of Ford aged 4, painted by Madox Brown. In this portrait he is painted as William Tell's son, and holds up the two halves of the apple that have been (thankfully) divided by the father's arrow, which remains stuck in the tree behind Tell's/Ford's head. Underneath the portrait, Ford has placed an inscription that is then echoed precisely by the words with which he introduces his memory – 'I seem to be looking at myself from outside'. In the painting it is obvious that Ford would be looking at himself thus, but he proves he also does this in prose.

Moser's analysis of this portrait is that 'the little boy [...] is looking out with very strange eyes',[22] and this is a fair description, except Ford himself emphasises instead the action of looking back in at himself, proving a split vision of himself as subject and object. He describes looking at himself alongside others, one a beloved grandfather, but also the father who has, in Ford's role as William Tell, fired an arrow at him, and who will shortly, in the written text, call him a 'stupid donkey' (p. ix). Ford here establishes the tone of the ostracised innocent, one suffering a self-analysed crisis of identity that will be so effectively and sexually developed when the grandmother too intervenes.

From that point, then, at the very beginning of the text, he pictures himself as a fragmented subject, one that is in addition guilt-ridden, death-threatened, stifled not just by the doves but by the men who came to call at Fitzroy Square. Ford writes that he can only breathe freely in a modern world without the 'Victorian Greats', and dwells a few pages further on in the narrative on the enormous stone urn that stood outside Madox Brown's house and seemed always to be about to fall on him. The threatened suffocation is emblematic, perhaps, of the panic attacks from which Ford used to suffer, as well as of the feeling of being overwhelmed, physically and emotionally, by these enormous male and female figures. Nothing, however, that he writes here about the 'Greats' is as replete with psychological and emotional energy as the memory of the doves.

Many of the 'Greats' did come to call on Madox Brown; over the years, as Teresa Newman and Ray Watkinson write, 'the Madox Browns entertained Browning and Tennyson, Mazzini and Charles Dilke, Mark Twain and Turgenev, Franz Listz and Cosima Wagner, as well as Swinburne and the younger writers Arthur O'Shaughnessey, Edmund Gosse and Oscar Wilde'.[23] The addition of members of the Pre-Raphaelite Brotherhood (to 'every luminary' of which, George Steiner asserts, Ford was 'connected by birth and relation'[24]), forms the group of men who frame Ford's Barbary-doves memory at its other extremity, the 'terrible and forbidding things' that squash the breath in his body. Far from granting him the benefit of clarity of vision, these men seem to maintain a position on the hill that precludes him from getting a toe-hold. 'These people', he stresses, still addressing Katharine and Christina, 'were perpetually held up to me as standing upon unattainable heights, and at the same time I was told that if I could not attain these heights I might just as well not cumber the earth'. Almost his last word on the subject in *Ancient Lights* affirms this sense of the intimidated and overwhelmed subject. Ford says it is finally 'astonishing how little I seemed to have changed since I was a very little boy in a velveteen coat with gold buttons and long golden ringlets ... I do not go into [my kitchen] because lurking at the back of my head I have always had the feeling that I am a little boy who will be either spoken to or spanked by a mysterious "They"' (p. 253). Looking back at himself, it is a Pre-Raphaelite vision that he sees, all ringlets and velvet and colours. He says that he hasn't changed. Ford's visual imagination, and the way he depicts and situates his position in the world, are essential to this narrative. (He treats himself as a protagonist similarly to the way he treats those others to be met shortly.) He makes meaning from the often sexualised situations in which he sees himself and others in his mind's eye, displaying the tendency to place himself in specific surroundings, with specific and vivid connotations. He watches, remembers and depicts the dramatic results. More positive results than those just detailed are discernible in this text, and in his fiction too.

Ford was desperately fond of his grandfather, with whom he went to live after his father's sudden death in 1889.[25] His effect upon Ford is extensively explored, and documented, by Moser, Saunders and Judd, among others (Judd avers that 'it would be hard to exaggerate the influence Brown had on his grandson'[26]) and also by Newman and Watkinson in their study of Ford Madox Brown. They state that 'Brown had become exceptionally close to his grandson Ford', partly because, after the tragic death of Brown's son Oliver in 1874, he looked to Ford to fulfil Oliver's 'literary genius'. 'Ford inherited Nolly's spiritual mantle', they conclude, just as he would 'inherit Rossetti's real cloak and stride about Bloomsbury in it, playing the last Pre-Raphaelite' (echoing Douglas Goldring's biography of Ford entitled *The Last Pre-Raphaelite*), a role that would later exercise Violet Hunt's memories of Ford.[27]

Madox Brown did indeed want 'Fordie' to write; he promised to illustrate the fairy story that Ford wrote for his sister Juliet after their father died, *The Brown Owl*. It is hard to ignore the significance of the title, especially when one enters the romantic, ancient world of the novel. Here is a land of magicians, kings and princesses; a king lies dying and extracts a promise from his beloved daughter to 'cherish the Owl'. She does not know what he means, but promises, and after his death the Owl appears, and is soon 'become a companion to her that would take the place of her father'.[28] The book is constructed as a series of emotionally demanding tableaux (think back to Leighton's view of art). Far from asking the reader to view the text from a complex set of perspectives, as in *The Good Soldier*, Ford asks instead for sympathy and sensitivity, to fantastical, Pre-Raphaelite-laced, impressions.

The Owl is loyal and kindly, powerful and wise, and is Brown's representative in Ford's imaginative universe. Madox Brown always held such a position, thus providing Ford with one of the 'static verities' of his life.[29] The book was published in 1891, following Brown's persuasions at T. Fisher Unwin via Edward Garnett. It thus owes its existence to him through several related channels, and Ford's name on the title page acknowledges the debt.[30] This begins to illustrate Ford's ability to experience his Pre-Raphaelite inheritance as stimulus to positive ends; Saunders writes that 'Madox Brown opened his eyes to visual impressions; Ford's impressionism in words thus pays perpetual homage to the painter'.[31] Two more fantasy stories were written by Ford before he set to his first biographical task: *Ford Madox Brown* was published in 1896.

According to Moser's analysis of these events and experiences, however, Brown's legacy expanded to contribute something very specific to Ford's burgeoning personality, and ultimately to that about which he would almost always write: 'young Ford had a much nearer, much more vivid guide to passion than his father's dull prose about twelfth and thirteenth century poets [*The Troubadours*]. From his colourful, garrulous painter-grandfather, Ford would have known a great deal, more perhaps than he wanted to know, of the real-life loves of his glamorous, sinister 'uncle', Dante Gabriel Rossetti' (p. 284). Moser thus focuses the attention once more on the extension of Ford's consciousness by those things that he experiences, even at second hand. In this case, as in Ford's memory of the doves, that consciousness (or visual imagination) is extended in primarily sexual directions. 'Thus I remember', writes Ford, seeing a new, sexual, tableau, 'in a sort of golden vision, Rossetti lying upon a sofa in the back studio with lighted candles at his feet and lighted candles at his head, while two extremely beautiful ladies dropped grapes into his mouth' (*Ancient Lights*, p. 5). The conduit for this consciousness was his grandfather, who was also, perhaps, an original cause of Rossetti's striking behaviour. Jan Marsh believes that the quality in Brown's work that fired Rossetti's poetic imagination was his 'intensely dramatic treatment of Byronic wickedness and illicit passion', appealing as it did to the young Rossetti encountering it in London exhibitions.[32] John Fuller has suggested that Rossetti was more interested in sex and beauty than in achieving a reputation for artistic greatness.[33]

This Pre-Raphaelite extravagance, painted as well as lived and talked about, became Ford's partly artistic, partly realistic, introduction to sexuality, and was a lesson learned with the ears and the eyes. Lessons

learned in this way, from this source, were also to do with attention to
the natural world, for though the Pre-Raphaelites were not naturalists,
they 'rooted their aesthetic in truth to nature' as a way of confronting
what was seen by some as an overly secular and industrial age.[34]
Stylistically, they dealt with this material with 'lucidity and minute-
ness'[35] (the start of the link to Ford's impressionism is clear here). Both
aspects of the aesthetic, the sexual and the natural, and the style, were
to prove crucial to Ford's development. He was to pursue such
intensely detailed, erotic, multiplicitous, licentious *and* regenerative
matter into his prose, in a way that was intended 'to make you see'. As
I proceed, in the rest of this chapter, to investigate this prose, and to
develop a sense of the visions that feed it, I will use as an illustrative
comparison Robert Graves's book on the mythological power of
womanhood, *The White Goddess*,[36] as well as Freud. Owing to the often
mythical subject matter (employed widely by modernist writers[37]),
Jung's theory is also consulted in an interpretation of Ford's fantastical
fictional visions – Jung wrote in a letter to Freud in 1900 of the need to
rekindle the religious, mythic urge, based on symbol.[38] Other evidence
(including that in this chapter) suggests this rekindling was already
extant.[39]

Positive fictions

Positive fiction I: The 'Half Moon'
In 1902 Ford wrote and published a book on the subject of his 'sinister'
uncle, Dante Gabriel Rossetti. It is a text that concentrates more than
anything on the women that Rossetti loved and the women that he
painted, finding Rossetti's primary artistic gifts to reside in his ability
to 'record a type of feminine beauty' whilst in 'raptly mystical, mysti-
cally sensual or sensually rapt' moods.[40] (I shall return to this book and
to this idea of female 'types' – as does Ford; in *The Good Soldier*,
Leonora expresses the belief that 'when Edward has exhausted a
number of other types of women he must turn to her'.[41]) Revealing the
continuing extent of Rossetti's influence on him, in 1909 he wrote and
published a novel, *The 'Half Moon'*, which takes as the source for its
main plot Rossetti's ballad, 'Sister Helen'. The plot of this ballad
concerns spurned love, hatred and jealousy; it explores, against a
weather-beaten, mystical back-drop, the female desire to kill a lover
rather than give up control of his heart. As I proceed, these sexually
attuned, lurid and dramatic roots will be clearly discerned in *The 'Half*

Moon'. Importantly, too, the typification of womanhood drives Ford's imagination in his novel.

In the dedication of The '*Half Moon*', to W. A. Bradley, Ford says something of another of his influences in this text, his interest in the historical period that inspired it: 'Fortunately for me the psychology of the Old World in the days of Hudson has always been very fascinating to me. It is, as you know, the subject to which more than anything I have devoted my attention: for at that date the Dark Ages were finally breaking up. There lingered many traces of that darkness...'.[42] Henry Hudson (c. 1565–1611) was an English explorer. He 'discovered' the North American bay, river and strait that bear his name. Such a figure helps Ford to establish a form common to many of his narratives: the concept of two opposing forces. In this instance they adopt the present-ing divisions of the Old World against the New, Catholicism (re-emergent with James I) versus a Protestantism that had been in the ascendant under the English queen, and Puritanism. And yet, it is nothing as abstract as the ruling faith and national politics that deter-mine the binary and the nature of Ford's quest into fantasy here: 'So, my dear Bradley [Ford concludes his preface], let this voyage go forth, with its cargo of human passions, faiths and endeavours, as it were crossing and recrossing the windy seas, linking and relinking the *old and the new worlds with chains and networks of desires and fears*' (p. xiv) [my emphasis]. In an unstable world, a world that Ford often depicts in his fiction, chains and networks must be interpreted as offering a sense of security, an antidote to fragmentation. This would help to explain the obvious relish with which Ford charts them when he can. These chains and networks of fear and desire, visible in this text and in the others to be discussed here, operate across time as well as across space; they are made of links of sex and myth.[43] The Old World comes into contact with the New, the past with the present, as they are fash-ioned. Evoking the discussion of the personal narrative, in Chapter 1, Ford's phrase here, 'linking and relinking the old and the new worlds', suggests the chains are forged from searches in the collective, as well as in his individual, memory.

The least disparate trace of 'that [Old] darkness' in The '*Half Moon*' is Anne Jeal (claimed by Ford in the preface to have really existed, and described as 'the most feared wench in the five ports'[44]). Jeal, a Catholic witch, makes an attempt to disrupt and then to destroy the new order. She makes this attempt with two distinct methods of attack: her sexu-ality and her faith. Ranged against Jeal's ritualistic and often frightening professions of faith is the biblical simplicity of the Puritan sect, personified by Magdalena Koop.[45] Ford takes care to establish these two in direct opposition of the most base kind, echoing Rossetti's 'Sister Helen', for they compete for the love of a man. His phraseology echoes this attempt at stark clarity: '[Magdalena] looked upon Edward Colman's drawing, and it was good; upon his smile – and it was good; upon the brown wood of the chests, and it was good' (p. 38). In this parody of the Creation myth, Magdalena represents one version of Eve, sanctioning male order, male creativity. An alternative version is found in the representation of Jeal, and Ford's portrayal of this second version seems to demand a psychoanalytic interpretation based on the Oedipal myth: '[Colman] smiled at the horse litter. For it had been instituted for the Mayoress, two years before, when Anne Jeal's father had for the fourth time become Mayor and Anne Jeal herself – her mother being lately dead – for the first time, Mayoress' (p. 31). Jeal has usurped her mother's place by her father's side, becoming mayoress to his mayor, and, with him, has assumed the leading role in local affairs. In addition to this symbolic act, she has altered the manner of her institution as mayoress, insisting upon the use of a litter, whereas in previous years a mule had sufficed.[46] In this way she proclaims her – unnatural – importance, and her essential (and desirable) difference from the calm and pious Koop. The witch, embodying, as she does, in Jungian terminology as well as Fordian, 'desires and fears', is the antithesis of the idealised image of womanhood.[47]

Ford has come to a period of history where, in a way similar to that in *The Fifth Queen*, there are big symbolic interests under which people must ally themselves as they see fit. What is further developed in this case are the gender specifics of the experiment: the symbolic interests are both gendered (female) and dramatically portrayed. Indeed, women work solely as symbols in this tale that is little more than an allegory – along Pre-Raphaelite lines.[48] Simplistically sketched, in broad strokes, the female characters are brazen or pious, fanatical or humble – 'Magdalena was beauteous, and large, and strong, and silent' (p. 46). They are there to be enjoyed in this simplicity (Ford's language is evidence of this), and *watched*, in a series of dramatic scenes, in their medieval setting. Here are the originals for Etta Stackpole, Katya Lascarides and Sylvia Tietjens, in Platonic, perfect, undiluted form. Ford has chosen the setting in order to be able to investigate the two key components to Jeal's challenge to the *status quo* (sex and religion) in this allegorical, visual and crudely drawn fashion. He is travelling in time to find a validation, and a perfection, of the essences of woman as he sees her, owing to a significant degree to his Pre-Raphaelite associations. What Weiss calls Ford's 'fascination with the idea of woman' is played out.[49]

Jeal is tried for heresy and witchcraft by six lords of the court of James I. Moser writes that Jeal is 'emphatically a Catholic witch' (p. 72) and despite the lords' religious allegiance to the Old World, her female arrogance must be punished. One of their number provides a further clue towards the unravelling of the symbolism within this text. He states, by way of explanation to his colleagues, 'My Lords, [...] if it is your pleasure, I believe that this is all a tale of a mare's nest' (p. 220). He locates Jeal and her tale in the shadowy world that Robert Graves investigates in *The White Goddess*:

> And what is a mare's nest? Shakespeare hints at the answer [but] a fuller account of Odin's feat is given in the North Country 'Charm against the Night Mare,' which probably dates from the 14th century:
>
> > Tha mon o' micht, he rade o' nicht
> > Wi' neider swerd ne ferd ne licht.
> > He socht tha Mare, he fond tha Mare,
> > He bond tha Mare wi' her ain hare,
> > Ond gared her swar by midder-micht
> > She wolde nae mair rid o' nicht
> > Whar aince he rade, thot mon o' micht.
>
> The Night Mare is one of the cruellest aspects of the White Goddess.[50]

The 'mare's nest' is the mare's lair, where she must be sought out. What becomes most clear in this ritualistic charm is the expressed necessity for restoring order, of the day over the night, the physically powerful male over the mysteriously powerful female. The Night Mare seemingly meets a violent end at the hands of the fourteenth-century warrior, except she doesn't, and becomes progressively less easy to manage through time. In her more modern form, as the 'nightmare', she possesses power over the nether regions of the human mind; she is of the unconscious world. (Remember Freud's writing on nature, in its illustration of the chaotic and mysterious female threat to male order.) Similarly powerful in *The 'Half Moon'*, the Night Mare reappears in a form in which Ford seems to revel: in the guise of a witch who has a tale to tell. Using magic, she attempts to destroy the hero and his Puritan wife; the personifications of manhood and of pure, chaste, simple religion are simultaneously attacked. Ford resorts to intertextuality to force the sense of outrage amongst the blustering locals home, borrowing from Shakespeare's reworking of the Lear myth: "'Sirs,'" Edward Colman said, "we are a great and glorious corporation, nevertheless our daughters, for lack of beating, twist us by the beard'" (p. 90). Colman could do no better in invoking moral indignation than to call in this way upon Goneril and Regan, the epitome of those who usurp the pattern.

Jeal's Catholicism is, of course, a highly significant fact, in historical and political terms (part of the reason for the nineteenth-century distrust of the Pre-Raphaelites was their 'High Church leanings'[51]). Ford intimates that it is more important in mythical terms, especially with regard to gender and to sex (bear in mind Dowell's puritanical description of Catholicism as a 'Scarlet Woman' in The Good Soldier[52]). Graves examines Catholicism in particular detail as a 'female-based' religion, standing in opposition to the patriarchal emphasis on the Trinity found in Protestantism: 'The popular appeal of modern Catholicism is [...] based rather on the Aegean Mother-and-Son religious tradition, to which it has slowly reverted' (p. 56), he states, sounding the subversive strains found in Ford's novel. The phrase 'slowly reverted' is synchronous with a chthonic drag, reversing the forward thrust of new religion. The forward thrust is identified by Graves as the Puritan revolution, the period setting of The 'Half Moon'. Graves defines this revolution thus:

> The Puritan Revolution was a reaction against Virgin-worship, which in many districts of Great Britain had taken on a mad-merry orgiastic character [...]. The iconoclastic wantonness, the sin-laden gloom and Sabbatarian misery that Puritanism brought with it shocked the Catholics beyond expression. It was a warning to them to strengthen rather than weaken the festal side of their cult. (p. 371)

He creates the sense of the male battling against the female and sexualised ritual – of a 'mad-merry orgiastic' nature – in the attempted repression of such religious traits. Catholics were warned 'to strengthen the festal side of their cult' Graves informs us, goaded to do so by the opposing quietude of the Puritans (perhaps Ford was also drawing on more immediate source material; Jay Winter describes the rise of nineteenth-century populist Maryan cults, particularly in Germany[53]). 'The cult of Mary', writes Marina Warner, 'is inextricably interwoven with Christian ideas about the dangers of the flesh and their special connection with women';[54] in The 'Half Moon' Jeal's Catholic, festal side is nothing so much as her subversive promise of sex. So alluring is this promise that many sought to deny the charge of witchcraft levelled against her, 'such as argued that witchcraft was limited to the old, the wrinkled or the hideous had it in their favour that Anne Jeal set the teeth watering of youths' (p. xii). Jeal's sexuality is rooted in her communication with her eyes and with her mouth, in the way she looks and in what she says.[55] She taunts Colman, keeping eyes on him that are 'dark, lustrous and intent as those of a cat', calling to him: '"Are the kisses of your fat wife sweet, Edward Colman? I warrant you have had none ere marriage from that Puritan. Whereas from me —"' (p. 82).

Ford's admiration of Christina Rossetti, about whom he writes in *Ancient Lights* (unsurprisingly, because of the family to which she belonged), is to a large degree based on her Koop-like ability to vanquish the festal side of her nature. The battle between the festive and the ascetic, the natural and the restrained, is identified by Ford as fundamental to her nature; it is translated by him into the religious sphere in a further parody of the battle between Jeal's instinctively high-church love of ritual and iconism and Koop's low-church simplicity and inward-looking faith: 'the trouble was, of course, that whereas by blood and nature Christina was a Catholic, by upbringing and by all the influences that were around her she was forced into the Protestant Communion' (*Ancient Lights,* pp. 60–1). As he proceeds, Ford makes it abundantly plain that his admiration is caused by a vicarious pleasure at her subjection of her humanistic, 'pagan' and instinctive nature (pp. 66–7). By conforming to type, that of the 'nun-like and saintly woman', Christina Rossetti solves a problem. The Catholic within her, described as her 'blood' – her life flow – and her 'nature', and simultaneously the possibility of sexual existence have been vanquished. One representation of the ideal woman has silenced another. In his fiction, moral intent of the kind Ford seems to display in his analysis of Christina Rossetti rarely intervenes. Despite his admiration, then, he proves that he *also* has something invested in the idea of the rebellious woman, the myth of the sexually potent Catholic witch – a woman much more likely to be of interest to Christina Rossetti's brother.

Ford took great pains, at times, to define himself as Catholic.[56] He is proud of this definition and revels in its festal side, creating Anne Jeal who will not die. It is, rather, Colman, the male protagonist who has bellowed 'I hate Papists!' (p. 52), who dies, beaten by women and their existence in a dramatic dimension that he cannot understand. Magdalena, in response to his loss, adopts a puritanical pose, claiming she will be with him always due to the power of their love. In opposition, Ford paints a picture of the ousted Jeal venting her primeval rage (once more express-ing herself vocally) at her lack of the man: 'every three weeks or so Anne Jeal was pervaded by such a fit of longing rage that she must go out at night into deserted places and scream, so that it was said in Rye that there was a new kind of ghost abroad' (p. 331). Does he believe she is a witch or a ghost? Perhaps. He could be alluding to the more modern form of the Night Mare, coming to assault the dreams of all good, self-denying, Protestant folk. But more significantly, she is symbolically, quintessen-tially, a sexual female – his use of the phrase 'every three weeks or so' could be said to invoke the menstrual cycle. Her screaming is an action no Puritan would have attempted; it is an individualistic expression of thwarted passion and desire no Puritan would have allowed herself. This is the dramatic, human legacy with which she leaves the reader. Ford's final suggestion that she is brought, semi-penitent, back within the ideo-logical fold is a clumsy one and does not succeed. The abiding image is of Jeal standing against Koop, vivid with the buzz of sexual energy: 'Anne Jeal was drawn in dark, and small, and quivered, as a wasp quivers above an apple' (p. 46), waiting to strike.

Whilst Christina Rossetti subdued the feminine, the natural, the 'Catholic' – as Ford defines them – parts of herself, in Ford's positive fictions it is these aspects of his characters that are vividly animated. In his definition of his own Catholicism (which came through his father's side of the family, though Francis himself was agnostic), they were equally vivid. Olive Garnett recorded a conversation with Ford in 1892, the year in which Ford was received into the Church.[57] In it he reveals his own feeling that 'Catholicism [...] satisfied his sensual religious needs'.[58] Douglas Goldring goes one step further in stating that 'the romantic, aesthetic, magical, superstitious, and poetic aspects of Catholicism caught and held his imagination'.[59] In The 'Half Moon' Ford is not concerned with representing the moral superiority of one form of the religious life over another; he is investigating the magical, poetical and superstitious aspects of Catholicism and, more generally, of women. Female 'types' are worked with by him to express and to contain the dualisms intrinsic to faith, sex and myth as seen and expe-rienced by him. The 'opposite types of feminine sexual passion' both have a heritage, then (a Pre-Raphaelite one), and a function.[60] These types, more of whom appear in the texts to come, can be understood as both a homage to his roots and a catalogue of regenerative, multiplici-tous and mythical experimentations.

Rossetti and The Troubadours

Jan Marsh published a book called *Pre-Raphaelite Women* in 1987. The following chapter headings appear in this text: 'Fallen Magdalenes'; 'Medieval Damozels'; 'Sorceresses'; 'Allegories and Icons'; 'Pale Ladies of Death'; 'Bohemians and Stunners'; 'Holy Virgins'; 'Nubile Maidens'; 'Doves and Mothers'.[61] It is this Pre-Raphaelite tendency to stereotype that Ford concentrates upon in his book on Dante Gabriel Rossetti.[62] In this criticism, however, he treats the tendency as one that is not under the artist's conscious control: it is the unconsciousness of this systematisation that interests him. Marsh's headings become comparatively reductive when examined alongside Ford's 'reading' of the painter: 'Rossetti at his best was a painter in, not of, moods. He was most successful when, having recorded a type of feminine beauty – or even repulsiveness – he afterwards found a name for it; stood back in fact from his canvas and only then discovered the moral of what he had been painting'.[63] Rossetti has been painting unconsciously. He is 'taken' by his material, inside it in some way, not critically distant from it, as he paints. Only afterwards can he consciously understand what he has created, and give it a name, bringing it forward into language (the multiple levels of existence are again symbolised by their relationship with speech). In the continuing description of Rossetti's paintings, Ford supplants Rossetti in his titular delineations: the 'Joli Coeur' is a 'rather sensual and quite young girl'; the 'Monna Vanna' a 'refined and delicately sensuous type'; the 'Lady with the Fan' a 'more or less animal type' and the 'Lady with the Gold Chain' a 'sort of odalisque'. Ford is comfortable with these symbols of womanhood. They certainly emanate from his association with Rossetti, his relationship with Madox Brown, and his affiliated tendency to visualise the world in symbolic ways, but they are also more deeply rooted, and to be analysed, in turn, as he analysed them in his artist subject. This analysis serves to turn the attention back to Ford's family, and to the function of his enlightening and invigorating unconscious.

Ford has consummately created in Anne Jeal a representation of the 'type' of the sorceress; Rossetti's ballad 'Sister Helen' had helped to focus the type, as had many other factors in the contemporary world and in Ford's responsive imagination.[64] Though Rossetti undoubtedly was significant, as was Ford's route to him, Ford's imagination was stimulated in other familial ways. A further examination of Graves will serve to reintroduce Ford's father, Francis Hueffer, to the discussion.

Moser's deduction was that Ford would have found in Rossetti a far more vibrant exponent of the possibilities of woman and passion than his father's 'dull' work on twelfth- and thirteenth-century poets – *The Troubadours*. However, an interesting correlation between Francis Hueffer's book and Ford's novel is discovered if Graves's exposition of the roots of the festal Mary cult is placed alongside the roots of Anne Jeal's magic. Jeal is here described from the point of view of a male, comparatively feeble sorcerer: 'In Anne Jeal he had met a practitioner of magic that came of an older and more cunning tradition than his. There were, he knew, some such witches in country places. They still held the secrets that knights of the Temple, who were all black necromancers and worshipped Satan [...] had brought back from the Crusades with women captives from the Saracens' (p. 254). Earlier in the text she is accused of knowing 'Saracen prayers' (p. 75). Graves places an alternative, but perhaps not altogether different tradition, in the same beginning: 'When the Crusaders invaded the Holy Land [...] they found a number of heretical Christian sects living there under Moslem protection, who soon seduced them from Orthodoxy. This was how the cult of Mary the Gipsy came to England [...]. The lyre-plucking, red-stockinged troubadours, [...] ecstatically adopted the Marian cult' (p. 348), conflating the history of the troubadours and the crusaders as does Hueffer in his text (see pp. 128–30). Ford knew the troubadours well because of his father's work, and it is possible there is a similar conflation at work in his mind as he writes *The 'Half Moon'* (though the vision of Catholicism he projects has more in common with Graves's approach). *The Troubadours* (1878) is a serious study, dedicated to providing a history of Provençal life and literature in the Middle Ages. But it would also have provided Ford's fertile imagination with other, more mainstream, images of the Virgin Mary (as sexually pure, and as the link between heaven and earth), and with pictures of 'the wayfaring singer, wandering through the beautiful land of Provence in search of praise and amorous adventure'. 'Provençal poets', Hueffer suggests, 'were naturally a restless tribe, ever in search of new lands and new loves' (compare this with Dowell's admission that 'with each new woman that a man is attracted to there appears to come a broadening of the outlook, or, if you like, an acquiring of new territory' (*The Good Soldier*, p. 79)), joining religious veneration of womanhood with more earthy perspectives. Hueffer makes a direct link between the duty of the medieval knight or crusader (some of whom were troubadours) to his lady, and that of the Catholic to

'immaculate womanhood', the pure woman, another Marian ideal.[65]
Hueffer's thoughts of womanhood, the subjects of his study, can also
be seen to shape those of his son (think of Magdalena in The 'Half
Moon').

As Graves writes it, the troubadours adopted what could be
described as a double-edged sword, and allowed themselves to be
'seduced' from Orthodoxy. But how this was dealt with, or defined,
depended on geography (in time – in relation to Old and New worlds
– as well as space). Whilst they were geographically free from England,
the knights of the Temple could relish black magic: it was the
Christians who indulged in the 'Marian cult'. It travelled with them,
and, in travelling, became known as something altogether different.
Back in England, where Orthodoxy ruled, the women were deemed to
be witches. When women associated with the cult reminded men of
what they would rather forget, they were persecuted, because they were
feared. In the Holy Land, in the time of the troubadours, they represented instead trangressive freedoms. Ford has invested both in these
transgressive freedoms and in their roots.

Graves traces the roots of female icons, or female goddesses, back to
antiquity. His claim is that they have not disappeared, but make their
presence felt in more subliminal ways – ways to which Ford proved
himself to be sensitive and which he then used to construct his 'chains
of desires and fears' between Old and New worlds. When Rossetti is
'without intent', in Ford's phrase, such evocations are the result of his
brush: lack of intent is a Fordian maxim for the writing of prose.[66] The
Fordian interest in such organised systems of female nature can be
consciously traced to much of his youthful experience, mostly of his
relatives; the meaning of these systems is both more ancient and
unconscious, and more psychologically valuable, than this implies.

Ancient sanities

C. F. G. Masterman's phrase 'ancient sanities' described an aspect of
spiritual life from which he felt modern man had been divorced.[67]
Ford, in his use of female symbols (as well as in his criticism of D. G.
Rossetti and in his analysis of his childhood) in his positive fictions, is
re-finding them. He himself acknowledges the gendered nature of both
this loss and the need, particularly when the subject is religion:
'Catholicism – with its female saints, with its female religious, with its
feminine element in the Divine Concord – has its chief safeguard in its
women. But in these islands, which have discarded alike female saints,

female religious, and the Mother of God as an object of worship, a comparative lukewarmness in attachment to established forms of worship has resulted'.[68] Jung says of the production of archetypal images that the 'main source... is dreams', but he goes on to add that 'another source for the material we need is to be found in "active imagination". By this I mean a sequence of fantasies produced by deliberate concentration'. (Think here also of Freud's 1908 essay on this subject, 'Creative Writers and Day-Dreaming'.)[69] The 'Half Moon', as discussed, and others that will shortly be considered, are the most fantastical of Ford's texts, those which, though not dreams, could be said to operate as a result of Jung's blurred distinction between the unconscious and conscious production of such material. The 'active imagination' of the imaginative author can be a source for archetypal images, for multiplicitous mythical forms then animated in fiction. This is one way of approaching and interpreting Ford's female characters which are the subject of this chapter.

Female types, and the reasons for them, have been definitively addressed by Jung in his delineations of the female archetypes, beginning with the anima:

> The anima is a personification of all feminine psychological tendencies in a man's psyche, such as vague feelings and moods, prophetic hunches, receptiveness to the irrational, capacity for personal love, feeling for nature, and – last but not least – his relation to the unconscious. It is no mere chance that in olden times priestesses [...] were used to fathom the divine will and to make connection with the gods.[70]

Ford's writing of women functions partly as a series of similar projections. His attention to multiplicity refers not only to modern visions but to mythical projections and to multi-faceted symbols. The fear induced in his male characters in the modern world by some of these projections of womanhood, as discussed in previous chapters, is countered by the visions of the fantasy worlds he creates.

Positive fiction II: The New Humpty-Dumpty

The New Humpty-Dumpty, written in 1912, has as its denouement the setting of a revolution. It is a cynical revolution, brought about as a side-effect, more than anything else, by the protagonists. Yet it is concerned with other worlds, with new lands, and in this way it echoes the cross-world voyage of *The 'Half Moon'*; as Ford stated in the preface to the earlier work, 'men were beginning to look out for truths of all kinds [...] perhaps above all, for lands in which Utopias might be found or founded' (or rediscovered) (p. vi). Ford travels in his writing, searching for 'chains of desires and fears', for ways to make manifest ancient and alternative wisdoms; Hudson travels to the New World, to the place that is now New York, just as Macdonald, Pett and their band of revolutionaries travel to Batahla in *The New Humpty-Dumpty*.

The concept of a utopia, of such a new world, was a prevalent one in the literature of the time. Ford was not alone in his quest for other 'truths' (or, more cynically, spaces for expansion). Essential to this re-animation of a fictional tradition was William Morris's *News from Nowhere* (1890). Morris is mentioned in *The New Humpty-Dumpty*, and Ford has this to say on the subject in *Ancient Lights*:

> In his *News from Nowhere* Morris tried to show us young things what a beautiful world we should make of it .... As far as I remember those young dreams, it was all to be a matter of huge-limbed and splendid women, striding along dressed in loose curtain-serge garments, and bearing upon the one arm such sheaves of wheat as never were, and upon the other such babies as every proud mother imagines her babies to be. (p. 119)[71]

Similarly to the way in which the Pre-Raphaelite legacy makes itself felt, Ford's work resonates with the effects of these youthful dreams. Big, physical, natural women, made busy by the wheat in one hand and the baby in the other, of nature and fertile, populate his mythical fiction. In terms reminiscent of the description of Magdalena in *The 'Half Moon'*, in *The New Humpty-Dumpty* Lady Emily Aldington fulfils the criteria: 'Lady Aldington herself suffered from no troubles of any physical kind. She was thirty-one. She stood five-foot nine in her stockinged feet. She rode ten stone, and she rode it for an hour and a half every morning of the year, wet or fine'.[72] The sheer size of her is admirable, and the reader is requested to appreciate her superiority over the weather, over her physical well-being, and over any horse which she chooses to mount.[73] Ford himself is impressed. His sentences are short and weighty, imbued with added strength by the repetition of the universal and totemic 'she'. Ford continues his foray into typification, for, whilst Lady Aldington is ideally strong and 'natural', fit and beautiful, she is simultaneously a 'little frozen white lamb' or sexually unawoken and undemanding. And it is no coincidence that she is also an aristocrat. Ford develops a theory concerning social class and its correlation with female sexuality as he proceeds. In the following extract, Lady Aldington is engaged in conversation with a friend; the subject is the affair which her husband has been conducting, and which he continues to pursue:

> 'It's still the same woman?' Madame Sassonoff asked.
> 'It's still the same,' Emily answered. 'I don't know what she's like. I know she was a barmaid. And I think I've gathered to-day that she has a cockney voice and drops her h's. And her extravagance must be extraordinary. I know in one way and another Aldington gets fifteen thousand a year out of me. Why, she has a house in Curzon Street...' And Lady Aldington's eyes filled with unmistakable tears. 'My dear', she said, 'what is the attraction of these creatures? Why is it that we women have to suffer? They appear to be nothing, these women. They are vulgar, they daub themselves with paint. And the men howl over them and suffer the pains of the damned. And if one offers to set them free to marry, they say "My God, no!" What does it mean? Isn't it the most abominable one can have offered to one? What *does* it mean?' (pp. 34–5)

Lady Aldington's frank speech in a moment of emotional unguardedness would seem to imply that what has, in fact, distressed her, has been the contravention of recognised boundaries to do with class and sex. She has learnt new information regarding this 'creature', who, as a sexual being and member of the lower classes, loses temporarily the right to be called a woman. 'She' (the female interpretation this time of the female Other) causes the women only grief and discomfort. When 'She' is poor, 'She' can be ignored; it is the treachery endemic in her possession of a house in Curzon Street, when added to her sexual status, that makes Lady Aldington cry.

Ford creates three distinct camps in this incident: the ladies Aldington and Sassonoff, the men and the creatures. Chaos only occurs when the strict guidelines governing behaviour in one category or another are contravened. Lady Aldington is a fine lady, and frigid. The 'creature' is lower class, and sexual, and the men have on this occasion begun to stumble between the two. Briefly, it looks as though Ford is heralding the world of *The Good Soldier* rather than describing his utopian, Pre-Raphaelite, dream. But Ford soon reveals that the added complication of class is not enough to disguise the true and only margins which exist: those between the sexually active woman and the sexually austere. Civilisation, society and the model of *The Good Soldier* recede. Lady Aldington falls completely in love with another woman's husband. Countess Macdonald, his wife, describes the new 'other woman' here, using, almost exclusively, identical imagery as that which

Lady Aldington employed, to describe *her*. Lady Aldington is no longer frigid; she has trangressed the boundaries by asserting herself sexually; she now is the creature. In conflict with Count Macdonald his wife demands: "'I want to understand what sort of painted fool it is that has taken a useless creature like you to her heart [...]. Why have these creatures such power?... They are idle, they are frivolous.... What are they compared to a woman like me? What do you see in them? How do they affect you? It's a mystery; it's all a mystery"' (p. 94). The sexual woman has been to the ladies Aldington, Sassonoff, and Countess Macdonald 'a mystery'. Ford's investigations, and in particular his illustration, of the nature of that mystery serve to reanimate the discussion of the Pre-Raphaelite inheritance and Ford's memory of the Barbary doves.

The 'dear dark forest'

The 'dark forest' is the most resonant symbol in this text. Ford's conceptualisation of such a place forms the centre of the novel; it is its heart and was Ford's chosen title.[74] At one level, the dark forest represents estrangement of self from self and self from other. The linguistic flag constantly employed to signify this recognition – 'The heart of another is a dark forest' – is repeated by many of Ford's characters. Ultimate loneliness is enforced by what Saunders describes as the 'sinister reserve of bitterness, envy, hatred, treachery and violence within apparently civilised conduct' that operates in this text (Saunders I, p. 326). The rules of civilised conduct exist to protect each of them from the realisation of such sinister motivations. And from sexuality. 'In this immense jungle that we live in', affirms Pett, revealing the back-drop of nature out of control, Lady Aldington is 'rather like a dark forest' (p. 70). The behavioural niceties protect her investigation, her exploration and navigation, and simultaneously circumscribe the mystery of what is within.

Moser states that 'sexual passion is the major source of the dark forest' (p. 108), the major force in Pett's 'jungle' and that which evokes the cries of 'mystery!' from those who are sexually abstemious. But sexual unions (as well as marital dissolutions) do occur, and, vanquishing civilisation, the tale finally buries itself in the containing confines of the differently conceptualised dark forest as discovered by Emily Aldington and Sergius Mihailovitch. The need for lonely protection from the terrifying heart of another disappears as these two lovers chart the contours of sexual union; the end point of Ford's fictional travel is much more Donne's 'new found land' than classical, civilised, utopia.

Ford constructs a pastoral scene towards the end of the text, nature, specifically *female* nature, triumphs, and, finally, Emily and Sergius find something that they have been looking for. Emily speaks: "'We've found it, really...'" And he said, "Yes! yes! The very centre of [the] dark forest!'" (p. 334). Linguistically, as well as symbolically, sex is thus signified by Ford in a manner that bespeaks equality between the two, joint discovery, joint delight – such a scene would have to be situated beyond the confines of civilisation.

This union is repeated in the final pages of the book, for as Sergius dies he turns his head into Emily's lap, saying: "'The dark forest! The dear dark forest'" (p. 432), in an act which, tragically, has the greatest sexual potential of any yet witnessed.[75] The final image of the book, caught up as it is with female symbolism, thus envelops it, becoming bigger than it, evoking Marlow's interpretation of the 'meaning of an episode' in Conrad's appropriately titled *Heart of Darkness*. Such meaning 'was not inside like a kernel but outside, enveloping the tale which brought it out only as a glow brings out a haze'.[76] The incident elicits a complete understanding, to which Ford's tale has brought the reader, of the containing and desirable strength that woman, that the symbolic image of woman as a dark forest, natural and sexual, represents. Clearly, the box with the doves into which the young Ford peered represents at one level the vagina. In his memory, he experienced it mainly as a worrying, castrating and yet enthralling image. In this novel, more powerfully positive aspects of that sight are revisited; the 'chains of desires and fears' reveal another link.

Positive fiction III: Ladies Whose Bright Eyes
Ladies Whose Bright Eyes (1911) is a novel that Max Saunders has described as an attempt 'to re-imagine the medieval past Madox Brown and Rossetti painted'.[77] It is the last of the positive fictions to be discussed in this chapter. The title evokes images of attractive, insightful women, as does the quotation from Milton's 'L'Allegro' from which it comes, one that also adds power and fantasy to the mixture. Ford's epigraph is as follows:

> Towered cities please us then
> And the busy haunts of men,
> Where throngs of knights and barons bold
> In weeds of peace high triumphs hold,
> With stores of ladies whose bright eyes
> Rain influence and judge the prize.

It comes from the section in Milton's poem that is dedicated to the imagined joys and delights that Euphrosyne/Mirth can bring the speaker.[78] Ford chose a medieval setting and a dream framework for this text. Each of these criteria denotes great scope for both investigating and revealing his fantasies concerning women, men and love. In modernist fashion, multiplicity is enshrined by Ford at the level of form, as well as of content: there are two time frames here, two levels of consciousness, two female protagonists, two castles and two stories (in the middle of the text the action tracks briefly the knightly, and amorous, exploits of the women's husbands). Sorrell's very aim is to allow himself to submit to the broadness, reliability and safety of a courtly, though passionate, idea of love. A dream fantasy, in which he travels to the fourteenth century, as a result of that quintessentially modern accident, a train crash, is his method for so doing. Trapped on board the train, amid the 'extraordinary rush of modern life',[79] Sorrell has been peeping at a nun, and talking with a Mrs Lee-Egerton, when the hurtling of the train turns suddenly into a 'fantastic hard jabbing' (p. 21). It crashes, and leaves Sorrell unconscious and hanging upside-down. His daydream of living in the Middle Ages, into which his consideration of the nun has transported him, and his admiration of Mrs Lee-Egerton ('she was very dark and very tall and very aquiline, and her eyes appeared perpetually to be searching into mysteries', p. 13[80]), create the world of his unconscious into which he 'wakes'.

Sorrell finds himself in a bright pastoral scene, a colourful nun on a donkey confronts him, the sun is high in the sky, and the sheep graze on shimmering pastures (Pre-Raphalite visual stimulation again). Though he knows he is near Salisbury, he begins to regret that he has always travelled everywhere so fast, oblivious to the small places between Bath and London, one of which he now imagines must be his location. Not for some time does he (incompletely) recognise that he has travelled in time as well as in space, finally coming to explain his existence in the year 1327 by the fact that the crash has shaken the soul out of his body. It doesn't take him long at all, though, to use his surroundings to bolster his fantasy life; he is, in some deep and real sense, at home. On his travels Sorrell isolates the type of woman who offers him fulfilment. The Lady Dionissia combines the comfort of a politically feudal system with miraculous and simplistic (Catholic) religious sanction, and for this he loves her:

> And these splendid and comfortable miracles of God and of the blessed
> angels of God and of the Mother of God, you, a poor sinful man [...] cry

out upon your fate and refuse to put your trust in God and the comfort
of society's hierarchical sanction: [. . .] a king shall give you a castle here,
and an emperor shall give you broad lands there [. . .]. And our lives shall
be very pleasant and restful, and you shall not ever be sad. (pp. 259–61)

The biblical simplicity of her language resonates with the added
strength of that used in The 'Half Moon' to describe Magdalena; this
protecting vision of woman evokes restfulness-in-plenty. His lover will
not be a sexual predator, but a provider of bounty and of peace. Her
physical presence will give him a different kind of rest.

The Lady Dionissia 'was tall, large-limbed, and of an exceeding and
most unusual fairness'. She is a further reincarnation of the utopian
ideal of womanhood. She also serves to divest Sorrell of his heretofore
very masculine, civilised, concentration upon order and self-assured-
ness: 'Mr. Sorrell found that his tongue was tied and he continued
gazing back at the Lady Dionissia as if the sight of her had struck him
with a disease of muteness' (p. 147). Dis-ease of this kind was prominent in Grimshaw's first taste of the unsettling nature of love: for Ford
it seems to symbolise the ultimate in recognition of the power of
woman. What is of crucial difference in this instance, and what stands
in opposition to this image of restriction, is the correlating natural and
instinctual freedom that Sorrell also discovers.

Sorrell is by trade, in the twentieth century, a publisher. Echoing one
of Ford's most painful beliefs about the public perception of literature,
Sorrell states at the outset of the text that publishing 'struck him still as
something connected with literature and in consequence as something
effeminate' (p. 8).[81] Nonetheless, it is plain that Ford believes that he
has to be shaken out of his publisher's reliance on facts and figures, one
that emasculates his body and deadens his soul. Tietjens is evoked in
Sorrell's differently conceptualised 'return to the body' (his own and
that of a beloved woman) in this text.

Within the medieval framework, and in the face of a woman such as
Lady Dionissia, Ford's male character finds the ability to embrace a
challenge, and does not need to fear it. He discovers his ability to act as
Dionissia's castle is attacked by outlaws: 'Suddenly they felt – and they
screamed aloud – that the devil was amongst them. . . . The men on the
left saw, enveloped in the clouds of smoke from the burning hovel, an
immense white horse, that fell in amongst them. Upon its back was a
terrible man all in red and white, waving a steel mace above his head
and calling out in an unknown tongue' (p. 153). There is much of
interest in this portrayal of a Fordian man. He is hugely, immensely

active, and finds the sanction to perpetrate his most deeply located maleness. Sorrell has regained his tongue – a tongue that exacerbates his threat to those he has come to destroy – and is using it to shout his strength as he masters an enormous horse and brandishes a murderous weapon. Order is indeed paramount in this society, but the power to perpetuate that order is apparently infinite; Sorrell can murder without fear of reprisal one who stands in contravention of its laws. In this vision of medieval times Ford finds the perfect combination of the order of civilisation (it is important that Sorrell is given power as a 'holy man', and starts his journey near the top of the feudal tree – and gets higher) with the freedom of nature. Returning to the quotation from Freud which described modern society as an enforcement of the 'renunciation of instinct' and continuing with him to imagine the lifting of these prohibitions: 'If, then, one may take any woman one pleases as a sexual object, if one may without hesitation kill one's rival for her love or anyone else who stands in one's way', the imaginary effects of modern society being rescinded are viewed as the Fordian concept of medieval living enshrined. Indeed, Sorrell points the way to a later Fordian protagonist who seeks what Sorrell has found. 'Am I no better than a eunuch or is the proper man – the man with the right to existence – a raging stallion forever neighing after his neighbour's womankind?' (*The Good Soldier*, p. 15), questions Dowell, beset by modern society, and unable to discover the raging stallion which for Sorrell has been released, experienced and known.

Ford has created within this novel the room for the propagation of the unconscious. Sorrell can be his deepest self. His fantastical journey into his unconscious is finally rewarded (though he weeps when he wakes in the twentieth century, he has been transformed). And it is this aspect of the travel, rather than that of actual, physical discovery, that Ford chooses to emphasise. This does not mean that what Sorrell sees, feels and tastes is not important: it is, because that sight, taste and sensation is part of the liberation of the unconscious. Once more, what he sees owes more to a Pre-Raphaelite conception of the world than to anything else, one that Ford tempers with modernist multiplicity. Whilst the heart of *The New Humpty-Dumpty* is the 'dear dark forest' and what happens in it, bespeaking one kind of reclamation, at the heart of this novel is light instead, prismatic, joyful and splendid light. Sorrell rides into Salisbury, and it is a sensational event: sights and sounds, people and colours, light and shade are related by Ford in a way that evokes the chaotic description of the railway station quoted at the outset of this chapter. He arrives at the cathedral:

> The immense pillars were painted a strong blue, and the little pillars running up them were bright scarlet; the high windows through which the sun fell were all in violent, crude and sparkling colours, and these colours, thrown down, seemed to splash a prismatic spray all over the floor, which was of bright yellow tiles.
> Mr Sorrell exclaimed:
> 'My God!' (pp. 233–4)

William Sorrell finds God in this cathedral, where also all life is to be found (Ford's use of the colours blue, red and yellow signifies the marriage of heaven and earth). Riotous humanity is praying and selling and talking and jostling and interacting in this holy, busy, living place. The 'prismatic spray' of light is important because it allows Sorrell to see all that is there. Light, separated out into its constituent colours, both mirrors his sight of all the levels of humanity and simultaneous experience of God, and indicates the fact that Sorrell would see, highlighted in red, orange, yellow, green, blue, indigo and violet, aspects that would remain hidden had the light remained 'whole'. Here is a sense in which kaleidoscopic vision (examined in the Introduction), central to Ford's ethic, can be seen working to the multiplicitous good.[82] Amid this riot of colour and communication, Sorrell finds the dean of the cathedral, a benevolent, wise man, one who advises sex outside marriage but also vows to help Sorrell's marital suit.[83] Close to God, with a wise man's blessing, and full of the rich and bright life-giving variety of the light and colour from the cathedral, Sorrell and the Lady Dionissia can then retreat to the pastoral idyll, also used in *The New Humpty-Dumpty*, to make love. The living heart of the novel gives way to its timeless, spaceless, yet also natural partner, where Sorrell 'felt as if he were sinking down between the myriads of stars into unknown spaces' (p. 262). He will know them now.

William Sorrell, the twentieth-century William Sorrell, obsessed by facts, decides as he comes back to his earthly body that he has not undertaken a spiritual journey at all. On recovering consciousness, he addresses his nurse, admonishing her that 'it must have been you that made me dream, and not my spirit that went back' (p. 360). This he believes he proves by a factual, historical inaccuracy he remembers from his travels. The woman who 'made him dream' is, by a beautiful irony, Dionissia – a descendant of the historically accurate Lady Dionissia that Sorrell 'met'. This contemporary Dionissia doesn't allow him the knowledge of history he believes to be his, and corrects him on his analysis. His collapse at this reimposition of the threat of woman-hood (as with Tietjens, facts are his lifetime's work) is anticipated, but it doesn't occur. Sorrell does not collapse. Grimshaw's comparative failure in the face of Katya is thus balanced and answered by one who has the increased strength of self-knowledge, fuelled by the self-explo-ration of dream fantasy.

Sorrell's dream, his unconscious production of archetypal form is thus fulfilled in reality; once his imagination has been freed he is re-constructed with 'ancient sanities' incorporate. He turns down a salacious, profit-making book, and instead decides to bring a morality to publishing, taking on loss-making, soul-benefiting poetry.[84] Words become possibilities to him, fantasy-bringers, and allow him to main-tain a relationship with the part of himself that is through the veil of his consciousness. Words make pictures, the pictures that help to form the 'chains of desires and fears' for Sorrell immediately, and for Ford more broadly (as in the case of the doves). The ancient sanities are defined by Dionissia, the pinnacle of female wisdom:

> 'In the summer it will be very pleasant; the birds will sing, and we shall walk in the gardens. And in the winter we shall go into our little castle, and we shall sit by our fire, and our friends will come and we shall pass the time in talking and devising. And all around us there will be the oceans of time and the ages of space, like mountains and seas and forests that it shall take us many months to travel through.'
> 'I've heard that before,' he said.
> 'Yes, certainly you've heard that all before', she answered with a gush of words. 'It's nothing new; it's the oldest wisdom or the oldest folly. You will find it in Chaucer... And you will find it in the Bible... You will find it baked in the bricks that the Assyrians used for books and in the old sands of the desert and the oldest snow of the poles. It's the only thing worth saying in life.' (pp. 362–3)

In their talking, Dionissia promises, they will devise new interpreta-tions of these old wisdoms.

Ford establishes, in ways such as this, a kind of imaginative reposi-tory in his positive fictions. In the series of texts investigated here he provides rich examples of the atavistic modernist consciousness; one that is plurally manifested, temporally complex and visually challeng-ing. Experimenting with his past, with the unconscious, and with the archetypal definitions one discovers there, creates in Ford's fiction a regenerative possibility to be encountered alongside the fragmenting forces more obviously endemic to modernism.

In the chapter that follows, the religious and existential aspects of Ford's regenerative quest are considered. In 1904 Ford published a poem called 'Grey Matter'. In it, one poetic voice asks of another,

> Where has either of us scope
> In this dead-dawning century that lacks all faith,
> All hope, all aim, and all the mystery
> That comforteth [?][85]

Continuing the analysis of his fantastical texts, *The Young Lovell* is compared with the poem 'On Heaven' in the attempt to answer Ford's own question, and a search is undertaken for the religious equivalent of the symbolic healing of women.

Notes

1 These are the last words of the text, and describe Grimshaw's vanquishment; see the end of Chapter 3 in this book.

2 Peter Childs writes that 'for the Modernists ... the point of using myth was to compensate for the dissatisfying fragmentation of the modern world, to create a controlling narrative that could be mapped onto' (*Modernism*, London, Routledge, 2000, p. 198). Schneidau makes a larger claim: 'in the imagination of the Modernists, atavism was rehabilitated, and became the matrix of a new energy in art', locating the source of this energy in the 'primordial past', and in the 'chthonic' religion of Greece (*Waking Giants: The Presence of the Past in Modernism*, Oxford, Oxford University Press, 1991, pp. 15–23). Both analyses focus attention on ways that modernist literature *combated* fragmentation.

3 Michael Levenson, *A Genealogy of Modernism* (Cambridge, Cambridge University Press, 1984), p. 56.

4 'Pon... ti... pri... ith' [1918], tr. Max Saunders, in Max Saunders (ed.), *Ford Madox Ford: War Prose* (Manchester, Carcanet, 1999), p. 32.

5 Quoted by Peter Conrad in *Modern Times, Modern Places: Life and Art in the Twentieth Century* (London, Thames & Hudson, 1998), p. 214.

6 Forster's depiction of King's Cross in *Howards End* (1910) is also conjured up in Ford's picture, especially because of the glorious yet fearful promise of the station. Once Aunt Juley has left for Howards End from its portals, 'no power on earth could stop her' (Harmondsworth, Penguin, 1989, p. 27).

7 Quoted by John Fuller in 'The Fine Arts' in Boris Ford (ed.), *Victorian Britain, The Cambridge Cultural History of Britain*, Vol. 7 (Cambridge, Cambridge University Press, 1992), p. 174.

8 Ford Madox Ford, *The March of Literature* (London, George Allen & Unwin, 1939), p. 723.

9 Ford Madox Ford, *Return to Yesterday: Reminiscences 1894–1914* (1931) (Manchester, Carcanet, 1999), p. 3.

10 *Outlook* 33, 17 January 1914.

11 *Daily News*, 14 January 1911, p. 7.

12 Ford Madox Ford, *A Call: The Tale of Two Passions* (1910) (Manchester, Carcanet, 1984), p. 121.

13 Conversely, at war, as Ford explores it in *No Enemy*, one's sight was almost permanently occluded. Ford writes that Gringoire had been able to notice 'only four landscapes' during 1914–18 (New York, Ecco, 1984, p. 23). Allyson Booth comments that the war could not be 'delineated' because it was 'too big to see from a distance [and] too confusing to see from up close' (*Postcards from the Trenches: Negotiating the Space Between Modernism and the First World War*, Oxford, Oxford University Press, 1987, p. 87.)

14 Ford Madox Ford, *Between St Dennis and St George: A Sketch of Three Civilisations* (London, Hodder & Stoughton, 1915), p. 39.

15 Ford Madox Ford, *Ancient Lights and Certain New Reflections* (London, Chapman & Hall, 1911), pp. viii–ix.

16 To make good her point to Orlando in *As You Like It*, Rosalind tells him that 'I will be more jealous of thee than of a Barbary cock-pigeon over his hen' (IV. i. 157). This is the best illustrative image she can find of primal, jealous behaviour.

17 Joseph Bristow, *Sexuality* (London, Routledge, 1997), p. 41. Ford read Otto Weininger's *Sex and Character* (1903); refer to the discussion in Chapter 2.

18 The pagan context provides a more helpful interpretation of the dove: as Aphrodite's bird, the dove comes to symbolise along with her the 'irresistible generative force' and the 'passionate desires which it kindles in all living creatures'. See the entries for 'Dove' and 'Aphrodite' in Jean Chevalier and Alain Gheerbrandt (eds), *The Penguin Dictionary of Symbols*, trans. John Buchanan-Brown (Harmondsworth, Penguin, 1996).

19 This is despite the house's intimidating nature; it is described by Teresa Newman and Ray Watkinson as a 'substantial Georgian town house, adorned with pilasters, rusticated stone facing and a large Roman urn cantilevered over the door [of which more later], which struck fear into visitors' hearts' (*Ford Madox Brown and the Pre-Raphaelite Circle*, London, Chatto & Windus, 1991, p. 146).

20 Bristow, *Sexuality*, p. 71.

21 Financially embarrassed by his brother, Tietjens, too, 'viewed his case from outside' (*Parade's End*, Harmondsworth, Penguin, 1988, p. 202).

22 Thomas Moser, *The Life in the Fiction of Ford Madox Ford* (Princeton, Princeton University Press, 1980), p. 284.

23 Newman and Watkinson, *Ford Madox Brown and the Pre-Raphaelite Circle*, pp. 146–7. They quote at length in their study from Ford's remembrances of his grandfather.

24 George Steiner, 'Gent', *New Yorker*, 47, p. 98.

25 Saunders traces the Freudian significance of this relationship, adding it to that of his grandmother: 'In Freud's "family romances", children fantasize about having grander parents than their actual ones. In Ford's case the family romance was actual: his grandfather had usurped Francis Hueffer as his male parent' (Saunders I, p. 26.)

26 Alan Judd, *Ford Madox Ford* (London, HarperCollins, 1991), p. 30.

27 Newman and Watkinson, *Ford Madox Brown and the Pre-Raphaelite Circle*, p. 191. Ford's feelings on inheriting Rossetti's cloak are detailed in *Ancient Lights*: 'Upon Rossetti's death, his inverness descended to my grand-father. Upon my grand-father's death it descended to me, it being twenty-three years old. I wore it with feelings of immense pride as if it had been – and indeed was it not – the mantle of a prophet' (p. 128). Violet Hunt talks of Ford's and Conrad's stylistic similarities to the Pre-Raphaelite aesthetic, and remarks on the extent of 'Pre-Raphaelite paraphernalia' at the *English Review* office. On a very different matter, she describes his marriage proposal to her as 'an assay in Pre-Raphaelite crudity of expression, as if a Madox Brown heavy oil painting ... had been suddenly turned into speech' (*I Have This to Say: The Story of My Flurried Years*, New York, Boni & Liveright, 1926, pp. 23, 68).

28 Ford Madox Ford, *The Brown Owl* (London, T. Fisher Unwin, 1892), pp. 5, 19.

29 This is the phrase used by Douglas Goldring (Ford's sub-editor at the *English Review*) to express the importance of Brown to Ford in *The Last Pre-Raphaelite: A Record of the Writings of Ford Madox Ford* (London, Macdonald & Co., 1948), p. 44.

30 Ford published this novel with Madox as a middle name.

31 Saunders I, p. 26.

32 Jan Marsh, *Pre-Raphaelite Women* (London, Weidenfeld & Nicolson, 1987), p. 39.

33 Ford (ed.), *Victorian Britain*, p. 170.

34 Ford (ed.), *Victorian Britain*, pp. 169, 166. Whereas in its earliest incarnation, the Pre-Raphaelite Brotherhood was heavily Bible-oriented, emphasising God's revelation of himself in nature and in scripture, by the 1850s the concentration had shifted to natural forms.

35 Michael Mason in a review of Kate Flint's *The Victorians and the Visual Imagination* in the *Times Literary Supplement*, No. 5108, 23 February 2001, p. 11.

36 Caroline Gordon notes that Graves's conclusions in *The White Goddess* 'shed light on aspects of Ford Madox Ford's work which have engaged my

attention for years'. These aspects are Ford's use of myth and archetypal patterns (*The Good Soldier: A Key to the Novels of Ford Madox Ford*, Davis, CA, University of California Library, 1963, pp. 9, 16).

37 Refer to note 2, and to Peter Faulkner, *Modernism* (London, Methuen, 1977), p. 18, where he states that using myth was one way that modernist writers could give coherence to their work.

38 Quoted in Mike Jay and Michael Neve (eds), *1900* (Harmondsworth, Penguin, 1999), p. 326.

39 See Childs, *Modernism* (p. 57) on the contribution made by Neitzsche, Darwin and Freud; see Peter Gay's chapter 'Offensive Women and Defensive Men' (*The Bourgeois Experience: Victoria to Freud*, Vol. 1, *The Education of the Senses*, Oxford, Oxford University Press, 1984) for a history of male fear of female sexuality and its mythic roots.

40 Ford Madox Ford, *Rossetti* (London, Duckworth & Co., 1902), pp. 136, 144.

41 *The Good Soldier: A Tale of Passion* (New York, Norton, 1995), p. 119.

42 Ford Madox Ford, *The 'Half Moon'* (London, Eveleigh Nash, 1909), p. vi.

43 They thus prove Ford was helping to fulfil Edwin Muir's invocation in 1918 to modern writers to 'resuscitate myth'. See Vassiliki Kolokotroni *et al.* (eds), *Modernism: An Anthology of Sources and Documents* (Edinburgh, Edinburgh University Press, 1998), p. 357.

44 The five ports, also known as 'The Cinque Ports' (Ford published a book under this title in 1900 after living in the area for five years), are a group of medieval ports on the south-eastern coast of England: Dover, Hastings, Hythe, Romney and Sandwich. Rye and Winchelsea were later added to the five.

45 It is possible that the model for this character is to be found in Magdalena Schabrowsky, Ford's 'second Slav romance', whom he met in Germany whilst a teenager. Ford describes her as 'coming back to him' as 'calm Purity', rescuing him from educational failure by acting as 'Copperfield's Agnes – Sister Agnes with her finger to her lips, pointing upwards' (*Return to Yesterday*, pp. 100–1).

46 The symbolism of Christ's Passion and concomitant humility is relevant here.

47 The quotation is taken from Gerhard Adler, *Etudes de psychologie jungienne* (Geneva, 1957), p. 18.

48 See Gay, *Education of the Senses*, pp. 202–3 for a discussion of Pre-Raphaelite images of female power.

49 Timothy Weiss, *Fairy Tale and Romance in the Works of Ford Madox Ford* (Lanham, MD, University Press of America, 1984), p. 4.

50 Robert Graves, *The White Goddess* (London, Faber & Faber, 1948), pp. 21–2.

51 Ford (ed.), *Victorian Britain*, p. 183.

52 *The Good Soldier*, p. 46.

53 Jay Winter, *Sites of Memory, Sites of Mourning: The Great War in European Cultural History* (Cambridge, Cambridge University Press, 2000), p. 63.

54 Marina Warner, *Alone of All Her Sex: The Myth and the Cult of the Virgin Mary* (London, Weidenfeld & Nicolson, 1976), p. 67.

55 I am reminded of Cixous' *Sorties* ('Where is she?') here, in which she lists a series of gender-related binaries, including 'Writing/Speech, Day/Night, Culture/Nature' (see Elaine Marks and Isabelle de Courtivron (eds), *New French Feminisms*, Hemel Hempstead, Harvester Wheatsheaf, 1981, pp. 90–8).

56 'I am a Tory because I cannot help myself', Ford averred in 1911, continuing, 'I am a Papist because it is the Faith of my Fathers' ('The Critical Attitude', *The Bystander*, 15 November 1911, p. 345).

57 It is necessary to acknowledge the complicated history of Ford's relationship with the church, however. Alan Judd calls him a 'kind of Catholic, or agnostic, or Catholic-agnostic' (*Ford Madox Ford*, p. 1).

58 From an entry in Olive Garnett's diary, quoted in Saunders I, p. 48. This entry is also quoted in full by Moser, *Life in the Fiction of Ford Madox Ford*, p. 13.

59 Goldring, *The Last Pre-Raphaelite*, p. 52.

60 Richard A. Cassell, *Ford Madox Ford: A Study of His Novels* (Baltimore, Johns Hopkins Press, 1961), p. 73.

61 Marsh, *Pre-Raphaelite Women*.

62 That ability perhaps extended in some degree to Ford's personal life. Arthur Mizener describes Violet Hunt as 'almost a Pre-Raphaelite beauty; she was auburn-haired, with large, liquid eyes and an expressive mouth that gave her a properly melancholy look' (*The Saddest Story: A Biography of Ford Madox Ford*, New York, Carroll & Graf, 1985, p. 145).

63 Ford Madox Ford, *Rossetti*, p. 144.

64 See the discussion in Chapters 1–3. Edward Carpenter wrote in 1894 that 'woman is the more primitive, the more intuitive, the more emotional; the great unconscious and cosmic processes of Nature lie somehow nearer to her' (*Woman and Her Place in a Free Society*, Manchester, The Labour Press Society, 1894, pp. 8–9). Joseph Bristow writes that 'countless images of *femmes fatales*' hung in 'many a *fin-de-siècle* art gallery' (*Sexuality*, p. 44). Peter Gay puts it more strongly still: 'no century depicted woman as vampire, as castrator, as killer so constantly, so programmatically, and so nakedly as the nineteenth' (*Education of the Senses*, p. 206).

65 Francis Hueffer, *The Troubadours: A History of Provençal Life and Literature in the Middle Ages* (London, Chatto & Windus, 1878), pp. 56, 59, 128.

66 See his discussion of Henry James' ethic, in which he praises James for having 'never committed the sin of writing what he "wanted" to write …

The novelist is not there to write what he "wants" but what he *has*, at the bidding of blind but august Destiny, to set down' (*Henry James: A Critical Study*, London, Martin Secker, 1918, p. 121). I discuss this in Chapter 3.

67 C. F. G. Masterman, *In Peril of Change* (London, T. Fisher Unwin, 1905), p. xiii.

68 Ford Madox Ford, *The Spirit of the People* (London, Alston Rivers, 1907), p. 115. Perhaps Ford's interest in his father's project is partly to do with its mitigation of this loss: 'Courtly love is in essence the result of the transfer of an attitude of religious adoration from a divine to a secular object – from the Virgin Mary to the lady worshipped by the troubadour'. Ian Watt, *The Rise of the Novel* (London, The Hogarth Press, 1987), p. 136.

69 C. J. Jung, *The Archetypes and the Collective Unconscious*, ed. Herbert Read, *The Collected Works of C. J. Jung*, Vol. 9, Part I (London, Routledge & Kegan Paul, 1968), pp. 48–9; Sigmund Freud, 'Creative Writers and Day-Dreaming', SE ix, pp. 141–53.

70 *Man and His Symbols*, ed. Jung and von Franz (London, Picador, 1978), p. 186.

71 Compare this with *The New Humpty-Dumpty*: 'Whereas [Count Macdonald's] views had completely altered, his wife's had remained exactly the same. She still dressed in clothes of sage green, her sleeves still swept the floor; around her neck was a rope of amber beads' (London, John Lane, 1912, p. 44). This description is usually interpreted by critics as a dig at Ford's wife Elsie, who was refusing to divorce him at this time. Aspects of the past were perhaps not so valuable in reality as they were in fantasy.

72 *The New Humpty-Dumpty*, p. 12.

73 Compare this with Sylvia's metaphorical mastery of horses in *Parade's End*. Her mounting of a chestnut stallion, her ability to maintain her seat, her occasional cruelty, her prevention of it consorting with its mate, all relate to her treatment of Tietjens and his relationship with Valentine. Sylvia's mastery opposes that of the Lady Aldington (*Parade's End*, pp. 708, 779–85, 798–808).

74 Freud's description of adult female sexuality as a 'dark continent' did not occur until 1926.

75 It is hard to avoid the idea that part of what Ford is signifying here is the desire is to reclaim the womb.

76 In *Heart of Darkness and Other Tales* (Oxford, Oxford University Press, 1996), p. 138. The metaphorical use of the forest in Ford's novel also evokes that of Conrad; what is found to be within depends very much on [s]he who discovers it: death and fear, or enlightenment. The sexual connotations are also present in *Heart of Darkness*.

77 Saunders I, p. 324.

78 John Milton, 'L'Allegro', in Helen Darbishire (ed.), *The Poetical Works of*

John Milton (London, Oxford University Press, 1958), pp. 420–4, ll. 117–22.

79 Ford Madox Ford, *Ladies Whose Bright Eyes* (London, Constable & Co., 1931), p. 5. The novel was first published in 1911, and was rewritten extensively for the American edition in 1935. I have used the original version, because of my attention to Ford's works of the time. Mizener states that Ford, in his revision, decided in part to 'bring his style into accord with his prose of the thirties' (*Saddest Story*, p. 485). For a detailed analysis of the discrepancies in these two editions, and of the reasons for Ford's rewrite, see Cassell, *Ford Madox Ford*, Chapter IV, 'Ford's Vision of His World'.

80 Compare this description with others already encountered in this chapter: of Magdalena, Emily Aldington, Morris's heroines.

81 This belief – one to do with remuneration and well as cultural currency – does dog Ford; see my discussion of it in the final chapter of this book.

82 Such use of light is an important part of Ford's technique in *The Young Lovell* too.

83 One must take account here of the fact that Ford was trying to divorce his wife Elsie at this time, in order to marry Violet Hunt.

84 Thus coming much closer to a work ethic of which William Morris would have approved.

85 Ford Madox Ford, 'Grey Matter' in Max Saunders (ed.), *Ford Madox Ford: Selected Poems* (Manchester, Carcanet, 1997), p. 23.

6

Visions in colour;
religious visions

According to the analysis in the last chapter, as William Sorrell travelled through the realised realm of his unconscious, what had been repressed in him was gradually translated into glorious action. His journey culminated, in the 'real' world of the text, in a poised harmony where talk, trust and fantasy, and the professional demands of publishing, could co-exist. (Feminine) nature and (masculine) civilisation were united. In *The New Humpty-Dumpty*, as Emily Aldington and Count Macdonald made love, they did so in a way that both signified the continuing power of nature in a world dominated by conceptions of 'civilised society', and celebrated the 'dark forest' as an image of female physicality.

Overall, as Ford investigated the legacies of the Pre-Raphaelites and his father in *Ancient Lights*, and revealed aspects of his creative unconscious in these positive fictions, Sorrell's and Aldington's self-expression was seen to have its mirror in Ford's own psychological reclamation. I interpreted his visions and memories as betraying not the typically modernist experience of 'fractured, divided sensibilities', but as a version of the more general, and positive, rediscovery of 'chains and networks of desires and fears' that modernism can also provide.[1] In *Ancient Lights*, Ford's greatest energy, his greatest visionary power, was related to his own unconscious psychological processes. The results of these processes, the stuff on the page, often constructed in scenes (like that of the doves) to be viewed by the imaginative reader, bespoke what had been forgotten, or repressed. Taken together, all these texts were seen to provide many such examples that were of collective significance, not just of significance to Ford. Modernism in the sense as applied in the last chapter, then, was closely tied to its atavistic tendencies, to its alliance with psychological discovery, and to its narrative techniques (whereby the past can be brought into the present and maintained there, or where exploration in time and space can occur).

The 'chains and networks of desires and fears' between the 'Old World and the New', were analysed in that chapter as formed partly of archetypal imagery, intended to counter repression, the deadening of instinct and the theological drive to defeminise the religious spirit. So the chains were various, complex and richly wrought. They were multiplicitous, but not fragmenting. Indeed, the plurality of the chains was actively sought by Ford, who evidently sometimes revelled in the fallout when the onward rush of the twentieth century was forcibly halted (perhaps by a train crash), so that what had been forgotten could catch up and re-establish a tangible, visible, knowable hold. In the material for consideration in this new chapter, that onward rush is still delayed, and the resulting hiatus further explored.

In this chapter concentration will remain on the enriching aspects of modernism as employed by Ford: on multiplicity and reclamation. Important though it was in *Ladies Whose Bright Eyes*, still greater focus here will be on how the action of 'seeing' (and also the experience of 'being seen') in Ford allows him to develop his devotion to these enriching aspects. Not for the characters here Dowell's 'mortifying' experience of having Leonora's 'lighthouse' glare turned upon him;[2] not for these characters either Ford's experience of looking at himself 'from outside' as a result of his grandfather's portrait of him as William Tell.[3] Indeed, this chapter could be considered as the culmination of the attention this book has given to the visual aspects of Ford's writing (and the modernist image of the kaleidoscope makes another appearance in *The Young Lovell*[4]). Ezra Pound wrote in his obituary of Ford that he 'was almost an *halluciné* ..., he saw quite distinctly the Venus immortal crossing the tram tracks'; Ford certainly thought he was, writing in 1915 that 'I see myself visions, every day of my life'.[5] This chapter will investigate what this capability means in Ford.

Like previous protagonists of the positive fictions, Lovell is subject to visions. His consciousness is stretched by Ford in a new attempt to visualise human imagination, human desire and the nature of love. Ford's climax to this latest text, in which the seer becomes the seen, is related, in important ways to do with this reversal, to the long poem Ford wrote at the same time, 'On Heaven'. This poem is investigated as a comparative text here. Central to Ford's representation of heaven in the poem is the reflecting, 'lonely old moon', which seems to threaten its existence. As the chapter proceeds, the moon's watchfulness is reconstructed as part of Ford's fantastical solution to the fragmenting experience of the divided self.

The Young Lovell

The Young Lovell was written and published in 1913; it was the novel before The Good Soldier. Though Saunders writes that both these texts are 'studies of the power of desire to enrapture and to endanger and of the conflicts between sexuality and society, passion and morality, pagan worship of desire and renunciation', the earlier of them is set in Northumberland in 1486 and concerns a young knight.[6] After wrestling his way through these conflicts and enjoying, in different ways, both sexuality *and* society, passion *and* morality, the knight finds he doesn't, ultimately, have to choose between them. More concerned with the power of desire to 'enrapture', the knight is different from the protagonists of The Good Soldier amongst whom that power ultimately wreaks havoc. The later of these studies is set in more contemporary times, of course, and is European, and in addition has nothing enriching to say about the power of passion and sexuality. As this is so, it is, perhaps, important to acknowledge that Ford had recently fallen in love again when he began The Young Lovell.[7] The 'curiosity, desire and hope' of this protagonist is quite possibly that felt by his creator at this time.[8] The text, though, provides clues to more interesting ways of sourcing the positive nature of this positive fiction.

La belle dame sans merci/the white goddess

According to Caroline Gordon, The Young Lovell is the climax of Ford's explorations into the mythical imagination; it is the best Fordian example of this kind of novel. She likes it mainly because the pictures it paints are convincing. She conflates two Fordian/Pre-Raphaelite representations of woman in her analysis of the novel, indentifying a *femme fatale* who means the credible departure of the eponymous hero from the 'real world': 'Ford's "Belle Dame Sans Merci" is as beautiful and as without mercy as any White Goddess needs to be in order to convince us that a man turned his back on the real world and followed her over hill and dale'.[9] Deliberately evocative of Graves's terminology, and also of the (romantic and) Pre-Raphaelite inheritance that was the focus of the previous chapter, this quotation draws attention to the depiction of gender in the debate between the real and fantasy worlds. According to Gordon's perspective on this text, fantasy = colourful woman, and man hovers on the border between that womanly world and the real one he unthinkingly inhabited before she came along. But once he sees her, he has no choice but to follow. Gordon also concentrates on the necessity for the wilful suspension of disbelief on the part of the reader, and isolates as the catalyst for this, as well as for Lovell's action, the extreme power in beauty and mercilessness of the female archetype. In her argument, the sight of the woman, as initially described by Ford ('on a green hill there stood a pink temple, and the woman on the back of the white horse held a white falcon. She smiled at him with the mocking eyes of the naked woman that stood upon the shell in the picture he had seen in Italy'[10]) is needed to convince the reader of the protagonist's entry into fantasy.

Astute as Gordon is in much of her analysis, I don't agree with her interpretation of the white goddess's function here. Lovell, as portrayed by Ford, has already crossed that border into fantasy, in a manner that disguises its existence, *before* seeing the white goddess. Similarly, Ford begins work in the first lines of the text, pre-white goddess, to persuade the reader to make a leap of faith. His method is more subtle than those employed in the other, recently examined, texts. The dramatic train crash of *Ladies Whose Bright Eyes* and the heavy Catholicism of the witch-like seductions of *The 'Half Moon'* are unnecessary here. For the first time in the discussion of myth, the desire to exploit and make fluid the border between fantasy and reality, and to employ and to know all the many layers of the mind, come from within the hero. Lovell is alert, conscious and shown to be in command of his diverse patterns of behaviour. Using him, Ford proves that deep and complex self-realisation does not have to be thrust upon his male protagonists, by white goddesses or by train crashes, but can be sought by them.

Vigil

Lovell is on the threshold of becoming a knight. In the time-honoured fashion, he appropriates this burgeoning to push himself first to the limits of his physical endurance. His decision to keep painful vigil (though traditional) is carefully shown to be his own. Lovell is a stern task-master, and yet late in the night he does break his vow: 'In the darkness Young Lovell of the Castle rose from his knees, and so he broke his vow. Since he had knelt from midnight, and it was now the sixth hour of the day, he staggered; innumerable echoes brushed through the blackness of the chapel; the blood made flames in his eyes and roared in his ears' (p. 1). These are the first words of the text. They

imply, in the 'blackness' and the 'flames', that Lovell will be punished
for his lack of integrity, for his precipitate act. But Ford isn't interested
in the morality of the case, and what would perhaps be more usually
inferred as a failed end (to devotion, to prayer and to knighthood) is
shown instead to be a wild and magnificent beginning. Lovell ceases his
devotional posture as the dawn breaks, and as he becomes conscious of
the great physical and mental strain that has beset him, as his senses
regain their feeling, and the blood starts to flow, he begins to recall the
events of the night. His recollection comes in its full vigour only as a
result of his decision to break his vow.

Lovell's transgression, then, the breaking of the vow and the flood-
ing return of his life's blood, mean he returns to the powerful things he
has seen in the night, things that must then be of some worth:

> Visions had come to him [...]. He had seen through the thick walls,
> Behemoth riding amidst crystal seas, Leviathan who threw up the smoke
> and flames of volcanoes. Mahound had passed that way with his cortège
> of pagans and diamonded apes; Helen of Troy had beckoned to him,
> standing in the sunlight, and the Witch of Endor, an exceedingly fair
> woman, and a naked one, riding on a shell over a sea with waves like
> dove's feathers. (p. 1)

It doesn't end here, for further sights are listed over another three
pages; the vibrant, vivid fantasies of the night are relived in their
entirety, after the fact. Ford wants Lovell to know, to remember and to
profit from these sights, sights that he presents as only available to
Lovell's conscious mind because he has interrupted his vigil before day
has broken. Interpreting them, it would appear that what Ford wants
them to teach Lovell is to do with his instincts, with the discovery of his
buried self (it is no accident that these visions come at night).[11]
Beautiful, naked women call to him; powerful, essential masculinity
tempts him into playing god. Ford also wants Lovell, and this is more
significant, to act on the instincts that the visions stir. To these ends, he
both emphasises his freedom of choice (Lovell chooses to watch, he
chooses this chapel and he chooses to break his vow) and simultaneously tempers the pervading aura of whirling dervishes and terrible
demons. They are powerful, but not vanquishing; they bring not death,
but freedom.

Ford illustrates Lovell's ability to intellectualise that which he has
seen as proof that he will not be overwhelmed by it; he shows no terror.
As indicated above, he can name those things that he has encountered,
somehow divesting them of their most dreadful power. Though he is

inhabiting a subliminal world, located in a haunted chapel, his consciousness assailed by many visions, none of these things is experienced as, say, Ford experienced, and visualised, the suffocating giants of the Victorian age.[12] Lovell explains the inexplicable with absolute surety; it is to be inferred that he will prosecute any further opportunity with equal vigour. Lovell fantasises, therefore, but he acts as well.

Lovell does not return to his vigil; rather he proceeds into the half-light of dawn, where the white goddess waits to join him on the new path he has chosen (having abandoned the devotional). Far from needing her to explain his journey, though, as suggested by Gordon, Lovell has shown that within his normally functioning psyche there is a vital, visual sensitivity to fantasy that would always make him susceptible to making such a choice. This remains true for the way in which he is seen to experience and to explain his world. Whilst the aura of ruption (for as a result of the sudden rise to his feet he staggers, and the blood rushes in his head) does in some ways echo that established by the disorientating, catalytic accident in *Ladies Whose Bright Eyes*, Lovell seeks no comparable excuse for what follows. He is more immediately at home in his environment even than Sorrell. Lovell 'fumbles' at the bar of the door, physically weak after his watch and his meeting with spirits, but he recovers his equilibrium immediately, and 'cast the door open, stepping out' (p. 5).

Seeing in colour

Lovell then disappears from the reader's immediate view, travelling with the white goddess, whilst Ford deals with the historical meat of the novel. (There is a kind of dual narrative that Ford manages brilliantly. Lovell does disappear, but edges into the action from time to time in a ghostly manner.) In his absence, his castle is overtaken by his brother, who is also knighted in Lovell's place whilst disguised, and betrothed to the Lady Margaret, Lovell's intended. Lovell is thus dispossessed in all materially imaginable ways. When he comes back into sight, however, it is in order that Ford can show his dispossession to be of no significance, because of a new and unique visual relationship to the world which he has formed.

In his absence from the main thrust of the text, Lovell has added to his imaginative and visual skills the ability to see in colour in particular ways. The colours will be familiar to readers of the last chapter:

> He considered the sleeve of his scarlet coat that was very brave, being open at the throat to shew his shirt of white lawn tied with green ribbons.

He saw that the scarlet was faded to the colour of pink roses. He looked
before him and, on a green hill-side, he was aware of a great gathering of
men and women bearing scythes whose blades shone like streaks of flame
in the sun. Also, at their head, went priests and little boys with lit censers
and lit candles. The day was so clear that, though they were already far
away, he could see the blue smoke of the incense. (pp. 52–3)

This is like painting by numbers. Having pushed aside other more
mundane ways of interpreting, or being successful in, the world
(through familial or political power, or knightly prowess, for example),
Lovell seems to work rather with a simplistic set of coloured keys.
These keys are both symbolic (of love: the pink roses; of innocence: the
white shirt) and brilliantly ordered (below: the green hillside; above:
the blue smoke). Seemingly oblivious to a realistic apprehension of the
dull greys and khakis, colours that don't appear in his kaleidoscopic
spectrum, Lovell sees only in colours that mean something. In addition, everything he sees is distinguishable from its surroundings: no
aspect of this world is hidden.[13] His perspective is long, though true.
Thus he reveals his visual existence to be made up both of perfect
perspective and coded apprehension. He paints a complete, interpretable, picture as he sees, simultaneously proving that Leviathan and
Mahound no longer stand for his instinctual life. The white goddess
will now do so instead.

The colour codes in operation, which support the act of his seeing,
are partly religious ones ('For the Young Lovell had talked always ... of
the Mother of God as the mystic rose, of the Tower of Ivory, and of the
dish that had the most holy blood of God'[14] (p. 128)). They are also
partly related (via religiosity) to the chivalric code. However, they
obtain in their greater part to his more recent experience of love, and
even the religious aspects are often 'corrupted', as it were, and become
equally applicable to sexual significations ('in short [the white goddess]
was all white and gold save for her red and alluring lips that smiled
askant, and he thought that he had never seen so bright a lady ... His
heart at the sight of her beat in great, stealthy pulses' (p. 47)). Although
it is true that Lovell's visual and fantastical imagination was emphasised from the outset of the text, at this point he didn't see much in
colour. Leaving the chapel having broken his vow, 'it was grey; the sea
grey and all the rushes of the sands' (p. 5); even during his recollection
of his nightmares, colour is not significant. Approach to the white
goddess changes that: 'he had a sense of brown, of pearly blue, of white,
of many colours; of many great flowers as large as millstones' (p. 11).

'White' can stand for the absence of colours; it can also, and does here, stand for the sum of them all.[15] The white goddess stands for the summation of all colours, then, and for their emotional equivalents too.

From the point when he encounters her, all that Lovell sees is translated into startling, nursery, Pre-Raphaelite shades of primary colours. Even his military procedures come to him in pictures with these shades: 'As he rode through the fields ... the siege of the Castle grew clear to him and like a picture, red and blue and pink' (p. 103). His experience of love, then, Ford suggests, enacts nothing more important in the Young Lovell than an explosion of visual capability across the spectrum, a capability that crucially includes a coded, interpretable apprehension at an elemental level.[16] There are those in the text who do not have access to this way of seeing, and they tend to be removed entirely from the secular life. These incapables are reminiscent of the fearful men of previous chapters (they fear the 'fairy' women whom they catch at the windows of their monkish cells), and act as a distinct foil to Lovell's colourful vision. Ford shows them bathed in the light that Lovell uses to such positive ends, but unable to apprehend it: 'at last, towards its setting, the sun shone blood red through all those windows of colours, ruby, purple, vermeil, grass green and the blue of lapis lazuli. All those colours fell upon the tiles of the floor that were hewn with a lily pattern in yellow of the potter. Twenty colours fell upon the figure of the Bishop, laying all in black upon his bed' (p. 206). The colours here, coming as they do at the end of a diatribe against women, show the variety of life, its richness, which have recently been miscalled and are being repressed.

Eventually, Lovell does recapture his castle, and is reunited with Margaret. Yet this is not the focus of the story, nor its point. And despite the way in which Lovell's coloured view of things develops the appreciation of Ford's positive fictions (how relaxing it must be to be able to see and understand the world with so little effort; how powerful is this conception of love[17]), it is in another of its aspects that this text contributes most to my analysis of modernist multiplicity in Ford. Here, it is in the experience of being seen, rather than in the act of seeing, that my interest lies.

Being seen

Lovell is a more complex character than he has appeared to be so far. What is usual to Ford, a diagrammatic split between an experiential self, and one which is critical (think for an example of the way Tietjens's mind is displayed at the point of his breakdown) is present in this text, though muted. Lovell may be a lover, but he is a religious man too. What is less immediately obvious, in comparison with those fictions previously studied, is the battle between these aspects of the self. Whereas Robert Grimshaw in *A Call* experiences a nervous breakdown due to the conflict between what he wants and what he thinks he should want, Lovell seems to suffer no such struggle. In addition, for the majority of the text, he seems to manifest no concept of guilt (after all, he has abandoned Margaret to a marriage with his brother, and his mother to imprisonment). *A Call* is a significant text here, partly because of the issues it raises in comparison with Lovell, but also because it is contemporaneous with Ford's foray into myth. What Grimshaw remains without, however, Lovell finds. The object of that search is an elusive one. Ford suggests it is the experience of being seen in one's complex, contradictory, wholeness; it is this that can make Lovell different from other men.

As Lovell rose to his feet in the chapel of his vigil, for a moment he lost his self-control. Ford's representation of this struggle (brief as it was) is crucial. At the second that Lovell becomes fully aware of his physical weakness, he becomes aware too of 'eyes ... peering into the chapel ... watching him'. They are 'kind eyes; eyes unmoved', and they make his heart 'beat enormously' (p. 4). These eyes project him into unexpected action. He stands, 'reeling and stretching out his arms, with prayers that he had never prayed before upon his lips', compelled to communicate himself in ways not to do with fantasy or desire. To whom do these eyes belong? Perhaps they are the eyes of judgement that beset the four protagonists of *The Good Soldier*? Perhaps they are the eyes of the white lady, waiting for him to join her? Neither of these options is convincing; the eyes make him want to backtrack, not to go forward. I think, rather, that they are the briefly glimpsed eyes of his faith. 'Unmoved', they don't seem human; 'kind', they bespeak Christian charity; rousing, they bring him to prayer like he has never prayed before. He cannot hide from these eyes; they see all, including him in the dark. In this sense of being seen and known, either by Christ or by Lovell's projection of his own religious faith, there is a comfort. Lovell wants to be seen, he decides in this moment, in his doubtful yet fantasy-fuelled confusion, rather than to be a seer.

Despite the strength of this experience, and the new kind of desire to which it introduces him, the struggle passes. Lovell argues himself out of his sense of guilt and regret, and reattaches himself to fantasy over religiosity: 'prudence came into his heart and he argued with himself. It was to himself and to no other man or priest that he had vowed to watch above his harness from midnight to dawning' (p. 5). Lovell reminds himself that he is beholden to no one and that the concept of devotional failure is of no account. The instant, the prayer and his feeling of being watched are all subsumed by the continuation of the action, and by his journey out into the kaleidoscopic light of the white goddess. Although the reader forgets these early aspects and progresses with the hero, it later appears the part of him they signified has not been fully vanquished. At the end of the text, once Lovell reclaims his castle, something occurs within him that reawakens the voice of guilt. It precipitates a similar examination of conscience as did the breaking of the vow. It both suggests that there is, conversely to what I have argued so far, a choice to be made about fantasy, and returns attention to the significance of being seen.

Ralph Griffiths characterises the fourteenth century as one of 'burgeoning interest in mystical and devotional writings, most of them in English from the latter part of the century [...]. The writers were frequently solitary figures commending the contemplative life to their readers'.[18] Lady Margaret is a proponent of the 'contemplative life.' Her reward for her purity, and for her self-reflection, is an extensive one:

> The Lady Margaret awakened from a slumber, and the sun had climbed far around in the heaven. Then she perceived a lady watching her through the trees and smiling. So beautiful and smiling a lady she had never seen. She stood between the stems of two white birch trees and leaned upon one, with her arm over her head in an attitude of great leisure. The Lady Margaret rose from her mattress and went towards that lady; she had never felt so humble, nor had her eyes ever so gladdened her at the sight of the handiwork of God. (pp. 154–5)

Margaret's experience is similar to that of Lovell at the outset of the novel; she, too, is seen by beneficient eyes. But she is more immediately able to profit from it. The signs are clearer to her, more comprehensible and enduring (the birch, for example, symbolically 'plays a protective role, it is the means by which heavenly influences come down'[19]); consequently she feels humbled, aware of her place in the scheme of things, and close to God. The notion of purification out of contemplation was at the heart of Lovell's initial decision to stand vigil before his knighthood. And yet he cannot take it far enough at first. At the end of the text, he can.

Lovell's sense of guilt for his abandonment of his knightly path and his betrothed reasserts itself as his mission is accomplished. The bright colours and the sense of exhilaration are edged aside in their turn by the voices of conscience and of religiosity that he silenced in the chapel. Though Lovell is fresh from the battle to retake his castle, this part of him requests the provision of a place to do penance for his sins, and by way of answer he is approved as inhabitant of a hermit's cell by an 'old monk' (p. 305). Without pomp or circumstance, without even the attribution of his name, Lovell enters the cell from which he will never emerge in his lifetime. The doubt as to his chosen course, his love for a woman of the spirit world, and his unchivalrous behaviour, are all to be atoned for. Lovell kneels before the monk and confesses. Having abandoned his fantasy life, and the white goddess, watched by the monk Francis, he is bricked into the 'kennel' by stone masons (p. 305).

So where is the experience of being seen? In a way, it is part of his confession: he lays himself open to the priest who can help him to atone; and it is part of Francis watching him disappear behind the masons' stones. But this is only the half of it. Ford manipulates this apparent finality with an astounding simplicity that both privileges complexity, not the necessity of singular choice so far suggested by the conclusion, and develops the idea of being seen. In the final pages of the novel Ford indicates that the hermit's cell does not complete his vision in this positive fiction: the ascetic half of his protagonist has a companion. Lovell's contemplation will be rewarded (though in a more pagan fashion than the Lady Margaret's), and his burden of choice removed.

As the rain falls upon the roof of the hermit's cell, the earthly confinement of Lovell's physical existence, the narrative suddenly shifts, to where the sun simultaneously shines on the Elysian fields in which his spirit shall always roam. Ford provides little further elucidation. In the first edition of the novel there is simply a sense break between paragraphs, and then the narrative proceeds: 'In a very high valley of Corsica the mistress of the world sate upon a throne of white marble'... (p. 306). The colours return, bronze and blue, scarlet and white. The self that embarked upon a journey into fantasy is pictured in a pagan celebration of all that is hedonistic whilst, simultaneously, the ascetic self is assuaged by permanent pensiveness, penance and self-castigation. Ford wrote to his publisher about the date and setting of the novel in March 1913. He stated that although it was 'running up to the beginnings of the Reformation', it was not 'in that sense concerned with religion'.[20] Perhaps the sense in which it is concerned with religion is in the dualistic realisation and manifestation of religious affiliation by the body and the mind. Two 'places', answering different needs, have been attained which will, in their equal status, render the need for further travel unnecessary. They are only put together, and made whole, by the reader of this text. Acting like the Venus of Lovell's imagination, the reader sees him whole, in his complex contradictoriness, enacting the awareness of his complete state that must be denied to him. Here is the essence of the positive fiction in this case.

Ford's modernist attention to the divided self thus culminates in the premise that each component must be given its own resolution, its own place for expression. There must be an individually tailored solution to the demands and the needs of each 'nature', to use Grimshaw's word.[21] Critically for Ford, too, these components, or natures, must be separate: 'that knight [in pagan bliss] thought never upon the weariness of Northumberland or upon how his mortal body lived in the little hermitage not much bigger than a hound's kennel' (pp. 309–10). Cognitive silence between one self and the other is of the essence, perhaps to quell the battles between the two that would ordinarily occur. Someone, somewhere, though, must see it all together to make it work. Someone must be in possession of all the fragments; in this case, it is the responsive and aware reader.[22]

The Young Lovell is an achievement because it presents the logical conclusion to some of Ford's metaphysical explorations. 'On Heaven' is the poetic attempt of the lover to find just such a conclusion. Arthur Mizener states that *The Young Lovell* 'represents an existence not unlike' that of this poem.[23] Yet the dual vision of a pagan heaven and an ascetic haven is augmented by the poem's quest for a place of peace, for a time of silence, in which the various parts of the self are answered and contained. Such a place, such a time, would serve to instil equilibrium in this new Fordian speaker, a speaker unbalanced in some familiar ways.

'On Heaven'

'You say you believe in a heaven', Violet Hunt challenged Ford, 'I wish you'd write one for me' (Saunders I, p. 395). And so he did, probably in the first months of 1914.[24] It was a 'plain, workaday heaven' she wanted, without beauty and without optimism. This perhaps encouraged Ford to produce what became a clear part of the modernist project in its attention to 'precise descriptive detail' rather than to transcendence;[25] it also makes it sound like a very different project from his positive fictions. And yet in what it became it is not so different from those other texts investigated in my recent chapters (perhaps because Ford ended up writing not just a heaven for Hunt, but one for Brigit Patmore, and ultimately one for himself as well). The fantasy *is* present, rubbing up against, and transforming, the realist materiality of a heaven that includes a 'swift red car', driven, one must assume, by Hunt.[26] Also present is Ford's concentration on the visual sense as the most powerful way of investigating aspects of consciousness, real or fantastic.

Lovell's dual existence is maintained, *ad infinitum*, by the power of Ford's pen and by the regard of the reader. As an important part of the conclusion to the text, it is made clear that there will be no communication between his active spirit (living out his fantasy) and the religiously contemplative mind in his body. In 'On Heaven', Ford attempts a more adventurous representation of what the multiple nature of the human spirit might look like. 'On Heaven' is a projection of a working heaven operating as an equation, balancing interspersed measures of fantasy *and* reality. If approached either as an attempt to escape reality or as an acute ear to the calling of time, the poem would fail. It is both, sometimes at the same time. The essence of it lies in the osmotic movement of Ford's words, of the speaker's memories and his hopes:

> That day the sunlight lay on the farms;
> On the morrow the bitter frost that there was!
> That night my young love lay in my arms,
> The morrow how bitter it was!

The voice which begins the poem in these lines is located not on one side or the other of these emotional landscapes, but on both sides at once. The rhythm of the lines, and the repetition of words, creates a boundary between them that is easily permeated, a kind of membrane through which bitter/happy osmosis can occur. Derek Stanford has called the poem 'not so much a time progression as a time continuum',[27] noting its tendency not to travel anywhere, but rather to exist as a series of layered elements which pass into and feed one another.[28] In this resistance to linear progression, too (a different kind of resistance from that of Lovell's conclusion), 'On Heaven' can be approached as an essentially modernist text.[29] The voice in this first stanza rejects inhabitation of one stratum or another, one time or another; grief and loss are almost immediately present even as touch and light are savoured. Exclamation marks, almost surprised at themselves, answer in their activity the impression of temporary joy.

The voice moves on to allude to the mythical incentive for this mixed geographical and psychological location, and then it alters, as the tangible narration begins. At this point the lilting, hypnotic beauty of the opening is temporarily lost; equilibrium falters, and the reader crashes through the membrane that has been part of the poem's balancing act, into reality. Heaven retreats.

The speaker is waiting; waiting in a place outside chronological time yet imbued with the trappings of somewhere he loves dearly. He is surrounded by the most comforting of stereotypical portrayals of 'small-town folk', when his beloved's red car, a powerful symbol of the twentieth century, interrupts the simplicity of his nursery rhyme existence to test his perception of heaven. And finds it wanting. The speaker is shown to have taken his 'Englishness' – his peculiar consciousness – to his heaven, and his lover cannot join him in a wild abandonment of earthly prudence, but can only try to remind him what heaven could be, were it not for himself. The consciousness that counters their joyous reunion is not transformative, nor is it even particularly acute. Unlike that of other characters from the positive fictions, it is also directed away from the self. It functions like that of the typical, nineteenth-century, realist narrator in omniscient mode:

> And the wrinkled old woman who keeps the café,
> And the man
> Who sells the *Libre Parole*,
> And the sleepy gendarme,
> And the fat *facteur* who delivers letters only in the shady
> Pleasanter kinds of streets;

The speaker watches, therefore, but he does not engage, or deliver a sense of another consciousness. His gently described sights do not mean anything to him. In love, in *his* fantasy, Lovell is shown what he must do by colour; there is the red of passion and the blue of reflection, and the bronze and silver of combat. All of it impacts directly on him. At this point in 'On Heaven', sights cannot be interpreted like this and are merely endured; the speaker seems both bored by his omniscience, and light years away from the truthful, modernist epistemological struggle that will be Dowell's territory. Indeed, in a parody before the event of that text, the old woman touches him on the wrist to coax the speaker, 'Why do you linger? – / Too many kisses can never be kissed!'[30] Doing the interpretative work for the speaker (and thus helping him to avoid the modernist morass in which Dowell is left), the old woman thus also reminds the reader that 'Englishness', as conceived of here, can be as crippling as Dowell's American Puritanism.

If the aim of this heaven is not action, then perhaps it is to escape such outdated omniscient consciousness; perhaps this will be how equilibrium is restored. Possibly, yes. Once the lover descends from the car and looks around (and now there is less of the bored omniscient narrator and more of the complex modernist consciousness in action), and the speaker joins her, spurred by the old woman, heaven comes back into view. The speaker looks inward, and starts to think about sex, realising that, despite his Englishness, his suppressed, 'forgotten', desires are now 'awake'. To act on them, he needs heaven to help with a different kind of forgetting; heaven must provide a sanctified moment to 'wash away past years'. The speaker's conception of his tainting past must be exorcised, and his painfully English conscious-ness dealt with, to leave him with only the physical, sexual experience of the now with his beloved. This is what he wants. But wouldn't that mean that the osmotic process, one that challenged the need to choose one time over another, one emotion over another (one that was so beautifully displayed in the opening lines), would be lost? It would, along with the sense that fantasy and reality must be interspersed. Ford doesn't let this happen.

With typical Fordian irony (and as simultaneously as the fact that the lines are written on a page will allow), the speaker is made aware instead that the memory of his 'past years' is necessary to him. It must come to remind him of what it is he has gained, of how it is he has moved, emotionally and psychologically, in order to be in heaven. Without that memory, Ford implies, heaven would fade. This need for complete vision is part of what makes this poem such a frustration, and so real. The perfection of the split between the ascetic and the aesthetic witnessed in Lovell, one that Ford has previously been seen to idealise in his perception of Christina Rossetti (see Chapter 5), is not on offer. In a much more realistic, and brave, approach to heaven, the speaker will not be able to ignore any part of himself. Ford will make him see it all. This necessity is managed by Ford in a different way from that in which he manages the same necessity for Grimshaw, say. His purpose here is not the same: Ford is experimenting with a new understanding of heaven, not trying to torture his poetic voice or simply display a fragmented soul. This new understanding is based on the fact that the experience of heaven is owed to the human, difficult, complex means of getting there, not to the ability to forget. In this way, in its attention to detail and its attention to the past, the poem again stakes its claim in the modernist tradition.

'You are conscious always of great pain', Ford writes, signifying the new understanding, '*Only* when it is over / And shall not come again'. This kind of speech pattern belongs to the opening of the poem. It describes an osmotic equation in which the present must be made open to the past. Great pain, it suggests, can only be dealt with in the joy to which it gives way. Existence in heaven necessitates reapproaching the past. The feeling of release from past selves is then paradoxically and inextricably bound up with the remembering of them. Fantasy has its roots in human reality; therefore these roots cannot be ignored. In keeping with the complex movements of the poem, the speaker is as yet unable to recognise this truth. He returns to his quest to forget what has come before.

Voice answers voice, qualification builds upon qualification as the words attempt to burrow into themselves to where the past self does not matter. The moment of togetherness, of unification with his lover, is all that there must be, if his attempt is to succeed:

> And, thank God, we had nothing any more to think of,
> And, thank God, we had nothing any more to talk of;
> Unless, as it chanced, the flashing silver stalk of the pampas
> Growing down to the brink of the Rhone,
> On the lawn of a little chateau, giving on to the river.
> And we were alone, alone, alone...
> At last alone ...

Each 'alone' is employed as a hammer, beating against what is a 'monstrous heap' of past reality, of old selves with their old responsibilities, coming back to haunt these two in heaven. That reality consists of their combined personal and familial entanglements ('in England' there is a husband, a wife, children and parents, uncles and grandparents), and when the 'alone' cannot beat any more it collapses, typically, into continuation dots. The hammer is unsuccessful in its task: the 'unless' of the third line represents the stubborn refusal of past selves – as of his acutely conscious 'Englishness' – to retreat. The speaker looks, as he celebrates the vacuum of no-memory, of no-speech, at the silver pampas as it flashes in its own momentary, dazzling glory. He looks to it, and as he does so he places himself outside the vacuum: his moment is no more. This movement of continual undercutting in which each point of arrival holds within it and suggests its mirror image (the day the night, the touch the bitterness, the present the past) is the basic nature of the poem. The resultant pressure seems to threaten to collapse it completely – and would, were it not for the strength of each apposite expression, the exquisite balance of the verse. Ford also anchors the poem in two ways I will go on to discuss (in addition to the time/space continuum he creates in his verse). Both represent recourse to externalities (by this I mean images or characters that skirt the confines of heaven). Both, in different ways, encourage the speaker to experience heaven in the complex form that is Ford's intention here, helping him finally to focus his attention on his past, on the opposed aspects of his self, as well as on his present.

Technique

Ezra Pound described 'On Heaven' as 'the best poem yet written in the "twentieth-century fashion"';[31] high praise indeed, but not surprising considering its combination of epic-resistant, imagistic, impressionistic style and technique. But Humphrey Carpenter challenges Pound's 'puff' in his reading of the poem: 'Ford was doing no more than putting into a nominal verse form (for 'On Heaven' is not very far from prose) the impressionistic narrative style he was developing in his fiction'.[32] The poem is impressionistic (and this is part of what Pound would have been celebrating[33]), but I disagree with Carpenter's reductive reading of this technique. In its search for the incandescent moment, one unmolested by the tides of human consciousness, 'On Heaven' is reminscent of the fragmented Victorian lyric of Matthew Arnold (Stanford too mentions the lyrical effect of the lines, p. 111). In the honesty of concern for what exactly it is that gets in the way, and the dedication to presenting it, one can see the progression from 'The Buried Life' to the 'twentieth-century [impressionist] fashion' for accuracy. Narrative would not cope easily with the plethora of multi-faceted, contradictorily self-conscious and diversely located counter-attempts at unselfconsciousness in love found here. It certainly could not cope with the speed at which the vision alters in this poem. Ford's 'dreary, lonely old moon' is both the first of the externalities that serve to anchor the poem, and an object of Ford's lyric.[34]

The moon
(That night my young love lay in my arms....

There was a bitter frost lay on the farms
In England, by the shiver
And the crawling of the tide;
By the broken silver of the English Channel,
Beneath the aged moon that watched alone –
Poor, dreary, lonely old moon to have to watch alone,
Over the dreary beaches mantled with ancient foam
Like shrunken flannel;
The moon, an intent, pale face, looking down
Over the English Channel.

But soft and warm She lay in the crook of my arm,
And came to no harm since we had come quietly home
Even to Heaven; [...])]

Ford *almost* separates the moon, the Channel and England from
heaven, but he does not quite do this. Though the moon does indeed
'watch alone', these lines of the poem hold it, what it sees, and heaven
all in an uneasy proximity. If they did not, we might feel that the
speaker had, like Lovell, found a place for pure indulgence. Yet the
'But' of awareness, in the last section quoted, signifies the speaker's
consciousness of the moon. He watches the moon as it watches, from
not such a very great distance, the beaches and the Channel, but also
the realm that has been appropriated for love. It is a painful image. One
possible interpretation of it would be in keeping with earlier analysis of
the poem: the moon helps to undercut their love-making, disrupting
their pleasure by a livid display of alternative and excluded consciousness. It sees all unrelentingly; the ultimate and unavoidable reminder of
the speaker's past in the specification of its longevity, it reflects his past
back at him. In this interpretation the moon would be said to echo part
of the speaker's own nature in the poem – the 'broken silver' that it sees
is related to the 'flashing silver' of the pampas – and the moon must be
read indeed as partly a vision of himself. But not like this.

   This image of the moon is not a disruptive one, not one that removes
their pleasure. It is a painful one, yes, of an ageing and lonely act of
witness. It is a vision by the speaker of himself, looking over his past
life, in England, across the 'broken silver' of the Channel. (Ford's
depiction of heaven is as a real place, a 'little town near Lyons', so it is
not surprising that the Channel, one means of attaining it, should
figure here.) The moon sees, and reflects, the 'monstrous heap' of

reality that is in 'England', sees and shows all, in fact. But, crucially, this vision of himself in his old age, this externalised image of his older self, also gives to the speaker, bequeaths to him, what he enjoys now, in the present. Its age, and its loneliness, serve to validate his current joy and union. Yes, it is a 'poor, dreary, lonely old moon', *but* 'soft and warm' she is also lying in the crook of his arm. The word 'but' signifies awareness, as suggested above; it also signifies a concomitant attention to the matter at hand. And so the image of the moon serves to instil in the undercutting, regressive movement of the poem some kind of sense. In the speaker's age and his infirmity there is also life and love. The moon manifests some of the speaker's attributes and reflects them back to him, but some of them it allows his youthful self to keep, and to use, for now. Still challenging the concept of linearity, the moon and the lover exist together, one conscious of the other, presenting alternative perspectives. The presence of the moon shows that he is complete, altogether, but free to manifest his constituent parts.

The second of the externalities Ford uses in this poem, that of the continually evoked 'God', is also significant because of what, and how, he sees.

God

Returning to Derek Stanford's analysis of the poem, he says that it is, 'for the most part', the

> present – a beautiful God-given present – which dominates one's sense of happenings in the poem; and this is why, in one respect, it comes closest to conjuring the idyllic element in a love-idyll. In equating the idyllic with Heaven, Ford has transformed the pagan background of the idyll into one which is specifically Christian. 'Heaven', spelt with a capital, obviates any ambiguity or synonymous use of the word for a more mundane scene or state of peace. (Stanford, p. 117)

The poem does stretch toward the idyllic, and it does equate the idyllic with 'Heaven'. However, the prominence Stanford donates to the 'present' in this reading is questionable. Until the final lines of the poem, this present is most noticeable by its absence for, as I have stated, the longed-for, peaceful, unconscious moment, sought for in love, doesn't ever really arrive ('you are conscious always of great pain/ Only when it is over / And shall not come again'). And nor should it, if my analysis up to this point has been right. The psychological factors which prevent the achievement of modified peace are those same factors which preclude existence in the desired present. However, there is a kind of active peace in this poem, one that is suggested by the above quotation. And there is also a kind of present. Stanford is accurate in his use of the phrase 'God-given present', for Ford's vision of God within the poem is that which ultimately provides both peace and a *critically modified* form of the present tense. God in this poem is Lovell realised in another, more complex, form:

> For God is a good man, God is a kind man,
> And God's a good brother, and God is no blind man,
> And God is our father [...]

> And God's a good mother and loves sons who're rovers,
> And God is our father and loves all good lovers.

In these new equations, wonderful in the simplicity of their plurality, multiplicity is enshrined. The present is found, or, rather, many presents are found and are fixed as the speaker celebrates, instead of retreats from, this different idea of family. In his fantasy, God replaces the cloying familial past that stood in the way of maintaining heavenly existence, but at the same time evokes that past, because of the forms in which he appears: the father, the mother, the brother. Without being partly a projection of himself, then, and with clearer potential in regard to what the speaker can see (of which more shortly), God echoes the function of the moon in the poem. God *is* one entity, and he is another as well: Ford barrages his reader with the certainty of it. And with God's realist, rather than transcendental, aspects (it is possible that Eliot's 'hooded' Christ in *The Waste Land* is a homage to this earlier, 'cloaked', presentation of the grounded God). In this vision of God, formal manifestations can be infinite, but the speaker's existential equilibrium can remain intact in the face of them. Poetic time, hierarchically resistant, as established by Ford, seems to support the vision in the way that one thing 'is' at the same time as another.

Interestingly, Robert Grimshaw's priest is familially linked, though less obviously so than Ford's God. The priest displays an immediate and then laudatory knowledge of Grimshaw's maternal family, and of his mother in particular: '"I knew her," the priest said. "She was a very good woman. You could not have had a better teacher".'[35] Once this knowledge has been revealed, Grimshaw's paralysed confusion in the face of this priest recedes: the priest adopts the role of teacher, given the right by Grimshaw's religious and filial respect. Grimshaw needs him, and his knowledge of 'other' parts of him, because no other agent will make him effectively, rather than destructively, see himself: 'It was pleasant to him to come into contact with this representative of an unseen world – to come for a moment out of the ring, very visible and circumscribed, in which he moved. It gave him, as it were, a chance to stand upon a little hill and look down into the misty "affair" in which he was so deeply engaged' (p. 221). As epitomised here, religious figures can provide stable visibility in Ford; they allow Grimshaw to step outside himself and look with a placid eye.

In the poem, God brings all of the speaker's past into the present and contains it effortlessly. He is more significant still in what he, in turn, sees. God's most important offering in 'On Heaven', in terms of the debates in this and previous chapters, is based on knowledge, on sight and understanding, as well as more simply on quiet – God smiles bene-ficiently and beatifically but is silent until the final lines. He evokes, in his majesty, the 'kind eyes' that looked down on Lovell in the chapel; he represents a next stage in the use of the reader as possessing all Lovell's fragments; the ultimate seer, he obviates the need for self-discovery, and thus induces an aware and active peace:

> Nor does God need to be a very great magician
> To give each man after his heart,
> Who knows very well what each man has in his heart:

Conspicuously different from the 'heart' as it appears in *The Good Soldier*, where it either threatens an attack, or conceals sexual desire or a lover's secrets, the heart here is known in its completeness, in its details, by God. Obviously a significant notion for Ford, this idea is developed in *Parade's End* when Christopher Tietjens has a vision of 'the Almighty' as a 'great English Landowner, [...] knowing all about the estate down to the last hind at the home farm and the last oak'.[36] This would include sight, and knowledge, of Christopher himself. In 'On Heaven' the speaker's God knows him, sees him; he has his life history in the palm of his hand.

The speaker does not actually meet God until towards the end of the poem. When he does, he mistakes him first for a priest and then for a lover. Within the context of this discussion, God is obviously both of these in the same way that he is able to incorporate, peacefully and simply, all those psychologically demanding and disturbing elements by which the speaker has found himself to be plagued. The crucial link between the images of the priest and the lover, in Ford's creative mind, is the ability to know peace of different kinds – as borne out by Lovell's dual climax. But God experiences, and communicates, both kinds.

Ford has come closer in the writing examined in this chapter to finding and knowing God's peace as embodied, and offered, by a priest, than to finding and knowing the peace posed by perfect communion with a lover. In the completeness of the multiple knowledge which the priest, or God, can reflect and provide, there is an active kind of peace. In the balance between the areas of that knowledge, there is the same kind of peace too. Lovell's monk gave him a cell. His need for asceticism and piety is thus silenced; his conflicting selves are divided and rendered powerless to torture him. In the poem, God's knowledge provides a peace-inducing sanction, forgiveness without the need for confession:

> For God's a good mother and loves sons who're rovers
> And God is our father and loves all good lovers.
> He has a kindly smile for many a poor sinner;

This knowledge is without judgement, and it implies sexual leniency on the part of God. As the poem closes, God approaches the table where the lovers sit, in silence. With his arrival, the poem ends.

Robert Grimshaw, seated in a churchyard next to Katya Lascarides, perceives the peace of God all around him. It is in the light, in the place, in his silence with Katya. A spoken misunderstanding disrupts his train of thought; his contemplation ceases, and the 'peace of God' (p. 136) is dispersed. In *The Spirit of the People*, a non-fictional work, Ford is discovered in his own encounter with that elusive entity, one which causes wonder, one which elicits a silent response: 'The priest has uttered the beautiful sentence which begins: "The peace of God which passeth all understanding keep your hearts...".. And then an absolute silence falls – a silence that seems to last a lifetime, an utter abandonment, a suspension of life'.[37] Words work as little more than symbols in the shaping of that which cannot be identified. This force takes Ford out of himself, defeats time and simultaneously allows all of his consciousness, his past, to come forward. The peace of God, this lifetime's silence and abandonment, is that for which he is continually aiming; if he cannot achieve it as a lover, he can achieve it as one who listens to what is deep within, and far beyond, at the same time. It would appear that the essence of that 'which passeth all understanding' comforts most strongly him who is most conscious. (Eliot, too, searches for it in *The Waste Land*, finding it in a translated rendering: 'shantih'.) *The Young Lovell* and 'On Heaven' have severally isolated ways in which consciousness can be organised to render effective that same essence, one that does not always have to pass understanding. This organisation challenges linear notions of time and space, and creates 'that sense of sudden [though hard fought for] liberation; that sudden freedom from time limits and space limits' that was dear to Pound, to Eliot, and to Ford also.[38]

In Chapter 7, my last chapter, having left behind the consideration of Ford's positive fictions and the more self-evidently modernist depictions of human consciousness and human suffering examined in earlier chapters, I move to focus instead on his non-fictional considerations of the world around him. I examine his modernist credentials, such as impressionism, in more formal terms, and also consider his belief in writing as a method to combat the experience of fragmentation: social, psychological and existential.

Notes

1 The first quotation comes from Peter Childs, *Modernism* (London, Routledge, 2000), p. 110; the second is from the preface to Ford's *The 'Half Moon'* (London, Eveleigh Nash, 1909), p. xiv.

2 *The Good Soldier: A Tale of Passion* (New York, Norton, 1995), p. 29. Dowell chooses his words advisedly; the look is 'mortifying' because it sees to the depths of his asexual, dead, soul. I discuss this moment in *The Good Soldier* in Chapter 2.

3 See Chapter 5.

4 See the Introduction for discussion of this central modernist image as employed by Ford.

5 Ford Madox Ford, 'Sologub and Artzibashef', *Outlook*, 35 (26 June 1915), p. 830.

6 Saunders I, p. 382.

7 With Brigit Patmore, originally a friend of Violet Hunt, and married to Coventry Patmore's grandson, Deighton.

8 Ford Madox Ford, *The Young Lovell* (London, Chatto & Windus, 1913), p. 4.

9 Caroline Gordon, *The Good Soldier: A Key to the Novels of Ford Madox Ford* (Davis, CA, University of California Library, 1963), p. 5.

10 An obvious reference to Botticelli's Venus.

11 Helen of Troy and the Witch of Endor are fairly common significations of desirable womanhood, and function as such here. Behemoth, the ox in the Book of Job, has been said to symbolise the 'animal, the brute force of the beast'; Leviathan (the 'monster that should not be aroused') features in the same book, and in Revelation and the Psalms. The name Leviathan is derived from Phoenician mythology, which applied it to a monster of primeval

chaos. Located in the sea, Leviathan could be said to symbolise the forces of instinct which lie dormant or controlled until some event unleashes them. See Jean Chevalier and Alain Gheerbrandt (eds), *The Penguin Dictionary of Symbols*, trans. John Buchanan-Brown (Harmondsworth, Penguin, 1996), pp. 81, 598–9.

12 Refer here to the early discussion in the last chapter.

13 As for Grimshaw, the ability to stand on a hill is important to Lovell. He has more permanent success at it though, often finding himself on 'high spots' from which to make sense of his world. (See the beginning of Chapter 5, and the end of this chapter, for a discussion of this attribute in Ford.)

14 Along with the tower of David, the 'Tower of Ivory' appears in the Litanies of Our Lady.

15 Kandinsky discusses the colour white: 'White is like the symbol of a world in which all colours, in so far as they are properties of physical substances, have vanished ... White acts upon our souls like absolute silence ... This silence is not something lifeless, but replete with life-potential ... It is a nothingness filled with childish happiness or, in better terms, a nothingness before birth, and before the beginning of all things'. One of Ford's most oft-repeated mantras to the women with whom he fell in love was 'du bist die Ruh' ('you are my rest'). Kandinsky's view (quoted in the *Penguin Dictionary of Symbols*) comes closer than usual to what Ford would have meant by this I think.

16 I would suggest that the significance of these colours is also related very closely to Ford's experience of his grandfather's and Rossetti's use of them. See the discussion of Ford's emotional and psychological debt to Ford Madox Brown and Rossetti in the previous chapter.

17 And how essentially opposed to the experience of women by Edward Colman, by Dudley Leicester (for whom Etta's red and black colourings signify only a particularly frightening beast, see Chapter 3), by Dowell, and by Tietjens, pre-Valentine.

18 Ralph Griffiths, 'The Later Middle Ages (1290–1485)' in K. Morgan (ed.), *The Oxford History of Britain* (Oxford, Oxford University Press, 1988), p. 244.

19 See the entry in the *Penguin Dictionary of Symbols*, p. 86.

20 Ford Madox Ford in a letter to J. B. Pinker, 17 March 1913, in Richard Ludwig (ed.), *Letters of Ford Madox Ford* (Princeton, Princeton University Press, 1965), p. 56.

21 In psychoanalytic terms, it is as though Lovell's *superego* and *id* have been externalised and realised in appropriate surroundings.

22 Crucial here are my earlier discussions of the fragmentation of modernism, and of the more common experience of the unresolved dissolutions of the self in modernist fiction (think of *Heart of Darkness*, say, or

Prufrock, or Mansfield's Bertha Young in the short story 'Bliss' (1918)).

23 Arthur Mizener, *The Saddest Story: A Biography of Ford Madox Ford* (New York, Carroll & Graf, 1985), p. 486.

24 Refer to Saunders's biography (I, p. 590, note 12) for a full discussion of the debate surrounding the dating of this poem. After posing summer 1913 as a possible date for it, Saunders, using Ezra Pound as the final authority, suggests the poem was completed by the beginning of March 1914. Despite the evidence for him writing it with Hunt in mind, Brigit Patmore was staying at Hunt's cottage at Selsey with Ford and Hunt as Ford wrote it.

25 This is how Michael Levenson analyses the poem (*A Genealogy of Modernism*, Cambridge, Cambridge University Press, 1984, p. 113), emphasising its reality – proof of Ford's impressionism as Levenson defines it.

26 Ford Madox Ford, 'On Heaven' in *On Heaven and Poems Written on Active Service* (London, John Lane, 1918). The poem is reproduced in full in Saunders's edition of the *Selected Poems* (Manchester, Carcanet, 1997), pp. 99–110.

27 Derek Stanford, '"The Best Poem Yet Written in the Twentieth-Century Fashion": A Discursive Note on Ford Madox Ford's "On Heaven"', *Agenda*, 27: 4/ 28: 1, Winter 1989/ Spring 1990, p. 117. Hereafter cited as Stanford.

28 Once again, Ford's exposure of narrative levels is witnessed. Compare my analysis here with Levenson's comments on *The Waste Land*: 'the fragments in *The Waste Land* merge with one another, pass into one another' (*Genealogy of Modernism*, p. 189).

29 See Allyson Booth, *Postcards from the Trenches: Negotiating the Space Between Modernism and the First World War* (Oxford, Oxford University Press, 1996), pp. 112–17 (she discusses Ford's technique in particular in this section); Joseph Frank, *The Widening Gyre: Crisis and Mastery in Modern Literature* (Indiana, Indiana University Press, 1963), pp. 56–9; and Woolf's use of time in *Mrs Dalloway*, for example.

30 This signal is of course an important one. It is how Leonora tries to show Dowell that Edward intends to have an affair with Dowell's wife (refer to my discussion of this scene in Chapter 2).

31 Ezra Pound, *Poetry*, June 1914.

32 Humphrey Carpenter, *A Serious Character: The Life of Ezra Pound* (New York, Delta, 1988), p. 163.

33 Though Pound defined imagism in opposition to both symbolism and impressionism in 1914, he also praised Ford at this time for his 'insistence on clarity and precision' and his 'vivid impression' ('Vorticism', *Fortnightly Review*, XCVI (1914), p. 461; 'Ford Madox Hueffer', *New Freewoman*, 1 (15 December 1913), p. 251). Here, as elsewhere, the devel-

opment of modernism is seen to be difficult to trace without uncovering inconsistencies.

34 As J. Hillis Miller points out in an essay on Conrad, the light of the moon has already been once refracted and thus fragmented: 'In Conrad's parable of the moonshine, the moon shines already with reflected and secondary light. Its light is reflected from the primary light of that sun which is almost never mentioned as such in *Heart of Darkness*' ('Deconstruction' in Ross C. Murfin (ed.), *Heart of Darkness*, Boston, 1996, p. 212).

35 Ford Madox Ford, *A Call: The Tale of Two Passions* (1910) (Manchester, Carcanet, 1984), p. 119.

36 Ford Madox Ford, *Parade's End* (Harmondsworth, Penguin, 1988), pp. 365–6. This image is developed to include the rest of the Trinity, Christ and the Holy Spirit, complete with different perspectives on the world-as-estate.

37 Ford Madox Ford, *The Spirit of the People* (London, Alston Rivers, 1907), p. 91.

38 Ezra Pound, 'A Few Don'ts', *Poetry*, 1: 6, March 1913.

7
'These fragments I have shored against my ruins'[1]

'Eliot was different from either Pound or Yeats in being a poet who brought into consciousness, and into confrontation with one another, two opposite things: the spiritually negative character of the contemporary world, and the spiritually positive character of the past tradition.'[2] Other analysts of modernism would qualify Stephen Spender's comparison here, but the oppositions he identifies are, of course, fundamental to an atavistic modernism (as is Eliot's language of fragments to modernism generally[3]). In the search for fragments with which to embrace and describe modernism, Eliot's poetic voice in *The Waste Land* (and in earlier poems too) probes the past. It does not superimpose that past which he discovers upon the present. Instead, the voice grants it new life, creating a conscious dynamic with which to confront poetically the early twentieth century. The literary consciousness that writes two such 'opposite things' is – or should be – itself a dynamic, in Eliot's own opinion, consisting of the 'man who suffers and the mind which creates'. The two elements are separate; indeed, he believes that 'the more perfect the artist, the more separate in him' they will prove to be.[4] Sensibility and creativity must stand apart; balance is simultaneously implied. One is reminded by this essential faith in duality of Ford's presentation of Lovell; it also signifies the crucial early modernist debates of subjectivism versus objectivism in the artist's stance.[5] (Not until Eliot 'got hold of' subjectivity, Levenson suggests, was it rejected as a modernist doctrine.)

The enriching and rewarding aspects of modernism (like myth, and self-discovery), as presented in Ford's positive fictions, were the subject of the previous two chapters. These chapters sought to amplify such commonly overlooked aspects of, or ways of approaching, modernist texts. They countered the fictional wisdom that Ford was seen to expound in more famous examples of his modernist texts, considered in earlier chapters, where the fragmenting experience of existence, in ways to do with sexuality and technology, faith and psychology, was paramount. Ford was closer to what Helen McNeil calls the 'characteristic modernist terror of Eliot', as discussed in the Introduction, in these more famous texts.[6] This chapter is to examine which aspects of modernism are manifested in Ford's faith in the act of writing itself: the regenerative or the terrible. It will consider Ford's creative dynamic, his techniques, and his literary rules for the writing of prose. Using a range of Ford's writing, it will address the question of which aspects of modernism ultimately hold sway in Ford's oeuvre, and will suggest some reasons for the answers that it provides.

Fordian doctrine[7]

This chapter, then, will concentrate on Ford's criticism, on his critical persona. In his genealogical analysis of modernism – as a literary movement – Levenson has chosen a similar method of approach to Ford, because 'it was in his critical doctrine that Ford was of most consequence in this [pre-war] period' (p. 49). True, perhaps, although Levenson does not examine enough of Ford's *writing* to give a complete picture of this doctrine at work. What, then, is Fordian modernist doctrine? Answers to that question have been provided in the textual analysis in previous chapters, but Ford's critical brain will be seen to provide some more ideas.

As part of an immediate answer to the question posed above, I want first to make a brief digression to consider Ford's role as an editor of modernist writing. This will help to provide a useful context for later discussion, as it was in his role as editor of the *English Review* from 1908 that some of his critical ideas were put into practice. As Nora Tomlinson writes of this period, 'Ford's capacity to recognise and endorse new ideas, his openness to new forms of writing is impressive'.[8] He published Hardy when others wouldn't ('A Sunday Morning Tragedy' was in the first issue in December 1908); he championed French writers, and thus forced consideration both of new literary techniques, and of sexuality 'without the distortions of bourgeois sentimentality'.[9] Following previous discussion in this book, these tenets could be condensed into the desire to tell life 'like it is' (experientially and epistemologically), not as it should be (morally or ideally): Ford was thus allied more with writers like Lawrence, Hardy and Conrad than with those like James and Galsworthy. Saunders writes that the *English Review*, publishing as it did Lawrence, Pound and Norman Douglas, as well as Conrad and James, both 'signalled the presence of English modernism' and quickly put Ford at the centre of literary London (Saunders I, p. 248). Commentators as various as Douglas Goldring, Arnold Bennett and Wyndham Lewis celebrated his achievements in what Ford described as the business of promoting 'either distinction of individuality, or force of conviction' in the writers he published. This statement of editorial intent, made by Ford in 1908, is a crucial one.[10] It displays the working of his literary consciousness as applied to the writing he wished to see being read (writing that would bespeak the differences between poets and novelists, and their distinct, multiple perspectives). It has also been used to site Ford in the Hulmean tradition of 'unrepentant subjectivity' in modernism, one that maintains there is value only in presenting individual consciousness. There is, of course, more to Ford than this.[11]

In keeping with the use of Eliot at the chapter's head, and with the discussion throughout this book, questions about the nature of Ford's modernist doctrine must be asked from a historical, as well as from a literary, perspective. History can mean one's personal past (one that is never approachable in complete isolation); it can mean a wider past; most often, it means a productive combination of the two. When Ford describes an instance, in *It Was The Nightingale*, of historical trauma, it is his modern, literary brain which has undertaken the writing of it. Ford is crossing a London road in the following extract, whilst using his wartime experiences to translate the action: 'It would be long before you regarded an omnibus as something which should carry you smoothly along the streets of an ordered life. Nay, it had been revealed to you that beneath Ordinary Life itself was stretched the merest film with, beneath it, the abysses of Chaos'.[12] Ford's apprehension of abysses of chaos, and Eliot's apprehension of ruin, demand a reconstruction of rules or forms within the new milieu which the writers perceive.[13] Eliot's climactic offering to the debate, *The Waste Land*, of 1922, was described by Ezra Pound as 'the justification of the movement, of our modern experiment, since 1900'.[14] (Ford had made other contributions, including 'On Heaven', also praised in extravagant terms by Pound.) The mythic, historical, contemporary, seen and heard fragments that Eliot assembled in *The Waste Land* owe much to Conrad, from whose work Eliot nearly took the epigraph for the poem.[15] These fragments are instructive when reading Ford. They form part of that doctrine Ford both ranges against, and uses to come to know, the abyss often used to describe modernist sensibilities (think of the catastrophist analyses of modernism detailed in the Introduction to this book).

Doctrine I: the novel

The first, greatest and most conclusive aspect of Ford's doctrine is the generic form of the novel itself.[16] Not, most immediately, the kind of novel that George Eliot and Charles Dickens used to write, for obvious reasons to do with omniscience and the nature of the modernist quest: in modernist novels, characters are not presented 'whole', but 'in the fragmentary way in which people appear'.[17] Ford really means another kind of novel, a post-railway-age novel, one that, though modern and realistic, perhaps overall need not be fragmentary. In modern times, Ford-the-catastrophist asserts in *The English Novel: From the Earliest Days to the Death of Joseph Conrad*, humanity has 'scrapped a whole culture; the Greek anthology and Tibullus and Catullus have gone the˙ way of the earliest locomotive and the first Tin Lizzie. We have, then, to supply their places – and there is only the novel that for the moment seems in the least likely or equipped to do so'.[18] The novel can both represent and shore up a catalogue of modern experiences, Ford thinks; he develops an argument in a similar vein. People no longer communicate (thanks to the 'habit of flux'): the novel can bridge that new disjunctive space and provide the knowledge, or perspective, of another that threatens to recede. Novels can give pictures of life, life as it looks from many angles; they can 'make you see'. The Great Figure, the heroic representation of mankind, has disappeared along with the allegiance to classicism, and the novel will replace their number – though with characters that look more like Christopher Tietjens.[19] In the face of the decline of revealed religion, the novel will function as a new (pluralist) faith.[20] This latter view is taken up and extended by Joseph Wiesenfarth, who likens Ford's visionary novelist to the religious guide: 'Ford's lecture ['The Literary Life', delivered at UCL some time between 1919 and 1922] shows the seriousness in which he held the vocation of writer, likening it to that of the priest. The call of the writer is to hand on the sacred fire [a phrase borrowed from Ford] of the imaginative life. [This] is the only sign of genuine immortality'.[21] There is little that Ford does not claim as the referential or representational or healing domain of the novel. Ford's theory of the genre inflates it as a sociologically, as well as a psychologically, applicable critical doctrine that acknowledges and combats fragmentation and collapse.[22] It is a way of living, of reacting to the splintering modern forces which rage through his world, splitting, metaphorically, self from self, but quite literally splitting self from other (from neighbour, from community). This chapter will continue to explore how Ford puts this essential, regenerative faith into practice. Experimentation with boundaries – as seen in Eliot's movement between past and present, as well as Ford's in many fictions – will be shown to be a primary method he employs.

Faith into practice: the novel at work

Joseph Conrad died in 1924. In his book on Conrad (one that Ford calls 'a novel', as well as many other things), published the same year, Ford attempts through narrative to maintain Conrad in life, involving him still in his literary imagination. In the following extract, Ford reconstructs the discovery of Conrad's death:

> The writer exclaimed, 'Look! Look!'... His companion unfolded the paper. The announcement went across two columns in black, leaded caps.... SUDDEN DEATH OF JOSEPH CONRAD. They were demolishing an antiquated waiting room on the opposite platform, three white-dusty men with pickaxes; a wall was all in broken zigzags. The writer said to himself, '*C'est le mur d'un silence eternel qui descend devant vous!*' There descended across the dusty wall a curtain of moonlight, thrown across by the black shadows of oak trees. We were on a verandah that had a glass roof. Under the glass roof climbed passion flowers, and vine tendrils strangled them. We were sitting in deck chairs. It was one o'clock in the morning. Conrad was standing in front of us, talking.[23]

The 'writer' (Ford talks about himself in the third person) refuses to allow the newly discovered dead to remain so. 'Look! Look!' he shouts, disturbing the peace – reading does mean seeing for Conrad and Ford. Then, in a beautiful literary transformation, a real/imagined resultant wall 'of silence' becomes the dramatic yet fragmented backdrop against which Conrad's continued life can be revealed. Against this wall a stage is set and the past appears. An instant of time – enough only for recognition of an exclamation mark – distinguishes one time, one level of reality, from the other. Ford wants us to come to believe with hallucinogenic certainty in the sight that he sees, a sight caused by the fragmentation of the surface of time present (one that simultaneously shores up the terrible experience of Conrad's loss).[24] He wants us to believe in it to the extent that he has justification for using the past continuous tense – the emphasis falling on the present continuous nature of the participles – 'standing, talking…'. To help, he uses light and dark, colour and shadow to enhance the picture-making upon which he is engaged, achieving a stillness in description, fuelled by short clauses, which grants precedence to the new time and space dimension with which he is working. The speed at which the passage is read slows gradually; chronological and formal time are challenged in the style of the passage as well as in its content. In Bergsonian terms, chronological time is clearly distinguishable here from 'duration', from Ford's experience of a vision of his past in the present (a vision that he seeks to share).[25]

As I have said, Eliot's original epigraph to *The Waste Land* was a quotation from Conrad. 'Did he live his life again in every detail of desire, temptation, and surrender during that supreme moment of complete knowledge?'[26] was his choice, one that emphasised, in modernist fashion, the retrospective vision (or memory[27]) and the importance of parallel form, of the past coming alive in the present. Despite the change in epigraph, Conrad's presence is still felt in the mix of 'memory and desire' in Eliot's third line. Parallel form, the past in the present, is also taken to extremes in the first lines of *The Waste Land* in which the dead return to life. Owing to the strength of his vision, his memory, of Conrad, the same boundary is obscured by Ford on his narrative stage. The obscurantist tendency continues in his attempt to define technically this writing; in *Joseph Conrad* he crosses many genre boundaries in the search for a correct narrative description, one that culminates in an extraordinary definition:

> This, then, is a novel, not a monograph; a portrait, not a narration: for what it shall prove to be worth, a work of art, not a compilation. It is conducted exactly along the lines laid down by [Conrad and Ford], both for the novel which is biography and for the biography which is a novel. It is the rendering of an affair intended first of all to make you see the subject in his scenery. It contains no documentation at all; for it no dates have been looked up […]. It is the writer's impression of a writer who avowed himself impressionist. (preface)

This is a work of fiction. It is to build towards the picture of a man, a three-dimensional image even – for the reader will 'see the subject in his scenery' – not a linear narrative. It will attempt to stand as an independent work of art. It will merge the confines of actual and imaginary.

It will resist the dictates of a supposedly universal time scale, and it will be an impressionist's impression of an impressionist. In addition, revealing its debt to its subject, it will make its appeal to those who encounter it 'through the senses' (as Conrad said that all art should) by springing them into a felt response. It is a formal riot, then, this book, and it certainly stands to assert Ford's freedom from 'traditional genre and form'.[28] Judging the text by the success of the first passage quoted, it achieves its aims: memory and desire create vision, the momentary experience of the past in the present. Ford has created in his vision of the novel, one shared to a greater or lesser degree with other modernists, an eminently plastic and various form.[29] He is unique in the way that he binds this to its spiritual, sociological and emotional regenerative promise.

Ford's often prevalent aim, when writing, is to capture the essence of Greek drama, as perceived by him.[30] The effect of his staging techniques has been examined more closely in reference to *The Fifth Queen*, in Chapter 2; here it is his success at manipulating boundaries in the development of his doctrine that is to be considered. In his work of reference (a contentious term for this book) *The March of Literature*, he confides that 'it is perfectly proper, then, for the chief actor on the boards at the moment to describe the beauty of the moonlight, the luminosity of the golden globes of the lemon and orange against the background of their dark foliages. That, indeed, is his function and the function of the poet who is behind him. He must make the hearers see the landscape with the eyes of the imagination'.[31] There are echoes of the initial extract from *Joseph Conrad* in the above quotation, in which Ford describes how dramatic words (rather than scenery) make an audience see. Verbal conjuring of the moonlight, shadows and rich vegetation produces the critical effect, the coming forward of the 'eyes of the imagination'; these are powerful eyes. The description of fecundity, luscious nature, here in the form of 'golden globes of the lemon', or in the Conrad extract in the deathly embrace of 'passion flowers' and 'vine tendrils', helps to stir the imaginative, responsive, senses to life. Nature, it seems, must be invoked over civilisation. How much more than usual the reader will be engaged, and convinced, by a text if the light can be seen with the eyes of the imagination, if ripe fruit can be touched and smelled, with similar imaginative sense, if a voice can be heard? All this is achieved in Ford's writing on Conrad. He has manipulated boundaries between reading and seeing, and witnessing and participating, in order to create a multi-sensory, highly realistic, experience; crucially, this experience stretches and extends the imagination, and human sympathy, of those who encounter the text. Ford's 'narrative visions', Max Saunders writes, 'need to be seen (to be believed)' alongside other technical bastions of modernism: 'Proust's re-experiencings of the past, Pound's visions of pagan metamorphoses, Joyce's "epiphanies", and Woolf's "moments of being"' (Saunders I, p. 386). The things that Ford makes us see do relate intricately to many of these other modernist techniques; in the extent of their appeal, in the ways in which they resonate, they also stand alone.

Ford and Conrad, in their creative work together, which from 1898 spanned nearly ten years of greater or lesser intensity, focused very precisely on questions of the form of the novel as a method, *the* method, of artistic expression. They were dedicated to the debate, as Ford states: 'We agreed that the novel is absolutely the only vehicle for the thought of our day. With the novel you can do anything: you can inquire into every department of life, you can explore every department of the world of thought' (*Joseph Conrad*, p. 222).[32] They thus proved a dedication to multiplicity, and perhaps also to the subjectivist movement signified in its early stages, according to Levenson, by Walter Pater's *Renaissance*, published in 1873. Of Pater's publication Levenson states that the literary 'step is a crucial one. It is not a move [...] in the direction of aestheticism. It is towards what we would better call psychologism: not life for art's sake, but life and art for the sake of a "quickened multiple consciousness" – consciousness as a source of value and a refuge from experience' (p. 19). Multiplicity of consciousness is enshrined in Ford's testimony to the novel – he admired Turgenev because 'he had the seeing eye to such an extent that he could see that two opposing truths were equally true'.[33] But does the novel also establish a new 'source of value' and create a 'refuge from experience'? Ford's writing on Conrad would seem to suggest so, for Conrad is to be maintained in life as Ford knew and loved him most. And yet, Ford's narrative has never been seen to offer a refuge; rather, it offers ways of reflecting and organising the plural nature of experience.

'The writer never in his life uttered one word of personal affection towards Conrad' (*Joseph Conrad*, p. 129), Ford admits. He uses his novel about him partly to revisit his past and invest it with feelings that have up until this point, the time of writing and the year of Conrad's death, been kept strictly under control. The novel served to fragment his control of his feelings. It also provided him with the only possible framework to organise those feelings. Ford is at the train-station when he discovers that

Conrad is dead; his literary eye and ear recreate immediately a vision of him and a conversation with him 'just now on this platform' (*Joseph Conrad*, p. 27). The memory is placed intentionally, perhaps fictionally. The train as modern totem, representing the death-knell to the old world, is vigorously appropriated by Ford, here and elsewhere, as the perfect symbol of modern fragmentation (or, rather, modern multiplicity). On the subject of the train, Robert Louis Stevenson wrote in 1895 that 'it seems to me ... as if the railway were the one typical achievement of the age in which we live, as if it brought together into one plot all the ends of the earth and all the degrees of social rank'.[34] In this way he manages to sum up much commentary on this issue. Briefly, in regard to Ford, trains appear perfectly on time when there is trauma at hand. Ashburnham's portentous indiscretion occurs on a train journey; this symbol of the modern age seems to sanction, if not to incite, his sexual impropriety. In *Ladies Whose Bright Eyes* Sorrell is catapulted into the past to enact his unconscious due to a railway accident. Tietjens and Macmaster conduct their most expressive and revelatory conversations – whilst behaving perfectly – as they watch England hurtle by. Dowell's lack of ability to control the running of trains, and the 'frenzy' this drives him into, is a thinly disguised parallel to the fact that he can neither understand nor harness twentieth-century sexual demands and existence (*The Good Soldier*, p. 39).[35]

Ford detailed his critical thinking about the image of the train in *The Soul of London*, published in 1905. Here he describes the rushing days, the endless meaningless activity of the social set, acknowledging eventually that 'each of these things sinks back into the mere background of your you. You are, on the relentless current of your life, whirled past them as, in a train, you are whirled past a succession of beautiful landscapes. You have "seen" such and such a social event as you have seen, say, Damascus, from a saloon window'.[36] This is a very different sight from that of Conrad established by Ford's prose. The train window becomes symptomatic of the space between the self and what it does in modern society: one travels, one watches, one does not engage. It suggests an endless mixture and catalogue of responses, none of which is permanent. In this, however, there is potential for the novelist: time and sight manipulated in this way mean the ability to experiment. The train (or its railway) represents fragmentation; it provides the pluralistic 'jumble of pictures', which phrase Herbert Butterfield creates, in a strikingly similar piece of railway writing from 1924.[37] But Ford's novels also employ it, as part of his modernist doctrine, as the obvious means with which to represent the multiple truths of modern consciousness (especially when visually represented, as in Ford's visions of the past). New ways of representing consciousness are endemic to the metaphorical journeys that it transcribes.

In Ford's mind, then, the novel can generate a more complete existence, in terms of what it enables one to see and to know. As a generic system, it can also enable one's communication of life, sometimes to the extent of usurping first-hand experience: 'Gossip is a necessity for keeping the mind of humanity as it were aerated and where, owing to a lack of sufficiently intimate circumstances [due to the railways, in part] in communities gossip cannot exist, its place must be supplied – and it is supplied by the novel'[38] (*English Novel*, p. 10). More often, however, the novel forms an added level to life, a new dimension. Ford says of himself as a young man, having read a line of Kipling, that life was edged gently aside by the novel: 'More plainly than the long curtains of the room in which I am writing I see now the browning bowl of my pipe, the singularly fine grey ashes, the bright placards as the train runs into the old-fashioned station.'[39] Kipling successfully courted the eyes of his imagination. Even now, as Ford writes, the sights he saw as he read that text return. It seems to be important, though, that he is writing as this occurs: his writing of the memory becomes a way of balancing, controlling and explaining the access he has achieved to an older self, to the past. One action incorporates, and sets the stage for, the other, just as writing brought Conrad back. It is no coincidence that a train has crept into the framework. It heralded Conrad's reanimation; it has heralded travel within the unconscious. Here it heralds the conjunction of times: the past and present; the conjunction of activities: reading and writing, living and reading; and the conjunction of levels of consciousness: the literary/fictional and the present/actual.

The novel is a mediator. It represents, as Ford thinks of it, a 'place' where plural truths can co-exist. It is at its best when it enables one to see, to hold, two seemingly exclusive truths of experience in conjunction, in equilibrium with one another (think here of Ford's praise of Turgenev). As Ford read Kipling, a moment was savoured not instantly, but continuously – it is a progressive example of what Joseph Frank believes modernism as a whole, as a movement, engenders as a response to an increasingly multiple consciousness. Frank has called this formulaic response spatial form. He states that in the 'juxtaposition of past and present, as Allen Tate has realized, history becomes ahistorical. Time is no longer felt as an objective, causal progression

with clearly marked out differences between periods; now it has
become a continuum'.[40] Ford's use of time seems to place him somewhere between Frank's definition of time and that of Eliot; he envisions
time as a fluid continuum where past and present can co-exist. His
writing on Conrad and his memory of his reading of Kipling have most
recently illustrated this point. But Ford also writes with a conception of
clearly marked-out periods, occurrences and movements in history
that he can identify and then novelistically exploit (think of *The Fifth
Queen*, *The 'Half Moon'* and *The Good Soldier*).

The new control and manipulation of different levels of time forms
only a part of what Frank analyses as possible through spatial form in
the novel. To begin his discussion, he embarks upon a detailed examination of the famous fair scene in Flaubert's *Madame Bovary*:[41]

> As Flaubert sets the scene, there is action going on simultaneously at three
> levels; and the physical position of each level is a fair index to its spiritual
> significance. On the lowest plane, there is the surging, jostling mob in the
> street, mingling with the livestock [. . .]. Raised slightly above the street by
> a platform are the speechmaking officials, bombastically reeling off plati-
> tudes to the attentive multitudes. And on the highest level of all, from a
> window overlooking the spectacle, Rodolphe and Emma are watching the
> proceedings and carrying on their amorous conversation [. . .].
> 'Everything should sound simultaneously,' Flaubert later wrote, in
> commentating upon the scene; 'one should hear the bellowing of the
> cattle, the whispering of the lovers, and the rhetoric of the officials all at
> the same time.' (p. 14)

Ford makes no secret of his debt to Flaubert (describing him as he who
'most shiningly preached the doctrine' of aloofness in authorial
creation[42]) and in a novel published in 1923, *The Marsden Case*, he uses
a similar dramatic structure to the one described above. This structure
is one that acknowledges plurality, and mirrors the pattern Frank
discerns.[43] The night club in *The Marsden Case* signifies the lowest spiritual plane; it is a den of iniquity, throwing the ground-level worry
about war into dramatic relief as the inhabitants act, flirt and gorge
themselves upon sexually evocative foods. 'We were at the bottom of
the stairs,' narrates Jessop, teasing the reader with his or her exclusion
as 'the fantastic vista of that home of orgies opened before us'.[44] The
luscious natural world is again part of the framework, as Madame leans
across the table towards Jessop and slowly peels and eats a 'Gargantuan
peach' (p. 94). The reader is supposed to try to taste it, as well as to
imaginatively see what Jessop sees. More overt, then, in its exploration

of sexuality than Flaubert's scene (Ford had written a few years earlier that 'the appeal of *Madame Bovary* is largely sexual'[45]), but just as imaginatively and tightly structured, is this use of spatial form to present the more paganesque realities of human experience.[46] Once again the novel, as Ford's modernist tool, is designed in recognition of modern, visualised, multiplicity. Reflective, it omits nothing in its representation of what it is to be human.

Frank concludes his discussion of Flaubert by remarking on the space that is created in the narrative by its structure (he is discussing the same extract). The manipulation of time, and of its many levels, now becomes central: 'For the duration of the scene, at least, the time-flow of the narrative is halted; attention is fixed on the interplay of relationships within the immobilized time-area' (p. 15). Frank finally judges the episode as a minor part of the narrative that is then rebsorbed. In the example of *The Marsden Case*, however, the preparation for, and the enjoyment of, that one evening, takes up almost a hundred pages of narrative. The time-flow is thus manipulated to a far greater degree, in a way that resists closure and climax simultaneously (compare this with my analysis of *The Good Soldier* in Chapter 2). This scene signifies not simply a Bacchanalian feast of delight, a facet of human experience which needs to be dwelt upon, but an escape into a peculiarly Fordian manner of evocation, where the narrative voice gestures towards sight, taste and touch, as well as (sometimes confusingly) knowledge. In so doing, it takes its time. The narrative voice controls the interplay between levels of consciousness in a way that correlates with its now moving, now immobilised, always turbulent, presentation of the narrative. This voice is a Fordian construct which is the subject of debate, and of which Dowell is the most successful proponent. Dowell is brought to mind by the difficulty Jessop has in progressing through the narrative, for Dowell's struggle with knowledge is similarly portrayed; 'I will try to continue my time-table', Jessop repeats (p. 111) after 'trying to put the events chronologically' (p. 45). (Of course, being in a modernist text means that he does not succeed.[47] Instead he puts events in the order in which they occur to him.) Dowell's explanation of such problematic dealings with chronology would be the one he offers in *The Good Soldier*: 'I have, I am aware, told this story in a very rambling way so that it may be difficult for anyone to find their way through what may be a sort of maze. [...] I console myself with thinking that this is a real story [and thus should be told as it would be experienced in "reality"]'.[48] There is a significant ambiguity here. One meaning is more interesting than the other: Dowell, but more significantly, Ford, intends the difficulty of the prose, and the story – '*so* that it may be difficult', for a reason, like the discovery of the way through a maze.[49] Ford is revelling in the conscious construction and design of a tale; the irony of the second sentence speaks for this: 'I console myself . . .'. Delay is endemic. Design is obfuscatory. Is this solely indicative of the 'reality' of such treatment of time, or does the distance thus established between author and tale further illuminate the discussion of the possibilities of the novel? Frank Kermode would say that it does:

> [Henry] James makes an elaborate plea for novels of which the technical disposition is such that they must be read twice. So he applauds Conrad's *Chance* [. . .] at least a book which by the elaborateness of its method makes a gap between producer and product, a gap, as he puts it, 'to glory in'. The existence of that gap ensures another, between the text and its reader, whose expectations are no longer subject to the usual kind of authoritative correction.[50]

It is hard to imagine a more successful illustration of that gap than Dowell's maze. An almost physical impediment prevents the reader from being carried away by the story, which would then by definition not be a real one, for life does not represent itself simply. Freedom is given to the reader by this systematisation of narrative, freedom from omniscience and from 'authoritative correction' – remember here Ford's praise of Flaubert. Freedom too is given to the writer, and Kermode continues his discussion by praising *The Good Soldier* as a pinnacle of the modern novel, enshrining multiplicity, expounding perfectly what he means by the 'turbulence of a text' (p. 103). He shows once more how Ford's grasp of the novel was such a glorious mirror to, and encapsulator of, modernism: 'Ford wanted to be the historian of a civilisation but in the Jamesian way. The dream of Flaubert – a shift of emphasis from story to treatment – is now at least half-realised, story is transformed into "affair", telling into "treatment". Nothing in the text is to be classifiable as formal or inert, merely consummable: everything is capable of production' (p. 106). Kermode signifies a riotously productive existence in Ford's novel, one alluded to in the analysis of *The Marsden Case*. The novel, as well as being the perfect expression of the age, would seem to give Ford the opportunity to glory in the gap alongside, though presumably less sedately than, James. I want now to move to look at other ways in which the novel, as considered by Ford, offers this opportunity. Emphasis remains on the regenerative aspects of modernism also revealed.

Whilst Ford was on leave from military duty at the battle of the Somme he made a visit to the theatre. Joining conversation with some French officers about the progress in the war he had a sudden vision, one that finds its way into *No Enemy*:[51]

> It was just at this point that I remembered Morgan and the old man of the bath-mill. I daresay you will think this merely a literary trick, when I say that I saw them.
> But I saw them: against an immense black mass fringed by flaming houses.[52]

'Nothing is more vivid', writes neuroscientist Susan Greenfield, 'than the pictures we can generate inside our heads'.[53] Ford/Gringoire offers confirmation of this judgement. Not only does he believe that he actually sees these two soldiers, now dead, because memory encourages it (and thus prove that the sight in his mind is more powerful than that in front of his eyes); he also imagines, simultaneously, the setting as it was when they died. The two-dimensional word 'point', signifying as it does a position in space as well as in time, serves as the introduction to another instance of parallel form. Speaking of the same incident, Ford explains this phenomenon elsewhere by stating simply, 'I think that is how the mind really works, linking life together' (*No Enemy*, p. 173). Ford does not believe, then, that the brain deals with experiences in a strict and chronological order; it receives information, but does not necessarily process it immediately. It will return the information to the fore when it becomes significant, or instructive, or possible to deal with it. (It is interesting to wonder whether this conception was exacerbated by his wartime experiences.)

Reading Stephen Crane's *The Red Badge of Courage* had a similar pictorial effect upon Ford. He read this book about the American Civil War whilst at the front:

> I had been reading, actually, *The Red Badge of Courage* by the light of a candle stuck on to a bully-beef case at my camp-bed head. And so great had been the influence of that work on me that, when at dawn I got out of my bed to see if a detail for which I was responsible was preparing carts to go to the Schiffenberg and draw our Mills bombs ... against and below hills and dark woods I saw sleepy men bending over fires of twigs, getting tea for that detail, it did not seem real to me. Because they were dressed in khaki. The hallucination of Crane's book had been so strong on me that I had expected to see them dressed in Federal blue.[54]

He has hallucinated, as he has encouraged his reader to hallucinate with him in his writing on Conrad. Both sections of war prose quoted above, written descriptions of transformative experiences, single out colour as a prime method of description, and both, more interestingly, use the word 'against' in their image-building. Conscious construction is evident. One facet, one level is set against another until the narrative becomes multi-dimensional, set on a stage; it creates a living, but written, picture. Picture-painting was a skill for which Ford's fiction was known (and this aspect of his prose has been a recurrent subject throughout this book). A contemporary review of *The Marsden Case* speaks of 'the incomparable charm and delicacy of portrayal, the sensitive, subtle revelation of the characters through the veriest fragments of speech or movement, or the pictorial power, which Hueffer possesses more than almost any other English novelist'.[55] Ford builds up the levels of portrayal of his characters partly by pictures. A multiplicity of these pictures, or portrayals, triggers to a reader's response, are held in equilibrium by his novels – in a way similar to that of his beloved impressionist painting.

Janice Biala (the painter who was Ford's last love; they were together from the early 1930s until the end of his life) was asked in an interview in 1979 whether there was any connection between Cézanne's aesthetic and that of Ford. She replied:

As a painter, I can't speak for a writer. But what does come to mind are the waterlilies of Monet. The waterlilies are floating on the water. They are blue and violet and pink. But when you look close, there are no waterlilies, no water, no trees – just blocks of paint. You step back – and once more the waterlilies are floating on the water shadowed by the drooping willow trees. In short you need a certain distance in front of any work of art. The artist is not concerned with scientific truth or facts.[56]

Colour works differently when the viewer is close to art from the way in which it works when you step back. One needs that gap, an objective distance, for the contents of that which is beheld to assemble and form themselves. The view from the railway-carriage window both indicates the multiplicity of modern life and offers a frame for it; Dowell's maze impedes rampant and unconscious progress through the narrative, making one aware of life's turbulence as well as of the novelist's ability to represent it. Ford's prose contains many views; one is not more real than another. It is the conglomeration of tenses and colours and words that matters. Again, as a technique for combating the disjunctive forces of modernism, whilst being true to its spirit, Ford's writing would appear to be highly successful. As a way of representing and containing the 'abysses of chaos', it is both honest and industrious.

Joseph Frank progresses a necessary step in the comparison between the writer and the painter:

> There is a striking analogy [...] between Proust's method and that of [...] Impressionist painters. The Impressionist painter juxtaposed pure tones on the canvas, instead of mixing them on the palette, in order to leave the blending of colours to the eye of the spectator. Similarly, Proust gives us what might be called pure views of his characters – views of them 'motionless in a moment of vision' in various phases of their lives – and allows the sensibility of the reader to fuse them into a unity. (p. 25)

It is logical in a discussion of this nature to incorporate the work of Proust – although in his desire to complete his analogy Frank is some-what reductive of Proust's intention. The gap between the reader and Proust allows the 'pure views' he creates to coalesce and make their multiple meaning. These 'pure views' are related to Ford's conscious picture-making, and thus are part of his modernist doctrine (think of Leonora 'looking into the pit of hell and seeing horrors there' though Dowell doesn't understand what her face tells him, and, differently, Kitty seeing Grimshaw and Katya embrace). Ford knew Proust was great; though he claimed not to have read him, he had an implicit understanding of his position in the tradition to which Ford had come. Frank's analysis of Proust's style is reminiscent of earlier discussion – the reader of *Joseph Conrad* must watch to see him and listen to hear him. However, Frank is most pertinent in his argument that the dialectic present in a painting can be found in similar dimensions in a piece of prose. Proust's 'moments', akin to those of Ford, are an instant out of time where that which is normally undetectable (though latent) can be appraised. These can be named 'pure views' or visions because Proust defined them as the product of a kind of supra-reality, a perfect conjunction of tenses.

Does Ford know and express this phenomenon theoretically, as part of his doctrine? Can it be actively solicited and consciously achieved; or is it a telling triumph of the unconscious? As can be seen in the following extract, an example of the Fordian 'moment', he is at least conscious of this technique. In *The Soul of London* Ford provides a glorious and picturesque rendition of the working of his layered, open and acquiring fictive mind. It is a picture of a mind which understands the 'moments', and the value of them, and which understands how to transgress the movement of time. For here, instead of sending one forward, time sends one below, and around, and above:

It is in the breaks, in the marking time, that the course of a life becomes
visible and sensible. You realise it only in leisures within that laborious
leisure; you realise it, in fact, best when, with your hands deep in your
trousers pockets, or listless on your watch-chain, you stand, unthinking,
speculating on nothing, looking down on the unceasing, hushed, and
constantly changing defile of traffic below your club windows. The
vaguest thoughts flit through your brain: the knot on a whip, the cockade
on a coachman's hat, the sprawl of a large woman in a victoria, the windshield in front of an automobile. You live only with your eyes, and they
lull you. So Time becomes manifest like a slow pulse, the world stands
still; a four-wheeler takes as it were two years to crawl from one lamp-
post to another, and the rustle of newspapers behind your back in the
dark recesses of the room might be a tide chafing upon the pebbles. That
is your deep and blessed leisure: the pause in the beat of the clock that
comes now and then to make life seem worth going on with. (*The Soul of
London*, p. 122)

Ford's punctuation in this beautiful passage, his imagery, and his
control of tempo all combine to mean that, as readers, as viewers of a
mind, we are presented with a lucid and calm visual image of what
could be chaos. Ford's fictive mind looks out, and finds inspiration in
whatever it lands upon. And yet it controls each impulse, holding 'the
knot on a whip, the cockade on a coachman's hat, the sprawl of a large
woman in a victoria, the windshield in front of an automobile' in an
immediate equilibrium. The line does not progress, in a linear fashion,
as does a normal list, towards a conjunctive clause; balancing commas
alone are utilised. This is reminiscent of Biala's prosaic account of
Monet's waterlilies as being 'blue and violet and pink': without hierar-
chy. Ford's writerly thoughts are evenly spaced, and he thus achieves a
panoramic vision. The back and forth, suck and release rhythm of the
tide, to which he directly refers, is endemic to the balance of the piece.
He bestrides it, uses it. The surface level of life, which he fragments, is
behind him in the rustle of the newspapers, a coarse splinter of rationality, of contemporaneity;[57] in front of him time broadens and
lengthens, allowing him a manipulation of textures and stimuli to the
extent that all, for a while, comes alive.

One of the more obvious achievements of this piece of writing is its
regulation of consciousness; Ford patterns his psychological processes
during a moment of this kind. He ascribes to natural and eternal – and
therefore highly secure – rhythms, the overall impression, but within
that he gains a unique independence and revelatory freedom. Such
writing counters with great force the suggestion that for Ford prose was

only about mirroring the soul. For Eliot, art involved 'selection, suppression, control and order'; Ford is usually approached, in criticism of the period, as adopting an antithetical position, a Hulmean position, one that collapsed in on itself by privileging individual experience as the sole aim of artistic representation.[58] But Ford acknowledges the need for both control and revelation. It is evident in the axiomatic Fordian paragraph above that he is not undertaking a simply private journey: *thoughts* are *sights*. What is more, he selects and orders that to which he responds, creating a system that controls it. It may be held simultaneously, rather than ordered preferentially, but much of *The Waste Land* is arranged in just such a manner. Ford has fashioned a critical doctrine for achieving equilibrium, a simultaneous awareness of the outside world and the inner response to that world.

It can be a protective equilibrium, for, as he states, 'You live only with your eyes, and they lull you'; whilst lending truth to the multiple and intricate levels of consciousness, the experience of them does not become too much to bear. His understanding of literary consciousness was that it could at times be a necessary intermediary between the external and internal worlds. 'I once heard', Ford writes, 'a couple of French marine engineers agreeing that although they had traversed the Indian Ocean many times and had several times passed through, or through the fringes of, typhoons, neither of them had ever been in one till they had read Conrad's *Typhoon*' (*English Novel*, p. 55). Taken literally, out of context, this is nonsense; taken in relation to the present discussion, it makes absolute sense. Experiencing war, as the writers examined in Chapter 4 proved, one can't know it; only afterwards does the knowledge come, often through writing. Likewise with these sailors and their reading of Conrad: his writing made them see and know what they had experienced. The desired capacity of the novel to show how things are, to help one to 'look things in the face', has more to do with reality than with navel gazing; though, as Ford would be the first to admit, there is no *one* reality (he uses Conrad's vision as an example here, after all). All the novelist can do is to show what he sees, or to use Ford's phrase, 'register a truth as he sees it', and hope it is resonant, along with other versions.[59]

This capacity of the novel is one that art too, as Ford thinks about it (perhaps more obviously), possesses. He uses the word 'modern' in his description, and criticism, of Holbein because 'artistically speaking [the phrase "with the modern eye"] means that Holbein, penetrating,

as it were, through the disguise of costume, of hair-dressing and of the
very postures of the body and droop of the eyelids, seized on the
rounded personalities – the underlying truths of the individuals before
him'.[60] Ford sees the realisation of who, and what, humanity most
basely and plurally is in the artistic representation of Holbein's
subjects; they appear in their most concealed secrets, for his brush finds
out their 'underlying truths'. And it is a 'modern' trait, one to be
embraced when searching for material: Paul Wiley cites examples of
'Ford's transference of Holbein's portraiture' in the *Fifth Queen*
trilogy.[61] The fictional mind will force the boundaries of the sight to
bring out what is deepest and most true in what it sees, as will the
artist's brush. It is, however, necessary to be continually aware of the
elliptical nature of sight in Ford: to see is not always simultaneously to
understand (think of Dowell, and of Sorrell). Sight must also, then, be
divided and manipulated for purposes of narrative. Real sight, like real
knowledge, can be delayed and buried further back in the unconscious,
waiting to emerge as, of course, Dowell's 'complete' knowledge eventually does. How does the novelist 'see' her or himself? How do
authorial levels of consciousness correlate to this concept of sight?
Answering these questions is crucial to coming to a full understanding
of Ford's modernist doctrine. In the following sections I will begin to
address them, considering Fordian impressionism as a vital part of the
discussion.

Doctrine II: the novelist, and impressionism

Up until this point in the discussion I have been primarily concerned
with the regenerative aspects and functions of the novel as Ford sees
them. Ford's extensive beliefs in the novel's healing and revolutionary
power, and his use of various techniques within his novels, have been
shown to work as hopeful, regulating, occasionally semi-transcenden-
tal, but most importantly realistic forces. The novel has provided him
with ways to counter and to represent the fragmentations and realign-
ments of the new age. From this point I will be shifting the emphasis of
the discussion, in order to focus on how the artist can most ably
achieve the visionary position necessary in order to write like this.

Ford provides a comprehensive image of the able writer in a letter to
Mrs. Masterman (married to C. F. G. Masterman) in January 1912. 'It
is for us [contemporary novelists]', he writes, 'to get at new truths or to
give new life to such of the old as appeal *hominibus bonae voluntatis*

[...] in the clear pure language of our own day and with what is clear and new in our own individualities'.[62] 'Getting at' what is new involves using oneself (one's distinct individuality) as a novelist, and 'clear pure language'. (Once you had 'got at' what is new, of course, as a modernist writer you then had to 'make it new' in the telling of it.) In his introduction to *The English Novel*, Ford's major image, and it is a recurring one, is that of a gradual but inescapable coming apart, or increasing disparateness, in English literary tradition. He exposes a deep pattern, one that possesses a 'refractory' nature (*English Novel*, p. 2); this nature is necessary, he concedes, for the incorporation of each new stage of writing. It seems necessary for writers to embody a similar level of refractoriness to do their job of accurately reflecting the times. If so, then a high level of self-awareness is required as literature moves into what is a particularly disjunctive age.

This sounds like a kind of reflexive fragmentation: as the times fragment, so must the self-aware, and thus genuine, novelist. Here we begin to encounter the kind of terminology associated with impressionism, a modernist doctrine with which Ford, perhaps more than any other modernist writer, is associated.

Impressionism

Consideration of the extent of self-consciousness necessary to a writer's professional existence caused a debate that pre-dated Ford, and modernism. It raged in the latter half of the nineteenth century, thanks to Matthew Arnold, amongst others,[63] but in the years before the First World War it became a quintessential part of literary life. In simple terms, on one side of the divide were the avowed impressionists, derided by Irving Babbitt as 'the last effete representatives of romanticism'. Levenson characterises impressionism 'as both a precise rendering of objects and an unrepentant subjectivizing' (p. 36): as attention to detail, in other words, in what one saw *and* in what one felt/remembered. (Saunders adopts a different moral framework, describing impressionism as 'a mode of getting people to see visions which have been prescribed' (Saunders I, p. 445).) Levenson's high moral tone, and Babbitt's plain offensiveness, are notable, and indicate the height of the contemporary cultural stakes over this issue. Opposed to the impressionists, on the other side of the divide, were those, like Babbitt, for whom art was primarily about self-transcendence and moral codes such as Duty (and we know from Chapter 4 how successful those were at surviving modern life).

The extreme expression of the belief in extensive self-consciousness (usually portrayed as an impressionist belief) is Anatole France's dictum,[64] quoted in disgust by Babbitt, that 'all of us judge everything by our own measure. How could we do otherwise, since to judge is to compare, and we have only one measure, which is ourselves'.[65] Babbitt, conversely, held a conviction that came to be shared by Eliot – that such individualism was entirely out of keeping with the business of literature, where rigorous and traditional uniform standards should be maintained. It was the impressionist writer who bore the brunt of his ire, for challenging uniformity and tradition. Despite its reactionary nature, Babbitt's attitude looms large in Levenson's genealogy of modernism (though he is omitted from other analyses of the time); it is useful partly because it encourages an analysis of the fragility necessary to Ford's kind of writing.

Things were not as simple as they look in the outline given above. The subjectivity/objectivity debate was often confused. Ezra Pound, for example, in 1914 both called Ford 'significant and revolutionary' and defined imagism as explicitly against impressionism, and the previous year opposed Ford's aesthetic to Yeats's 'subjectivism'.[66] The confusion, added to the simplistic and violent terms in which the battle was waged, mean that Ford's own view of impressionism is hard to place here. However, Levenson's statement that impressionism was about a 'precise rendering' comes close to Ford's realist, watchful, intention, and added to that must be Ford's idea that all the novelist had to offer was one – usually complex – view of the thing to be rendered. For who, as he might have said, knows and sees all?

For Ford, impressionism was about the development of the novelist's ability to 'make you see'. V. S. Pritchett describes Ford's 'ingenious system of getting at the inside of things by looking at the surface alone',[67] which sounds as though it is not doing justice to the multiple dimensions in which Ford works – until one considers the nature of the surface itself. It would, of course, be a reflective one. In the seminal essay 'On Impressionism' (1914), Ford writes that 'Impressionism exists to render those queer effects of real life that are like so many views seen through bright glass – through glass so bright that whilst you perceive through it a landscape or a backyard, you are aware that, on its surface, it reflects a face of a person behind you'.[68] Ford seems to be looking through one of the many windows in Henry James's House of Fiction ('so many views'). In that early thinking on impressionism, James was concerned to represent the multiplicity of perspectives possible from the multiplicity of windows. James's windows are different shapes and sizes; they are peopled by countless individuals with their countless takes or views. Ford works, in detail, impressionistically, with similar windows. But Ford is not just talking about looking *through* the windows, he is talking about looking *at* the windows. In an added twist that turns James's House of Fiction into something more Fordian, a vital ingredient must then be added to the impressionist's vision: the embodied, because reflected, past. Memory, then, is what is in front of the impressionist as he beholds the world – it is the stuff of impressionist fiction. Ford proved in his writing about Conrad that this permanent access to the past can work smoothly, clearly, and that readers' imaginations can be similarly engaged. But the picture can become more complicated even than it already is, when access to the past is blocked, or is incomplete.

In Sussex, post-war, Ford is haunted:

> In Red Ford, whilst the crock boiled over the sinking fire the cottage was filled with a horde of minor malices and doubts. The stairs creaked; the rafters stirred; in the chimney the starlings, distressed by my fire, kept up a continuous rustling. The rest of that empty house I had only dimly seen by the light of one candle. It was unknown ground. I had a sense that the shadows were alive with winged malices and maladies and that the dark, gleaming panes of the windows hid other, whispering beings that jeered behind my back, hanging from the rose stems in the outer night. (*It Was the Nightingale*, p. 116)

The brightly, cheerfully reflective glass of 'On Impressionism', called to account for double vision, denotes the mind's capability for being in two places (at least) at once. Those are places of time as well as of space: the person he sees, and will in turn show, is 'behind' Ford, in his envisioned past. Somewhere else can also be sometime else, but both are within easy reach. The clouded, obfuscatory glass of Red Ford is a postwar mutation. It threatens Ford with what he does not, any longer, know about himself and, in turn, about the world. His paranoia feeds on ghosts that whisper and jeer; he cannot quite hear them (his hearing was damaged also in the war); he cannot quite see them either, for his glass has become dark. So Ford's doubts about his failing memory, and thus his continuing life as a novelist of history, centre on the changing glass that *has* described for him his impressionist's view of the world. It is the ability, quite literally, to reflect, that is now challenged. When the glass is clear Ford can revel in his regenerative, recovering, impressionist techniques; he can rejoice in multiplicity. When the glass is not clear that multiplicity becomes a terror, enacting the fragmentation of his hold on the past and on himself in front of his eyes. The impressionist's glass has been seen throughout this book to function powerfully in both states.

Impressionism is about lending a detailed, containing and representative truth to the multiple aspects of human consciousness; it is about 'making you see', and know, truths. Impressionism also depends on the novelist's ability to see, and to remember, in order to create the invigorating detail that for Ford constitutes 'good prose'. It depends on the novelist's ability to see, and to remember, in order that *a* picture (which would then of course have to be compared with *another* example) is presented. The critical doctrine at work here is primarily regenerative, then, so long as memory allows; others do not agree, as the following debate illustrates.

Trevor, in his foreword to Stang's book, *The Presence of Ford Madox Ford*, states that 'Ford shatters the surface of things and even out of the fragments creates an extra pattern of truth'.[69] He uses violent imagery to reflect the crucial nature of the issue, and the level of pain involved. As Levenson has said, 'Consciousness [...] enfeebles' (p. 33): it is hard to be aware. Ford strews about him, in his fiction, many versions of this maxim, most horrifically perhaps in the bed-ridden torture of Robert Grimshaw, or in Tietjens's stumbling, blind, madness. There is a splintering involved in showing humanity how it is, a temporary privileging of individual consciousness, but out of that splintering *can* come something else (think of Tietjens, finally, of Sorrell, and of the speaker in 'On Heaven'). Trevor believes that though Ford fragments the surface, he then uses those fragments to build a more complete picture. His word is 'pattern', after all.

For Levenson, however, there is no pattern in Ford. He places Ford in the tradition of James and Conrad, where he belongs, yet thinks him an unworthy, careless inheritor:

> Both James and Conrad depended heavily on a conscious subjectivity – nothing could be clearer. But in both writers there remained a crucial *separation* between consciousness and the objective world. It is worth repeating James's well-known description of Conrad's method: namely that it was 'a prolonged hovering flight of the subjective over the outstretched ground of the case exposed'. In Ford, the 'hovering' relation breaks down. [his emphasis] (p. 116)

James's 'gap to glory in' re-emerges as a significant metaphor in the discussion. Levenson sees collapse in Ford's writing, but no subsequent restructuring of newly gained information or ideas. He sees a chaotic obfuscation of boundaries, in the main due to Ford's non-observance of a strict line between objective and subjective visions (though he doesn't say where this line might be located).

If Levenson's analysis is accepted, then simultaneously the diminutive interpretation of Ford's 'impressions', of his Proustian 'moments', gains credence. It is a diminutive interpretation that is given voice by Michela Calderaro, who is, nonetheless, attempting to do justice to the difficulty of the relationship between what is outside the author and how it is reflected in his writing. 'The only answer to a fragmented world', she argues, 'is a narrative which represents only fragments, only impressions of life'.[70] Eliot's narrative persona in *The Waste Land* has no such redundant conception of the uses of fragments. 'His' fragmented impressions and truncated thought processes are a form of truth and are, equally importantly, a form of stability. They are a logical response to external chaos (Stan Smith writes that the Thunder's 'DA DA' is 'both chaos and cure'[71]). This chaos is alluded to equally effectively and revealingly in Ford's host of often contradictory impressions, impressions which are fragments of the whole and which reject the notion of one truth and one reality. As with the refractory nature of real life, so with impressionism; there is not one vision of life any more than there is one visual representation of a field full of poppies.[72]

These techniques that Calderaro names as 'only fragments, only impressions' are the crucial elements of Ford's art. Throughout this book, Ford has been seen to show how life is for his characters in multiple series of fragments and impressions: because that *is* how life is. The same can be said for his approach to the novelist. In Ford's opinion, it is the novelist who is most attuned to impressions, and who is thus most aware of his or her fragments, as indicated in the letter to Mrs Masterman, who will write in the best way. Philip Davis puts this equation in a slightly different order, 'imagination is a function of memory and personality', but the point is similar: one's creative abilities are inextricably linked to one's self-image and one's views of the past (which of course one would have to be able to remember).[73]

In the frank, though dramatic, appraisal of self that the Fordian novelist must undergo, there is access to an understanding of the fragments of life. This understanding can in turn be used to show life as it is, fragmented and multiplicitous, which is itself a way of shoring up the experience of modern life, as in Ford's picture of Conrad. C. H. Sisson demonstrates, in his afterword to *The English Novel*, how far self-awareness is necessary to Ford's approach, stating that Ford has delivered 'Ford's history' of the novel, one full of enthusiasm and reck-lessness and provocation. Ford has not disguised his stance: 'I shall present to you my *reflections* on the English Novel – ... and the pattern that, *for me*, it seems to make down the short ages during which it has existed [my emphases]' (*English Novel*, p. 5). Returning to the letter that he wrote to Mrs C. F. G. Masterman, this technique of reflection, and making patterns, is partly what constitutes the 'new faith'. The defensive tone in this passage is notable, however; it is one that, when investigated, begins to tip the balance away from the regenerative aspects of his critical doctrine examined thus far.

Ford found difficulty in isolating a public, theoretical language for what he did, and, more significantly here, for the man who did it. There is little in his critical definition of his style and form which is as concrete as that, say, of Conrad (though Conrad too contradicted himself on the matter of objectivity versus subjectivity). Evidence of this appears in *The Critical Attitude* as Ford traces his experience of theory:

> The moment you become constructive your theory is an integral part of yourself and you will defend it according to the intensity of its hold on you until you are worsted in correspondence in the public press or until you have earned the faggot and the halo of martyrdom. It is perhaps foolish – it is certainly perilous for the imaginative writer to attempt to occupy the position of a man of intellect. (p. 101)

In the long and breathless first sentence Ford's frustration at being, as he imagines, publicly misunderstood is made plain. The need to be artistically creative, in his terms, and in those impressed upon him since he was a small child (see Chapters 1 and 5), meant understanding of self, meant being creative and exaggerated, meant using and explor-ing one's whole personality in thought, in theory and in fiction. Anti-impressionist polemic that neglected to see how this stance could also correlate to realism meant that by 1914–15 this position entailed condemnation at best, and at worst professional death.

Levenson's implication is that Ford is included in the fringes of the movement traced from Bergson to Hulme of 'anti-intellectualism' (p. 62) and anti-materialism.[74] Despite this assertion, as I have suggested, Ford often rigorously formulated his beliefs. 'It seems pretty certain,' he wrote in January 1914, 'that we of 1913 are a fairly washed-out lot and that we do desperately need a new formula'. Continuing, he offered an antidote: 'what we want most of all in the literature of to-day is religion, is intolerance, is persecution, and not the mawkish flap-doodle of culture, Fabianism, peace and good will'.[75] In the semi-fascistic tone that he adopts here, one can see his sheer frustration at the apparent mutual exclusivity (which he cannot control) of the 'imaginative writer' and the 'man of intellect'. He wants to be seen to be fighting hard for regulation, and objective status, and for his critical doctrines, but he sounds as though he thinks the battle he is fighting is lost.

It is not only his intellect that Ford believes is belittled by his cultural and literary surroundings. It goes deeper than that. He proceeds to decry the emasculating effects of the paltry remuneration offered to the imaginative (impressionist) writer, as public proof of his public worth. He then further forces his point to suggest a 'stigma of effeminacy' (think back to Babbitt) attached to his branch of the profession, one that he had not managed to elude twenty-seven years later: 'Imaginative writing is a despised, an as if effeminate, occupation, and the imaginative writer a something less than a he-man – and one whom you could not introduce to your wife'.[76] The vitriol he feels for those who judge his occupation is felt in this outburst, as well as his own sense of insecurity. The threat to his sexuality is endemic in the terri-tory he has chosen, as it is often interpreted. It is a territory of watching rather than doing; of writing rather than building; of merely existing as opposed to making money; of showing rather than directing and of implying rather than making plain. He seems to confuse his images a little in the above extract, for this man is most certainly one whom you could introduce to your wife. Dowell, in his eunuch speech, shows that he experiences his lack of sexual knowledge in a way that resonates in Ford's lack of public status; Dowell also approximates Ford's concur-rent anxiety about the public perception of the writer's sexuality. The emasculating effects of the business that Ford was in, coupled with the kind of writing that he produced, are perhaps related to Ford's many attacks on the academy. The nature of his profession, as well as the nature of his writing, determined what is emerging as Ford's difficulty in 'staying with' the regenerative aspects of modernism.

Ford wanted to encourage debate. He wanted this debate to proceed along the best Greek lines and he considered it essential to his mode of writing. 'If I choose to write those extreme statements', he avers without equivocation and with honesty, after a particularly stunning passage of subjective thought in *The English Novel*, 'it is because I want the Reader mentally to object to them the names of Swift, Keats,

Thackeray, Browning [...]' (*English Novel*, p. 25). Sondra Stang
outlines the confusion and lack of imagination implicit in the general
non-understanding of this fact: 'Ford liked to tell stories that stretched
possibility, to see how far he could go. He expected resistance, skepti-
cism, interpretation; what he got was belief or disbelief, indignation,
and even a sense of outrage'.[77] Ford is seeking reaction, response,
testing his ground in open debate, playing with ideas in some senses.
He wants people to use their imaginations, to follow with him along the
path of 'stretched possibility' where reality is a notion which demands
experiment. He makes this aim theoretically explicit in 1907: 'Let me
here very particularly impress upon the reader that these remarks are
intended as a purely personal view. They are matters to promote argument; they are views, not statements of fact, spoken with any *ex
cathedra* weight. They are intended to arouse discussion, not to
instruct; they are part of a scheme according to which one thinker
arranges his ideas'.[78] What he received in response, in general, was
literal 'belief or disbelief'. His hope for the expression of an equal
opinion, one that could similarly claim an element of truth, was not
often fulfilled. Modernism has fragmented, he suggests; fragments of
words, of visions, of experiences and ideas must be used to rebuild the
bigger picture. Surprising though it is in modernist times, response was
often one-dimensional instead.

One must adopt an impressionistic technique to read Ford – one
that appreciates the reasons for his dramatic distance, for debate, for
non-linear representations of reality, for the isolation of moments out
of time and their special significance – if one is not to misunderstand
or to condemn him. All of these techniques are described by elements
of his modernist doctrine. Biala used her comparison of impressionist
painting with Ford's writing (based on the 'considerable distortion'
necessary 'for the purposes of a greater reality') to 'explain some of
those famous "lies" of Ford'.[79] His use of facts was often liberal, highly
subjective, and simply annoying, but this use is part of the impressionistic and empiricist holistic doctrinal system I have been exploring
throughout this chapter.[80] Ford stipulates rules concerning the writers
of fiction, as well as the novel as genre, which govern, and which
combine to form a doctrine pertaining to his faith in fiction. These
rules connote freedom as well as being true to the core of modernism:
being a memory-fuelled, spatially aware, dialectically astute writer is of
the modern essence. The question of whether these rules combined
finally attest more effectively to the fragmentations and ruptures of

modernism, or to its regenerative aspects, will form the last section of this chapter.

Memory and modernism

In a series on the human brain broadcast in 2000, Oxford professor and neuroscientist Susan Greenfield made the startling claim that the 'visual brain relies as much on what comes from our memories as on our eyes'. She went even further than this in the book that was published shortly afterwards: 'we see things with our brains, not our eyes [...]. What we see must depend on the unique contents of our personalised brains – our memory'.[81] Ford's modernism has been seen throughout this book to be intertwined with what he remembered and with what he (and his characters) saw. Why? Part of the answer is provided by Ford's image of the glass of impressionism, signifying as it does the interplay, the rejuvenation, of past meeting present in the watchful, memory-fuelled, writer. Part of the answer is also provided by Schneidau, who in his analysis relates modernist consciousness as a whole very closely to memory, and via memory to narrative. He writes that 'consciousness seems to turn stimuli and perceptions into a running, subverbal but latently articulate narrative, a "story" of our lives'.[82] Ford remembered in ways that made the subverbal verbal, even if incompletely (as I argued in Chapter 1). This also meant that he found ways of obscuring the boundaries between subject and object. 'Ford was nearly all his characters', attests Janice Biala; 'he was Tietjens and Leonora, Sylvia and The Young Lovell, but probably not Florence, who was a cheat. How else could he understand them?'.[83]

Such expressions of Ford's critical doctrine are as far as it is possible theoretically to travel from Eliot's maxim: 'the more perfect the artist, the more completely separate in him will be the man who suffers and the mind which creates'. Consciousness, says Eliot, must not filter into the creative sphere, though interestingly he concentrates upon suffering nonetheless. This echoes the previous suggestion that consciousness somehow enfeebles and cripples a man, and perhaps goes some way to explain why Levenson seems to rate Conrad's system for writing more highly than he does Ford's. Levenson isolates Conrad as existing upon the middle ground between Eliot's idealism and Ford's impressionism, for, as he states: 'If Conrad shares Babbitt's desire for order, he also shares Pater's conviction that consciousness is the source of meaning and value' (p. 35). It must be *ordered* consciousness, however, with a clear distinction between subject and object. Ford does not fully recognise such a distinction and this, ultimately, is the crucial factor.

When Robert Lowell asked Ford a question, whilst assisting him on the production of his final work, *The March of Literature*, Ford proved the extent to which he merged the boundary between fictional subject and object. Lowell reports: 'I once asked him the young writer's question "What does a writer need more than anything else?" and he said memory'.[84] Lowell's memory of his association with Ford, and Ford's answer, reanimate Davis's equation: 'imagination is a function of memory and personality'. Quotations from *Ancient Lights*, in the Introduction and Chapter 1, were placed there partly to invigorate the powerful murmur of the past. Ford continually 'went back' in this way. The need for memory must be considered to be prior to any aspect of critical doctrine, but what effect did Ford's more than usually tenacious, transfigurative and critical belief in its centrality have?

Herbert Butterfield links memory to fragmentation: 'The memory of the world is not a bright, shining crystal, but a heap of broken fragments, a few fine flashes of light that break through the darkness'.[85] Memory is not a singular entity then, a uniform whole, but a plurality of fragments. What works for the world as a subject with many alternate memories, works for the individual. Butterfield could be describing a Proustian moment as it flashes out and finds a relevant historical happening in memory to make it more real; he could be describing Ford's multitudinous levels of consciousness which all remember one version of the truth. He is saying that memory fragments and tears apart the notion of a solid existence; it refracts, not reflects, light in many opposing directions. The more memory one possesses, then, or the more keenly one seeks for it, the more fragmented one becomes.[86] There is immediate, contemporary and historical support for this contention.

In *Return to Yesterday*, Ford's reminiscences of these currently significant years, 1894 to 1914, he returns to the discussion of memory often (indeed the title alone indicates the temporary preference for existing in the past – temporary because the narrative is interspersed with 'memories' of the present as well). He claims that an 'amazing memory' (p. 127) saved his school career as he was naturally lazy and badly behaved; he states that his 'once prodigious memory' (p. 290) (referring again to pre–1914) was what helped him to build his characters. The loss of memory incurred due to 'shell-shock' during the war does not seem to be to the detriment of this volume of reminiscences (and so the fear of losing his access to 'impressions', given such vivid life in *It Was the Nightingale*, was not permanent), for, in a particularly resonant 'memory', he achieves a very effective sense of a still-affecting past:

> From 1903 to 1906 illness removed me from most activities. The illness was purely imaginary; that made it none the better. It was enhanced by wickedly unskilful doctoring [...]. I suffered from what was known as agoraphobia and intense depression. I had nothing specific to be depressed about. But the memory of those years is one of uninterrupted agony. Nothing marks them off one from the other. They were lost years. (p. 266)

This passage relates to his first period of serious mental illness, in the early 1900s (see Chapter 1). In it, he reveals a plurality of selves that are a mixture of fictive, experiential, critical and narrational creations. The first verb construction is a passive one, indicating a resigned 'me' in relation to an illness the strength of which at this point he does admit. It has affected him, it has brought him low, and this too is signified in the delayed personal pronoun that appears towards the end of the sentence. The next phrase introduces his critical persona: it is not particularly sympathetic, nor does it seem overly involved – with the second phrase of that sentence the original affected persona is reawoken. Yet the distanced tone of it – 'that made it none the better' – means that it does not counter the harshness of its partner; an uneasy co-existence is thus established. Ford is both an unsurprised and a resigned victim. He hated his doctors, and there is a confusion of bitterness and dismissiveness in the pronouncement that the illness was 'purely imaginary' (an unwitting acknowledgement of the existence of the unconscious). What follows a little later is the first 'straight verb', and by this I mean one which is unqualified or unmediated by another persona or reality: 'I suffered', he says, and this stands out from the page. Immediately, however, the critical self is reintroduced with a distancing, convoluted phrase, 'from what was diagnosed as ...', as he besmirches the reputation of his doctors. In some sense, he relinquished control of his own understanding in a sad and pathetic fashion – but the 'narrative' self performs the role of maintaining an alliance between his resignation and his control. The depression is non-specific (again he does not quite understand an element of what he is describing), but, conversely and finally, the memory is highly specific: 'the memory of those years is one of uninterrupted agony'. Each word, in comparison with the recent meanderings, has an explosive, moving simplicity.

The agony may be uninterrupted, but he has shown that it is also pluralistic. He remembers the uneasy, mutual exclusivity of the knowledge that the illness was imaginary, and the feeling of the pain. He remembers his distaste. He remembers his lack of respect for his doctors and simultaneously the suffering caused him by that which they were attempting to define . A more accurate statement at the close of that paragraph would have been, 'the memory of those years is one of uninterrupted agonies' – and the memory itself means it is uninterrupted still.

Conrad recognised a kind of ultimate significance in what he depicts in this instance as an intransitive power of memory. He wrote, in 1921, that 'the permanence of memory is the only form of permanence in this world of relative values'.[87] He finds it to be a stabilising factor, then, brooding over all, although it brings with it its own structural fragmentation. Levenson suggests that Conrad is one of the century's first proponents of consciousness and pluralism, in opposition to his Victorian predecessors with their comparatively singular vision. Levenson's example of this singularity is the narrative voice of George Eliot; he argues that the 'consistency of a single omniscient voice' stands in contradiction to Conrad's 'distinct voices, distinguishable points of view' (p. 8). I would agree that Eliot's narrative voice can be omniscient and singular, but she balances this tendency with representations of the complexity of human existence that would rival those of any modernist. One of the powerful ways in which she illustrates this knowledge of complexity in her great novel, *Middlemarch*, is through the representation of the fragmentative effects of memory, a representation that later proves fundamental to Ford. Here, George Eliot provides a different tradition for the development of spatial form; it is one that privileges memory above all:

> It was not that [Nicholas Bulstrode] was in danger of legal punishment or beggary: he was in danger only of seeing disclosed to the judgement of his neighbours and the mournful perception of his wife certain facts of his past life which would render him an object of scorn and an opprobrium of the religion with which he had diligently associated himself. The terror of being judged sharpens the memory: it sends an inevitable glare over that long-unvisited past which has been habitually recalled only in general phases. Even without memory, the life is bound into one by a zone of dependence in growth and decay: but intense memory forces a

man to own his blameworthy past. With memory set smarting like an reopened wound, a man's past is not simply a dead history, an outworn preparation of the present: it is not a repented error shaken loose from the life: it is a still quivering part of himself, bringing shudders and bitter flavours and the tinglings of a merited shame.[88]

Joseph Frank examined scenes from Flaubert's *Madame Bovary* as examples of spatial form. Eliot's passage exhibits perfectly the criteria necessary, and deals more purely than Flaubert's fair scene with time and its relationship to space. Eliot represents, ideally, the non-progressive, even retrogressive and dispersive, properties of novelistic language – in a way that proves that it can, as Frank pointed out and as Ford has shown, hold all together. The sentences are layered with the use of colons, and balance each other almost perfectly in weight and length until the final assault on the comprehension. The phrasing is non-hierarchical because Eliot is evoking, and displaying, a dialectic, although her image is more multiple in form than this description allows. The 'light' of memory, a concept that Butterfield also employed, reanimates all; it sets all a-'quiver' with life; it makes specific that which has been merely general and it exposes multiple surfaces when one has very comfortably believed in the existence of just one – 'dead history.' It is almost dangerous.

Eliot makes a bold statement of allegiance to a theory of the unconscious – 'even without memory, the life is bound into one by a zone of dependence in life and decay'. She superimposes on this theory, and clearly favours, the consciousness-raising properties of memory. Memory makes conscious that which one sought to protect oneself from and that which one sought to render ineffective and dead. At the same time, it ruptures linearity, the false premise that life, and consciousness (and therefore narratives that represent life) can progress in an orderly fashion: one dead past becomes many living ones; one idea of self is proved to be false; one level of existence multiplies tangibly and visibly.

Ford's theory of impressionism, consciously or unconsciously, owes much to George Eliot. Subsequent to the passage from *Middlemarch*, quoted above, comes the following particular and then general observation as to the function of human memory:

Into this second life Bulstrode's past had now risen, only the pleasures of it seeming to have lost their quality. Night and day, without interruption save of brief sleep which only wove retrospect and fear into a fantastic present, he felt the scenes of his earlier life coming between him and

everything else, as, obstinately when we look through the window from a
lighted room, the objects we turn our backs on are still before us, instead
of the grass and the trees. The successive events, inward and outward were
there in one view: though each might be dwelt on in turn, the rest still
kept their hold in the consciousness. (pp. 663–4)

Regulation has broken down. Memory and desire, or fear, as the terrible face of desire is known, are shown to assail a human mind.
Obstinately, the past, what is behind Bulstrode, forces itself into the
present, taking over for the time. Ford's impressionist writer tried to
see the same grass, from a proximate window. Here is the evidence of
his debt to her ('impressionism exists to render those queer effects of
real life that are like so many views seen through glass so bright that...
you are aware that, on its surface, it reflects a face of a person behind
you'). What was seen in the window could be liberating, part of the
modernist representation of plural truths. Or it could be as terrible as
that which looms in front of Bulstrode, plainly, or disguised. More
often, perhaps because of what Ford had to remember, or couldn't, it
was terrible.

   One's ability as a writer depended, Ford thought, on being able to
feel the shudders of revolution, to taste the bitter flavours and to suffer
the quiverings that Eliot describes. It meant remembering. It meant, in
another novelist's thoughts for the novelist's progeny, leaving behind
something more than 'the colours and figures of his own hard-won
creation'. That something more was 'the still voice of that inexorable
past from which his work of fiction and their personalities are remotely
derived'.[89] Manifesting Conrad's credo meant that the art of writing for
Ford itself both demanded and provoked a refracted sense of self – for
the personal narrative is never complete – as well as reflecting the
truths of the modern world.

   In 1937, two years before Ford's death, Lowell remembers Ford as

   always writing and writing! He was at work on his last book, The March
   of Literature, and re-reading the classics in their original tongues [...]
   writers walked through his mind and through his life – young ones to be
   discovered, instructed, and entertained, contemporaries to be assembled,
   telegraphed, and celebrated, the dead friend to be celebrated in anecdote,
   the long, long dead to be freshly assaulted or defended.[90]

Writing was Ford's only constant amid a chaotic personal existence. It
could be imagined, using my earlier analysis, that this was because Ford
thought the rules of writing could ease the rules of living, because

regeneration was to be found in the novel. It must be understood slightly differently now. For Ford, it took great courage to write and, simultaneously, he could do nothing else; it provided the only true, modern, representations of life. But in order to write, one had to remember, and break apart one's own defences.

As Ford was recovering from his breakdown in 1903/4 in Basel, Switzerland, he stayed with a professor, a man who continually wept for the loss of a daughter (*Return to Yesterday*, p. 266). The professor had filled his house with clocks to disguise the silence; clocks of all kinds that struck at all hours in different ways. Reading his whole analysis of the time that he spent there, Ford's description of the omnipresence of the clocks seems to work on my memory as the reading of Kipling, amongst other things, has worked upon his. Two truths, two memories, come together. The first is the stay at Basel in a period of personal, portentous, fearful instability; he feels as though he is out of his mind, yet, surrounded by clocks, he is held by the space in between the pulses of the passing of time. This sense of being held can be imagined because of the second memory, his portrayal of the fictive, impressionist, acquisitive mind in *The Soul of London*, working in 'the breaks, in the marking time, [...] in the pause in the beat of the clock'. One memory reanimates, or sets the stage for, the other.

As the two, equally important, memories converge it can be seen how personal misery becomes entwined with fictional creativity, how intricately the most raw difficulties of a fragmented age are allied to the possibility of displaying them completely. What fragmenting modernism means, in Ford's hands, is seen too. Ford's belief in the novel is such that he can do nothing but try to remember 'uninterrupted agony' and write, to give the memory the recognition it, and his time, both demand.

Notes

1 T. S. Eliot, *The Waste Land* (New York, Boni & Liveright, 1922), l. 430.
2 Stephen Spender, *Eliot* (Glasgow, William Collins, 1982), p. 9.
3 See the Introduction in this book.
4 T. S. Eliot, 'Tradition and the Individual Talent' in Frank Kermode (ed.), *Selected Prose of T. S. Eliot* (London, Faber & Faber, 1975), p. 41.
5 These debates form the parameters of Michael Levenson's analysis of modernism, *A Genealogy of Modernism* (Cambridge, Cambridge University Press, 1984). They were also prioritised by modernist writers

themselves (think of Woolf advocating exploration of the inner life). See Randall Stevenson's summary at the beginning of Chapter 2 of *Modernist Fiction: An Introduction* (Hemel Hempsted, Prentice Hall, 1998).

6 In the introduction to H.D.'s *Her* (London, Virago, 1984), p. vii. The 'Eliot-esque' experience of modernism is countered, McNeil suggests, by H. D.'s rewriting of these terrors.

7 I use this phrase in a slightly tongue-in-cheek manner, after the fashion in which Ford would use such terminology. Nonetheless, Levenson writes of the 'doctrines' of modernism (*Genealogy of Modernism*, p. vii), including impressionism, and I am thinking here about Ford's theoretical statements on matters like impressionism.

8 Readers interested in this aspect of Ford's career are referred to Nora Tomlinson's PhD thesis (this quotation is taken from p. 8), 'The Achievement of Ford Madox Ford as Editor' (Open University, 1995), which takes issue with his reputation as a great editor; it has lots of useful discussion.

9 Saunders I, p. 242.

10 It was made in a promotional circular, and is quoted by Violet Hunt in *I Have This to Say: The Story of my Flurried Years* (New York, Boni & Liverright, 1926), p. 26.

11 For example, in texts already considered, there are the detailed contexts provided by *A Call* and *The Fifth Queen*, the archetypal journey that is *The 'Half Moon'*, and the multiple investigation of consciousness in *The Good Soldier*.

12 Ford Madox Ford, *It Was the Nightingale* (1934) (New York, Ecco, 1984), p. 64.

13 The metaphorical motif of the wasteland in its transition through the works of Eliot and of Ford is part of the subject of Radell's study, *Affirmation in a Moral Wasteland: A Comparison of Ford Madox Ford and Graham Greene* (New York, Peter Lang, 1987). On the subject of communication between Ford and Eliot, Hugh Kenner has written, 'if Ford and Eliot talked it is not recorded (though they must have; surely they must have)'. Letters were exchanged between them in the 1930s. Hugh Kenner, 'The Poetics of Speech' in Richard Cassell (ed.), *Ford Madox Ford: Modern Judgements* (London, Macmillan, 1972), p. 169.

14 Ezra Pound to Felix E. Schelling, July 1922, Letter 189 in D. D. Paige (ed.), *The Letters of Ezra Pound 1907–1941* (New York, Harcourt Brace, 1950), p. 180.

15 Regarding Conradian 'fragments', he writes in the preface to *The Nigger of the 'Narcissus'* (1897), on the task of the creative artist that 'to snatch in a moment of courage, from the remorseless rush of time, a passing phase of life, is only the beginning of the task. The task approached in tenderness and faith is to hold up unquestioningly, without choice and

without fear, the rescued fragment before all eyes in the light of a sincere mood'.

16 Henry James's conception of 'The Novel' as 'Art Form', his 'extreme reverence for the medium in which he worked' was what Wells disliked in him – Ford's notion is different, as we shall see. Christopher Gillie, *Movements in English Literature 1900–1940* (Cambridge, Cambridge University Press, 1975), p. 6.

17 From May Sinclair's review of extracts of Dorothy Richardson's *Pilgrimage* (published in the *Egoist* in 1918). Vassiliki Kolokotroni *et al.* (eds), *Modernism: An Anthology of Sources and Documents* (Edinburgh, Edinburgh University Press, 1998), p. 352.

18 Ford Madox Ford, *The English Novel: From the Earliest Days to the Death of Joseph Conrad* (London, Constable, 1930), p. 19.

19 He published an essay called 'The Passing of the Great Figure' in 1909. It should be borne in mind that Ford may have had ambivalent feelings about this passing: the 'Great Figures' were those who in their Victorian majesty also made him feel threatened, and suffocated, and overwhelmed (see Chapter 5).

20 For the full exposition of Ford's argument, see *The English Novel*, pp. 10–34. Refer to the Introduction for my discussion of the historical basis for such an argument regarding faith.

21 Joseph Wiesenfarth (ed.), introduction to 'The Literary Life: A Lecture Delivered by Ford Madox Ford', *Contemporary Literature*, 30: 2, Summer 1989, p. 171.

22 In much more recent writing on the role of the novel, specifically in the eighteenth century, Ford's view of its sociological relevance is upheld: 'A lot of the pleasure available, especially to young readers, involved recognizable situations in the contemporary world where decisions about marriage and a course of life were practical ones no longer dependent just on the demands of parents or community; where individual needs and desires counted as much as convention and tradition.' The language J. Paul Hunter uses, of conventions and demands, and of the individual as opposed to society, evokes that which Ford employs to address *his* time and the role of the novel in it ('The Novel and Social/Cultural History' in J. Richetti (ed.), *The Eighteenth Century Novel*, Cambridge, Cambridge University Press, 1996, pp. 22–3).

23 Ford Madox Ford, *Joseph Conrad: A Personal Remembrance* (1923) (New York, Ecco, 1989), pp. 27–8.

24 Here some history of Ford's relationship with Conrad is necessary. Saunders describes their meeting at Edward Garnett's as 'the crucial literary event in both men's lives' (Saunders I, p. 100). Later in 1898 they began to collaborate, to write together (sometimes living together as well); though this tortuous, fascinating, energetic process produced joint novels,

it more immediately affected and improved their individual work. Perhaps as a predictable outcome of the intensity with which they worked together, their relationship deteriorated seriously throughout 1909, and they ceased to see one another for periods. However, Conrad remained one of the three most significant men in Ford's life (in addition to Ford Madox Brown and Arthur Marwood).

25 Henri Bergson, French philospher, published *Time and Free Will* in 1889. Peter Childs summarises an influential view of time given in this work as follows (influential particularly on modernist writers such as Woolf and Joyce): 'Bergson argued that psychological time was measured by *duration*, defined as the varying speed at which the mind apprehends the length of experiences according to their different intensities, contents and meanings for each individual' *(Modernism*, London, Routledge, 2000, p. 39). Bergson's theories also impacted greatly on T. E. Hulme, who first appeared in modernist circles, in England, in 1907 (Levenson, *Genealogy of Modernism*, p. 39).

26 Here, Marlow is considering the death of Kurtz in *Heart of Darkness*.

27 Conrad is writing in imaginative ways of the 'flash-back', or speeded-up replaying in the visual imagination, of a life lived.

28 The quotation is from Bradbury's definition of the term 'modernist' in Roger Fowler (ed.), *A Dictionary of Modern Critical Terms* (London, Routledge & Kegan Paul, 1987).

29 Conrad also asserts, in his preface to *The Nigger of the 'Narcissus'* (this preface can be taken as a statement of early modernism), that novels should aspire to the 'plasticity of sculpture, to the colour of painting, and to the magic suggestiveness of music'. Ford's attention to and development of these ideas have been seen in action throughout this book.

30 Ford's interpretation of a modern breach in knowledge of the classics (*English Novel*, p. 19) is also assuaged in this way.

31 Ford Madox Ford, *The March of Literature from Confucius to Modern Times* (London, George Allen & Unwin, 1947), p. 348.

32 In an essay written seventeen years later, Mikhail Bahktin proves that this thought pattern, regarding the capacity of the novel rather than the single-minded reassurance it offered in the nineteenth century, is still current: 'The novel has become the leading hero in the drama of literary development in our time precisely because it best of all reflects the tendencies of a new world still in the making; it is, after all, the only genre born of this new world and in total affinity with it' ('Epic and Novel', in M. Holquist (ed.), *The Dialogic Imagination*, Austin, TX, University of Texas Press, 1986, p. 7).

33 Ford Madox Ford, *Mightier than the Sword* (London, George Allen & Unwin, 1938), p. 208.

34 Robert Louis Stevenson, 'The Desert of Wyoming', quoted in Mike Jay and Michael Neve (eds), *1900* (Harmondsworth, Penguin, 1999), p. 251.

35 I have written an essay on this topic. Called 'Ford's Training', it will shortly be published by Rodopi in *Ford Madox Ford's Modernity* ed. Max Saunders and Robert Hampson.

36 Ford Madox Ford, *The Soul of London* (London, Alston Rivers, 1905), pp. 120–1.

37 Herbert Butterfield, *The Historical Novel* (Cambridge, Cambridge University Press, 1924), p. 24.

38 This image of an airing is a common one in Ford: 'Crowds of intelligent and wealthy people [...] go to that ballet-house to be made better men. They are made better men because the subsoil of their emotions has been vainly, irrationally, but very really disturbed. And any farmer will tell you that the most important thing in agriculture is to stir and aerate the soil beneath the crust. That is the real value of all the arts' ('The Critical Attitude', *Bystander*, 20 December, 1911, p. 639). Ford's use of the word 'disturb' is crucial to the discussion, and to his repetition of this metaphor.

39 Ford Madox Ford, *Return to Yesterday: Reminiscences 1894–1914* (London, Victor Gollancz., 1931), p. 4.

40 Joseph Frank, *The Widening Gyre: Crisis and Mastery in Modern Literature* (Indiana, Indiana University Press, 1963), p. 59. Refer too to my analysis of 'On Heaven' in Chapter 6.

41 Peter Childs has described Flaubert's works as one of the 'literary roots' of modernism (*Modernism*, p. 14).

42 *English Novel*, p. 123. Saunders describes Flaubert as one of Ford's 'literary ancestors' (Saunders I, p. 17).

43 See H. Robert Huntley's article, 'Flaubert and Ford: The Fallacy of Le Mot Juste', *English Language Notes*, 4: 283–7 (June 1967), for another critical language here. He concentrates on Flaubert's use of 'chords' and the 'pitch of prose', of 'binary sentence structure' and 'syntactic construction', and how Ford uses and adapts it.

44 Ford Madox Ford, *The Marsden Case* (London, Duckworth, 1923), p. 88.

45 Ford Madox Ford, 'On Impressionism', *Poetry and Drama*, 2 (June and December 1914), p. 167. This essay is reproduced in full in the Norton edition of *The Good Soldier*.

46 Bakhtin's writing on the carnivalesque addresses the place of eating and drinking in human ritual. Feeding and laughing generates an energy that he defines as potentially revolutionary: no wonder Ford puts this scene underground. See 'Carnival Ambivalence' in Pam Morris (ed.), *The Bakhtin Reader* (London, Edward Arnold, 1994), p. 194ff.

47 Saunders describes the book's 'double perspective – reaching tentatively and painfully back across the devastated zones of memory to the hysteria of the war's eve' whilst it presents on the surface the post-war social scene (Saunders II, p. 111).

48 *The Good Soldier: A Tale of Passion* (1915) (New York, Norton, 1995), pp. 119–20.
49 As I suggested in Chapter 2: so we are protected from the full force of this tragedy.
50 Frank Kermode, 'Novels: Recognition and Deception', *Critical Inquiry*, 1, (1974–5), p. 106.
51 This text is described by Ford as 'reminiscences of active service under a thinly disguised veil of fiction' (Saunders II, p. 357).
52 Ford Madox Ford, *No Enemy* (New York, Ecco, 1984), p. 200.
53 Susan Greenfield, The Brain Story II, 'The Mind's Eye', broadcast 1 August 2000, BBC2.
54 *Mightier than the Sword*, pp. 163–4.
55 P. Renny, *Golden Hind* 1: 38, July 1923.
56 Janice Biala, 'An Interview with Janice Biala' in Sondra Stang (ed.), *The Presence of Ford Madox Ford* (Pennsylvania, University of Pennsylvania Press, 1981), p. 223.
57 In a commentary on Picasso's 'Bowl with Fruit, Violin and Wine Glass' (1912), Brony Fer suggests that 'an aspect of contemporary life may be signified by the inclusion, or intrusion, of a "real" bit of newspaper, but the representation of modernity hinged also on the fragmentation of the whole'. Francis Frascina *et al.* (eds), *Modernity and Modernism: French Painting in the Nineteenth Century* (New Haven, Yale University Press, 1993), p. 11.
58 See Levenson, *A Genealogy of Modernism*, pp. 48–62.
59 Ford Madox Ford, 'English Literature of Today – II' in *The Critical Attitude* (London, Duckworth, 1911), p. 102. This book is made up of the essays Ford wrote in a series of the same name in the *English Review* in 1908–9.
60 Ford Madox Ford, *Hans Holbein the Younger: A Critical Monograph* (London, Duckworth, 1905), pp. 159–60. Compare this with Ford's analysis of Rossetti, detailed in Chapter 5. In this earlier assessment of a painter, Ford isolates his unconscious – his 'underlying truth' – as that which paints.
61 Paul Wiley, *Novelist of Three Worlds: Ford Madox Ford* (Syracuse, Syracuse University Press, 1962), p. 112.
62 Frank Macshane (ed.), *The Critical Writings of Ford Madox Ford* (Nebraska, University of Nebraska Press, 1964), p. 150.
63 Christopher Gillie (*Movements in English Literature*, p. 4.) calls it Hebraism versus Hellenism, or 'conscience' versus 'consciousness', following Matthew Arnold's coinage in *Culture and Anarchy* (1869). Arnold identified two basic attitudes of mind, one moral and practical, the other cultural and aesthetic, to which he gave these names. Later debates harked back to Arnold's terminology, and to his analysis, even whilst developing them.

64 Anatole France's *L'Ile des Pingouins* was reviewed by Conrad for the first edition of Ford's *English Review* in 1908. France himself contributed in 1909.

65 Irving Babbitt, *Masters of Modern French Criticism* (1912) (Westport, CN, Greenwood Press, 1977), p. 345.

66 Ezra Pound, *Poetry* (June 1914), and 'Status Rerum', *Poetry* (January 1913), p. 125.

67 Quoted by Sondra Stang in her introduction to *The Ford Madox Ford Reader* (London, Paladin, 1987), p. xiv.

68 Ford, 'On Impressionism', in Stannard (ed.), *The Good Soldier*, p. 263.

69 In Stang (ed.), *The Presence of Ford Madox Ford*, p. xii.

70 Michela Calderaro, *A Silent New World: Ford Madox Ford's Parade's End* (Editrice Bologna, Cooperativa Libraria Universitaria, 1993), p. 13.

71 Stan Smith, *The Origins of Modernism: Eliot, Pound, Yeats and the Rhetoric of Renewal* (Hemel Hempstead, Harvester Wheatsheaf, 1994), p. 142.

72 At the beginning of *The English Novel* (p. 6) Ford writes about stumbling across a painter creating an image of poppies which, from the painter's position, looked black. From another point of view they were 'dark-purple shot with gold'.

73 Philip Davis, *Memory and Writing: From Wordsworth to Lawrence* (Liverpool, Liverpool University Press, 1983), p. xvi.

74 Frank Macshane judges Ford's critical stance as 'anti-academic'; Max Saunders states that Ford's 'virtues are not academic ones' (I, p.vii).

75 Ford Madox Ford, *Outlook*, 33 (3 January 1914), p. 15.

76 *Mightier than the Sword*, p. 158.

77 Stang (ed.), *Presence of Ford Madox Ford*, p. xviii.

78 Ford Madox Ford, *The Spirit of the People* (London, Alston Rivers, 1907), p. 67.

79 Stang (ed.), *Presence of Ford Madox Ford*, p. 223.

80 Many of the objections to Ford's 'abuse' of facts were full of invective. Contemporary examples are provided by Richard Aldington in *Life for Life's Sake* (London, Viking, 1941), p. 30 ff. Modern comparisons are found in Humphrey Carpenter's Pound biography, *A Serious Character* (New York, Delta, 1988), p. 110. Other critics relate this tendency to Ford's impressionism.

81 Susan Greenfield, *Brain Story* (London, BBC, 2000), p. 79.

82 H. Schneidau, *Waking Giants: The Presence of the Past in Modernism* (Oxford, Oxford University Press, 1991), pp. 15–23.

83 In Stang (ed.), *Presence of Ford Madox Ford*, p. 219. Ford himself said a writer must 'live with' his subject, for 'a long, long, time' before beginning a novel (*English Novel*, p. 140).

84 In Stang (ed.), *Presence of Ford Madox Ford*, p. 204.

85 Butterfield, *The Historical Novel*, p. 15.

86 The presence and absence of memory work in the same way: as signifiers of plurality in questions of identity. Personal narratives can be fractured by being made aware of the gaps in memory – refer to the discussions of war and psychoanalysis and their relationship with writing in the first chapters – as well as of the contradictory, many-layered nature of memory itself.

87 Joseph Conrad, 'Henry James', in *Notes on Life and Letters* (Garden City, NY, Doubleday, 1921), p. 13.

88 George Eliot, *Middlemarch* (Harmondsworth, Penguin, 1985), p. 663.

89 Joseph Conrad, *A Personal Record* (London, J. M. Dent & Sons, 1923), p. 24.

90 Robert Lowell, introduction to *'Buckshee' (Last Poems)* by Ford Madox Ford (Cambridge, MA, Pym-Randall Press, 1936), p. xi.

Bibliography

Editions of Ford's books used

Ancient Lights and Certain New Reflections, London, Chapman & Hall, 1911.

Between St Dennis and St George: A Sketch of Three Civilisations, London, Hodder & Stoughton, 1915.

The Brown Owl, London, T. Fisher Unwin, 1892.

Buckshee (Last Poems) by Ford Madox Ford, Massachussetts, Pym-Randall Press, 1936.

A Call: The Tale of Two Passions (1910), Manchester, Carcanet, 1984.

The Critical Attitude, London, Duckworth, 1911.

The English Novel: From the Earliest Days to the Death of Joseph Conrad (1929), London, Constable, 1930.

The Fifth Queen: and How She Came to Court, London, Alston Rivers, 1906.

The Fifth Queen Crowned, London, Eveleigh Nash, 1908.

Sondra Stang (ed.), *The Ford Madox Ford Reader*, London, Paladin, 1987.

Max Saunders (ed.), *Ford Madox Ford: Selected Poems*, Manchester, Carcanet, 1997.

Max Saunders (ed.), *Ford Madox Ford: War Prose*, Manchester, Carcanet, 1999.

The Good Soldier: A Tale of Passion (1915), New York, Norton, 1995.

The 'Half Moon', London, Eveleigh Nash, 1909.

Hans Holbein the Younger: A Critical Monograph, London, Duckworth, 1905.

The Heart of the Country, London, Alston Rivers, 1906.

Henry for Hugh, Philadelphia, J. B. Lippincott, 1934.

Henry James: A Critical Study (1914), London, Martin Secker, 1918.

A House, London, The Poetry Bookshop, 1921.

It Was the Nightingale (1934), New York, Ecco, 1984.

Joseph Conrad: A Personal Remembrance (1924), New York, Ecco, 1989.

Ladies Whose Bright Eyes (1911), London, Constable, 1931.

The Letters of Ford Madox Ford, ed. Richard Ludwig, Princeton, Princeton University Press, 1965.

The March of Literature from Confucius to Modern Times, London, George Allen & Unwin, 1939.

The Marsden Case, London, Duckworth, 1923.

Mightier Than the Sword, London, George Allen & Unwin, 1938.

Mr Apollo, London, Methuen, 1908.

Mr Fleight, London, Howard Latimer, 1913.

The New Humpty-Dumpty, pseud. 'Daniel Chaucer', London, John Lane, 1912.

New Poems, New York, William Edwin Rudge, 1927.

No Enemy (1929), New York, Ecco, 1984.

On Heaven and Poems Written on Active Service, London, John Lane, 1918.

Parade's End, Harmondsworth, Penguin, 1988.

Privy Seal, London, Alston Rivers, 1907.

The Rash Act, London, Jonathan Cape, 1933.

Return to Yesterday: Reminiscences 1894–1914 (1931), Manchester, Carcanet, 1999.

Rossetti, London, Duckworth, 1902.

The Soul of London, London, Alston Rivers, 1905.

The Spirit of the People, London, Alston Rivers, 1907.

This Monstrous Regiment of Women, London, Women's Freedom League, 1913.

Thus to Revisit, London, Chapman & Hall, 1921.

When Blood is their Argument: An Analysis of Prussian Culture, London, Hodder & Stoughton, 1915.

Women and Men, Paris, Three Mountains Press, 1923.

The Young Lovell, London, Chatto & Windus, 1913.

Ford's articles/reviews used

'Literary Portraits XX: Authors' Likenesses and a Caricaturist', *Tribune*, 2, 7 December 1907.

'London Town and a Saunterer', *Tribune*, 2, 21 December 1907.

'The Critical Attitude', *Bystander*, 15 November 1911.

'Joseph Conrad', *English Review*, X, December 1911.

'Church, State and Divorce', 'The Critical Attitude' series in the *Bystander*, 24 January 1912.

'Impressionism – Some Speculations', *Poetry*, 2, August 1913.

'On Impressionism', *Poetry and Drama*, 2, June and December 1914, repr. in Stannard (ed.), *The Good Soldier*, New York, Norton, 1995.

'Sologub and Artzibashef', *Outlook*, 35, 26 June 1915.

Review of Sinclair Lewis in *Bookman*, 69, April 1929.

'Pure Literature', *Agenda*, 28/29, 1989–90.

'The Literary Life: A Lecture Delivered by Ford Madox Ford', ed. Joseph Wiesenfarth, *Contemporary Literature*, 30: 2, Summer 1989.

'A Day of Battle', *Yale Review*, 78: 4, Summer 1989, p. 499.

Other works cited

Abel, Elizabeth, *Virginia Woolf and the Fictions of Psychoanalysis*, Chicago, University of Chicago Press, 1993.

Ackroyd, Peter, *T. S. Eliot*, London, Sphere Books, 1986.

Adler, Gerhard, *Etudes de psychologie jungienne*, Geneva, 1957.

Aldington, Richard, *Life for Life's Sake*, London, Viking, 1941.

Alvarez, Al, *The Savage God: A Study of Suicide*, London, Weidenfeld & Nicolson, 1977.

Ash, Edwin, *The Problem of Nervous Breakdown*, London, Mills & Boon, 1919.

Babbitt, Irving, *Masters of Modern French Criticism* (1912), Westport, CN, Greenwood Press, 1977.

Barbusse, Henri, *Le Feu [Under Fire]* (1916), tr. Fitzwater Wray, London, Dent, 1988.

Barker, Pat, *Regeneration*, Harmondsworth, Penguin, 1992.

Barker, Pat, *The Eye in the Door*, Harmondsworth, Penguin, 1993.

Bakhtin, Mikhail, *The Dialogic Imagination*, ed. M. Holquist, Austin, University of Texas Press, 1986.

Bergson, Henri, *Time and Free Will: An Essay on the Immediate Data of Conciousness* (1889), London, George Allen & Unwin, 1971.

Berlin, Isaiah, *Four Essays on Liberty*, Oxford, Oxford University Press, 1979.

Bloom, Harold, *The Western Canon*, London, Macmillan, 1995.

Booth, Allyson, *Postcards from the Trenches: Negotiating the Space Between Modernism and the First World War*, Oxford, Oxford University Press, 1996.

Booth, Wayne C., *The Rhetoric of Fiction*, Chicago, University of Chicago Press, 1973.

Bradbury, Malcolm (ed.), *Modernism 1890–1930*, Harmondsworth, Penguin, 1991.

Brandell, Gunnar, *Freud: A Man of His Century*, Brighton, Harvester Press, 1979.

Bristow, Joseph, *Sexuality*, London, Routledge, 1997.

Brittain, Vera, *Testament of Youth*, New York, Macmillan, 1933.

Brontë, Emily, *Wuthering Heights*, Harmondsworth, Penguin, 1961.

Butler, Christopher, *Early Modernism: Literature, Music and Painting in Europe 1900–1916*, Oxford, Clarendon Press, 1994.

Butterfield, Herbert, *The Historical Novel*, Cambridge, Cambridge University Press, 1924.

Calderaro, Michela, *A Silent New World: Ford Madox Ford's Parade's End*, Editrice Bologna, Cooperativa Libraria Universitaria, 1993.

Cannadine, David, *The Decline and Fall of the British Aristocracy*, London, Macmillan, 1996.

Carpenter, Edward, *Woman and Her Place in a Free Society*, Manchester, The Labour Press Society, 1894.

Carpenter, Humphrey, *A Serious Character: The Life of Ezra Pound*, New York, Delta, 1988.

Cassell, Richard, *Ford Madox Ford: A Study of His Novels*, Baltimore, Johns Hopkins Press, 1961.

Cassell, Richard (ed.), *Ford Madox Ford: Modern Judgements*, London, Macmillan, 1972.

Casson, Herbert N., *The History of the Telephone*, Chicago, A. C. McClurg, 1910.

Chevalier, Jean, and Alain Gheerbrandt (eds), *The Penguin Dictionary of Symbols*, tr. John Buchanan-Brown, Harmondsworth, Penguin, 1996.

Childs, Peter, *Modernism*, London, Routledge, 2000.

Churchill, Winston, *The World Crisis 1911–1918*, London, The New English Library, 1964.

Conrad, Joseph, *Notes on Life and Letters*, Garden City, NY, Doubleday, 1921.

Conrad, Joseph, *A Personal Record*, London, J. M. Dent & Sons, 1923.

Conrad, Joseph, *Heart of Darkness*, in Cedric Watts (ed.), *Heart of Darkness and Other Tales*, Oxford, Oxford University Press, 1996.

Conrad, Peter, *Modern Times, Modern Places: Life and Art in the Twentieth Century*, London, Thames & Hudson, 1998.

Cook, Cornelia, 'Going Beyond Modernism', *English*, 33, Summer 1984.

Cook, Cornelia, '*Last Post*: "The Last of the Tietjens Series"' *Agenda*, 27/28, 1989/1990, pp. 23–30.

Dangerfield, George, *The Strange Death of Liberal England*, London, Constable, 1936.

Davis, Philip, *Memory and Writing: From Wordsworth to Lawrence*, Liverpool, Liverpool University Press, 1983.

Dunker, Patricia, *Hallucinating Foucault*, London, Serpent's Tail, 1996.

Dyer, Geoff, *The Missing of the Somme*, London, Hamish Hamilton, 1994.

Eliot, George, *Middlemarch*, Harmondsworth, Penguin, 1985.

Eliot, T. S., *The Waste Land*, New York, Boni & Liveright, 1922.

Selected Prose of T. S. Eliot, ed. Frank Kermode, London, Faber & Faber, 1975.

Elliott, Anthony, *Psychoanalytic Theory: An Introduction*, Oxford, Blackwell, 1994.

Faulkner, Peter, *Modernism*, London, Methuen, 1977.

Ferguson, Niall, *The Pity of War*, Harmondsworth, Penguin, 1998.

Ford, Boris (ed.), *Victorian Britain, The Cambridge Cultural History of Britain*, Vol. 7, Cambridge, Cambridge University Press, 1992.

Forster, E. M., *Howards End*, Harmondsworth, Penguin, 1989.

Foucault, Michel, *The History of Sexuality, Volume 1: An Introduction*, Harmondsworth, Penguin, 1990.

Frank, Joseph, *The Widening Gyre: Crisis and Mastery in Modern Literature*, Indiana, Indiana University Press, 1963.

Frascina, F., *et al* (eds), *Modernity and Modernism: French Painting in the Nineteenth Century*, New Haven, Yale University Press, 1993.

Freud, Anna (ed.), *Sigmund Freud: The Essentials of Psycho-Analysis*, Harmondsworth, Penguin, 1991.

Freud, Sigmund, *Standard Edition of the Complete Psychological Works*, tr. and ed. James Strachey *et al.*, London, The Hogarth Press, 1953–74.

Freud, Sigmund, *The Interpretation of Dreams*, ed. Angela Richard, *The Penguin Freud Library*, Vol. 4, Harmondsworth, Penguin, 1991.

Fussell, Paul, *The Great War and Modern Memory*, Oxford, Oxford University Press, 1975.

Gay, Peter, *The Bourgeois Experience: Victoria to Freud*, Vol. I, *The Education of the Senses*, Oxford, Oxford University Press, 1984, Vol. II, *The Tender Passion*, Oxford, Oxford University Press, 1986.

Gay, Peter, *Freud: A Life For Our Time*, London, J. M. Dent & Sons, 1988.

Gilbert, Martin, *The First World War*, London, Weidenfeld & Nicolson, 1994.

Gillie, Christopher, *Movements in English Literature 1900–1940*, Cambridge, Cambridge University Press, 1975.

Goldring, Douglas, *The Last Pre-Raphaelite: A Record of the Writings of Ford Madox Ford*, London, Macdonald & Co., 1948.

Gordon, Ambrose, Jr., *The Invisible Tent: The War Novels of Ford Madox Ford*, Austin, University of Texas Press, 1964.

Gordon, Caroline, *The Good Soldier: A Key to the Novels of Ford Madox Ford*, Davis, CA, University of California Library, 1963.

Graves, Robert, *The White Goddess*, London, Faber & Faber, 1948.

Graves, Robert, *Goodbye to All That*, Harmondsworth, Penguin, 1973.

Greene, Graham, 'Ford Madox Ford' (1962) in Philip Stratford (ed.), *The Portable Graham Greene*, Harmondsworth, Penguin, 1985.

Greenfield, Susan, *Brain Story*, London, BBC, 2000.

Harrison, Charles, and Paul Woods (eds), *Art in Theory 1900–1990*, Oxford, Blackwell, 1995.

Haste, Cate, *Rules of Desire: Sex in Britain World War I to the Present*, London, Pimlico, 1992.

H. D., *Her*, London, Virago, 1984.

Hergenhahn, B. R., *An Introduction to the History of Psychology*, Pacific Grove, CA, Wadsworth, 1992.

Hillis Miller, J., 'Deconstruction' in Ross C. Murfin (ed.), *Heart of Darkness*, Boston, 1996.

Hueffer, Francis, *The Troubadours: A History of Provençal Life and Literature in the Middle Ages*, London, Chatto & Windus, 1878.

Hunt, Violet, *I Have This to Say: The Story of my Flurried Years*, New York, Boni & Liveright, 1926.

Huntley, H. Robert, 'Ford, Holbein and Dürer', *South Atlantic Bulletin*, 30, May 1965.

Huntley, H. Robert, 'Flaubert and Ford: The Fallacy of Le Mot Juste', *English Language Notes*, 4, June 1967.

Hynes, Samuel, *The Edwardian Turn of Mind*, Princeton, Princeton University Press, 1968.

Hynes, Samuel, *A War Imagined: The First World War and English Culture*, London, Pimlico, 1992.

James, Henry, *The Portrait of a Lady*, Harmondsworth, Penguin, 1970.

James, Henry, 'The Art of Fiction' in William Veeder and Susan Griffin (eds), *The Art of Criticism: Henry James on the Theory and the Practice of Fiction*, Chicago, University of Chicago Press, 1986.

James, William, *The Principles of Psychology*, New York, Holt, 1890.

James, William, *Psychology: The Briefer Course* (1892), New York, Harper, 1963.

Jameson, Frederic, *The Political Unconscious: Narrative as a Socially Symbolic Act*, London, Methuen, 1981.

Jay, Mike, and Michael Neve (eds), *1900*, Harmondsworth, Penguin, 1999.

Josipovici, Gabriel, *The Lessons of Modernism*, London, Macmillan, 1977.

Judd, Alan, *Ford Madox Ford*, London, HarperCollins, 1991.

Jung, Carl, *The Archetypes and the Collective Unconscious*, London, Routledge & Kegan Paul, 1968.

Jung, Carl (ed.), *Man and His Symbols*, London, Picador, 1978.

Jung, Carl, *Freud and Psychoanalysis*, London, Routledge, 1984.

Jung, Carl, *Modern Man in Search of a Soul*, London, Routledge, 1985.

Keegan, John, *The Face of Battle*, London, Pimlico, 1993.

Kermode, Frank, 'Novels: Recognition and Deception', *Critical Inquiry*, 1, 1974–5.

Kolokotroni, Vassiliki, Jane Goldman and Olga Taxidou (eds), *Modernism: An Anthology of Sources and Documents*, Edinburgh, Edinburgh University Press, 1998.

Kristeva, Julia, *Tales of Love*, New York, Columbia University Press, 1987.

Kurzweil, Edith, and William Phillips (eds), *Literature and Psychoanalysis*, New York, Columbia University Press, 1983.

Lawrence, D. H., *Fantasia and the Unconscious and Psychoanalysis and the Unconscious*, London, Heinemann, 1963.

Lawrence, D. H., 'Why the Novel Matters' in Anthony Beale (ed.), *Selected Literary Criticism D. H. Lawrence*, London, Heinemann, 1967.

Levenson, Michael, *A Genealogy of Modernism*, Cambridge, Cambridge University Press, 1984.

Ludwig, Richard, 'The Reputation of Ford Madox Ford', *PMLA* 76, December 1961.

Macdonald, Lyn, *1914*, Harmondsworth, Penguin, 1989.

Macshane, Frank (ed.), *The Critical Writings of Ford Madox Ford*, Nebraska, University of Nebraska Press, 1964.

Manning, Frederic, *The Middle Parts of Fortune* (1930), Harmondsworth, Penguin, 1990.

Marcus, Steven, *Freud and the Culture of Psychoanalysis: Studies in the Transition from Victorian Humanism to Modernity*, Boston, George Allen & Unwin, 1984.

Marinetti, F. T., 'Destruction of Syntax – Imagination without Strings – Words-in-Freedom' in Umbro Apollonio (ed.), *Futurist Manifestos*, London, Thames & Hudson, 1973.

Marks, Elaine, and Isabelle de Courtivron (eds), *New French Feminisms*, Hemel Hempstead, Harvester Wheatsheaf, 1981.

Marsh, Jan, *Pre-Raphaelite Women*, London, Weidenfeld & Nicolson, 1987.

Masterman, C. F. G., *In Peril of Change*, London, T. Fisher Unwin, 1905.

Masterman, Lucy, *C. F. G. Masterman: A Biography*, London, Nicholson & Watson, 1939.

Milton, John, *The Poetical Works*, ed. Helen Darbishire, London, Oxford University Press, 1958.

Mitchell, Juliet, and Jacqueline Rose (eds), *Feminine Sexuality: Jacques Lacan and the Ecole Freudienne*, London, Macmillan, 1982.

Mitchell, Juliet, 'Sexuality and Psychoanalysis: Hysteria', *British Journal of Psychotherapy*, 12:4, 1996.

Mizener, Arthur, *The Saddest Story: A Biography of Ford Madox Ford*, New York, Carroll & Graf, 1985.

Morgan, K. (ed.), *The Oxford History of Britain*, Oxford, Oxford University Press, 1988.

Morris, Pam (ed.), *The Bakhtin Reader*, London, Edward Arnold, 1994.

Moser, Thomas, *The Life in the Fiction of Ford Madox Ford*, Princeton, Princeton University Press, 1980.

Newman, Theresa, and Ray Watkinson, *Ford Madox Brown and the Pre-Raphaelite Circle*, London, Chatto & Windus, 1991.

Nietzsche, Friedrich, 'The Use and Abuse of History' in Oscar Levy (ed.), *Complete Works of Friedrich Nietzsche*, vol. 5, ii, *Thoughts Out of Season*, Edinburgh, T. N. Foulis, 1909.

Nordau, Max, *Degeneration*, London, Heinemann, 1895.

Paglia, Camille, *Sexual Personae: Art and Decadence from Nerfertiti to Emily Dickinson*, Harmondsworth, Penguin, 1991.

Pareto, Victor, *The Mind and Society*, London, Jonathan Cape, 1935.

Paterson, Isabel, review of Ford in *New York Herald Tribune Book Review*, 4, 26 February 1933.

Phillips, Adam, *On Flirtation*, London, Faber & Faber, 1994.

Pick, Daniel, *War Machine: The Rationalization of Slaughter in the Modern Age*, New Haven, Yale University Press, 1993.

Porter, Roy (ed.), *The Faber Book of Madness*, London, Faber & Faber, 1993.

Pound, Ezra, 'Status Rerum', *Poetry*, 1, January 1913.

Pound, Ezra, 'A Few Don'ts', *Poetry*, 1, March 1913.

Pound, Ezra, 'Ford Madox Hueffer', *New Freewoman*, 1, 15 December 1913.

Pound, Ezra, 'Vorticism', *Fortnightly Review*, XCVI, 1914.

Pound, Ezra, 'Wyndham Lewis', *Egoist*, 1, 15 June 1914.

Pound, Ezra, 'Affirmations... VI. Analysis of this Decade', *New Age*, XVI, 11 February 1915.

Pound, Ezra, 'Ford Madox (Hueffer) Ford: Obit.', *Nineteenth Century and After*, CXXVII, August 1939, pp. 178–81.

The Letters of Ezra Pound 1907–1941, ed. D. D. Paige, New York, Harcourt Brace, 1950.

Pound, Ezra, *Selected Poems 1908–1959*, London, Faber & Faber, 1990.

Radell, Karen, *Affirmation in a Moral Wasteland: A Comparison of Ford Madox Ford and Graham Greene*, New York, Peter Lang, 1987.

Read, Herbert, *Art Now: An Introduction to the Theory of Modern Painting and Sculpture*, London, Faber & Faber, 1933.

Renny, P., review of Ford in *Golden Hind*, 1: 38, July 1923.

Richardson, Dorothy, *Pilgrimage*, London, Virago, 1979.

Richetti, J. (ed.), *The Eighteenth Century Novel*, Cambridge, Cambridge University Press, 1996.

Rivers, W. H. R., 'Why is the "Unconscious" Unconscious?', *British Journal of Psychotherapy*, London, 1918.

Rivers, W. H. R., *Instinct and the Unconscious: A Contribution to a Biological Theory of the Psycho-Neuroses*, 2nd edn, Cambridge, Cambridge University Press, 1922.

Said, Edward, *Beginnings: Intention and Method*, Columbia, Columbia University Press, 1985.

Sartre, Jean-Paul, *Existentialism and Humanism*, London, Methuen, 1984.

[Sassoon, Siegfried] *Sherston's Progress*, London, Faber & Faber, 1936.

Saunders, Max, *Ford Madox Ford: A Dual Life*, vols I and II, Oxford, Oxford University Press, 1996.

Schneidau, H., *Waking Giants: The Presence of the Past in Modernism*, Oxford, Oxford University Press, 1984.

Scott-James, R. A. *Modernism and Romance*, London, John Lane, 1908.

Seymour, Miranda, *A Ring of Conspirators: Henry James and his Literary Circle 1895–1915*, Boston, Houghton Mifflin, 1989.

Showalter, Elaine, *The Female Malady: Women, Madness and English Culture, 1830–1980*, London, Virago, 1993.

Slobodin, Richard, *W. H. R. Rivers*, Stroud, Sutton Publishing, 1997.

Smith, Stan, *The Origins of Modernism: Eliot, Pound, Yeats and the Rhetoric of Renewal*, Hemel Hempsted, Harvester Wheatsheaf, 1994.

Spender, Stephen, *Eliot*, Glasgow, William Collins, 1982.

Stanford, Derek, '"The Best Poem Yet Written in the Twentieth-Century Fashion": A Discursive Note on Ford Madox Ford's "On Heaven"' in *Agenda*, 27/28, 1989/90.

Stang, Sondra, *Ford Madox Ford*, New York, Frederick Ungar, 1977.

Stang, Sondra (ed.), *The Presence of Ford Madox Ford*, Pennsylvania, University of Pennsylvania Press, 1981.

Stansky, Peter, *On or About 1910: Early Bloomsbury and its Intimate World*, Cambridge, MA, Harvard University Press, 1997.

Steiner, George, 'Gent', *New Yorker*, 47.

Stevenson, Randall, *Modernist Fiction: An Introduction*, Hemel Hempstead, Prentice Hall, 1998.

Sturrock, John (ed.), *Structuralism and Since: From Levi-Strauss to Derrida*, Oxford, Oxford University Press, 1979.

Tallack, Douglas (ed.), *Critical Theory: A Reader*, Hemel Hempstead, Harvester Wheatsheaf, 1995.

Tate, Trudi, *Modernism, History and the First World War*, Manchester, Manchester University Press, 1998.

Taylor, A. J. P., *English History 1914–1945*, Oxford, Oxford University Press, 1965.

Tomlinson, Nora, 'The Achievement of Ford Madox Ford as Editor', PhD thesis, The Open University, 1995.

Tracy, David, 'Fragments: The Spiritual Situation of Our Times' in John D. Caputo and Michael J. Scanlon (eds), *God, the Gift and Post-Modernism*, Bloomington, Indiana University Press, 1999.

Trotter, David, *The English Novel in History 1895–1920*, London, Routledge, 1993.

Turgenev, Ivan, *Fathers and Sons*, Oxford, Oxford University Press, 1991.

Unger, R. M., *Passion: An Essay on Personality*, New York, The Free Press, 1984.

Warner, Marina, *Alone of All Her Sex: The Myth and the Cult of the Virgin Mary*, London, Weidenfeld & Nicolson, 1976.

Watt, Ian, *The Rise of the Novel*, London, The Hogarth Press, 1987.

Weininger, Otto, *Sex and Character* (1903), New York, AMS Press, 1975.

Weiss, Timothy, *Fairy Tale and Romance in the Works of Ford Madox Ford*, Lanham, MD, University Press of America, 1984.

West, Shearer (ed.), *The Bloomsbury Guide to Art*, London, Bloomsbury, 1996.

Wiesenfarth, Joseph (ed.), 'The Literary Life: A Lecture Delivered by Ford Madox Ford', *Contemporary Literature*, 30: 2, Summer 1989.

Wiley, Paul, *Novelist of Three Worlds: Ford Madox Ford*, Syracuse, Syracuse University Press, 1962.

Williams, Meg Harris, and Margot Wadell, *The Chamber of Maiden Thought: Literary Origins of the Psychoanalytic Model of the Mind*, London/Routledge, 1991.

Wilson, Trevor, *The Myriad Faces of War*, Cambridge, Polity Press, 1988.

Winter, Jay, *Sites of Memory, Sites of Mourning: The Great War in European Cultural History*, Cambridge, Cambridge University Press, 2000.

Woolf, Virginia, *Orlando*, Harmondsworth, Penguin, 1975.

Woolf, Virginia, *Moments of Being: Unpublished Autobiographical Writings*, ed. Jeanne Schulkind, London, Chatto & Windus, 1976.

Woolf, Virginia, *The Diary of Virginia Woolf*, vols 1 and 2, ed. Anne Olivier Bell, Harmondsworth, Penguin, 1979, 1981.

Zanuso, B., *The Young Freud*, Oxford, Blackwell, 1986.

Other works consulted

Ackroyd, Peter, *Eliot*, London, Sphere Books, 1986.

Angier, Carole, *Jean Rhys*, Harmondsworth, Penguin, 1992.

Bergonzi, Bernard, *Heroes' Twilight: A Study of the Literature of the First World War*, London, Constable, 1965.

Carroll, John, *Humanism: The Wreck of Western Culture*, London, HarperCollins, 1993.

Conrad, Joseph, *The Mirror of the Sea*, London, Methuen, 1947.

Durkheim, Emile, *The Elementary Forms of the Religious Life*, London, George Allen & Unwin, 1915.

Eliot, T. S., *For Lancelot Andrewes: Essays on Style and Order*, London, Faber & Gwyer, 1928.

Eliot, T. S., *Knowledge and Experience*, London, Faber & Faber, 1964.

Frazer, J. G., *The Golden Bough*, London, Macmillan, 1987.

Freud, Sigmund, and Albert Einstein, *Why War? A Correspondence Between Albert Einstein and Sigmund Freud*, London, Peace Pledge Union Publications, 1933.

Goffman, Erving, *The Presentation of the Self in Everyday Life*, Harmondsworth, Penguin, 1990.

Goldring, Douglas, *South Lodge: Reminiscences of Violet Hunt, Ford Madox Ford and the 'English Review' Circle*, London, Constable, 1943.

Haslam, Sara, 'A Question of Knowledge: Ford, James, *A Call* and "The Beast in the Jungle"', *Henry James Review*, 21: 1, Winter 2000.

Hillis Miller, J., *The Disappearance of God: Five Nineteenth Century Writers*, Cambridge, MA, Harvard University Press, 1975.

Hulme, T. E., *Speculations: Essays on Humanism and the Philosophy of Art*, ed. Herbert Read, London, Kegan Paul, 1936.

Keegan, John, *A History of Warfare*, London, Pimlico, 1994.

Lee, Hermione, *Virginia Woolf*, Harmondsworth, Penguin, 1996.

Lukes, Stephen, *Emile Durkheim, His Life and Work*, Harmondsworth, Penguin, 1973.

Macshane, Frank (ed.), *The Critical Heritage: Ford Madox Ford*, London, Routledge & Kegan Paul, 1972.

Mangan, J. A., and J. Walvin (eds), *Manliness and Morality: Middle-Class Masculinity in Britain and America 1800–1940*, Manchester, Manchester University Press, 1987.

Masterman, C. F. G., *The Condition of England*, London, Methuen, 1909.

Said, Edward, *Culture and Imperialism*, London, Vintage, 1994.

Sayers, Janet, *The Man Who Never Was: Freudian Tales* (London, Chatto & Windus, 1995.

Soskice, Juliet, *Chapters From Childhood*, London, Selwyn & Blount, 1921.

Tate, Trudi (ed.), *Women, Men and the Great War: An Anthology of Stories*, Manchester, Manchester University Press, 1995.

Tawney, R. H., *Religion and the Rise of Capitalism*, London, John Murray, 1936.

Tolstoy, Leo, *War and Peace*, Harmondsworth, Penguin, 1981.

West, Rebecca, *The Return of the Soldier*, London, Virago, 1980.

Weston, Jessie, *From Ritual to Romance*, Cambridge, Cambridge University Press, 1920.

Index

Introductory note:

As Ford Madox Ford is the main subject of this book, he does not appear as an index entry. All entries must be considered to relate to Ford, to a greater or lesser extent. Discussion of his works is indicated in the index under individual book titles. Major characters are named also, and the book in which they appear is given in brackets. Modernism and the First World War, as subsidiary subjects of the book, do appear as index entries, but should be considered to relate to many other entries too (for example: John Dowell is a consummate example of a modernist narrator; the war receives significant treatment in *Parade's End*, *No Enemy* and *It Was the Nightingale*).